MariaDB Cookbook

Over 95 recipes to unlock the power of MariaDB

Daniel Bartholomew

BIRMINGHAM - MUMBAI

MariaDB Cookbook

First published: March 2014

Production Reference: 1120314

Published by Packt Publishing Ltd.
Livery Place
35 Livery Street
Birmingham B3 2PB, UK.

ISBN 978-1-78328-439-9

www.packtpub.com

Cover Image by Aniket Sawant (aniket_sawant_photography@hotmail.com)

Credits

Author
Daniel Bartholomew

Reviewers
Pradeesh Parameswaran

Sergei Petrunia

Acquisition Editors
Vinay Argekar

Amarabha Banerjee

Rubal Kaur

Content Development Editor
Anila Vincent

Technical Editors
Menza Mathew

Shali Sasidharan

Copy Editors
Karuna Narayanan

Laxmi Subramanian

Project Coordinator
Venitha Cutinho

Proofreaders
Simran Bhogal

Maria Gould

Ameesha Green

Paul Hindle

Indexer
Priya Subramani

Production Coordinator
Shantanu Zagade

Cover Work
Shantanu Zagade

About the Author

Daniel Bartholomew has been using Linux since 1997 and databases since 1998. He is a frequent contributor to various magazines, including *The Linux Journal*, *Linux Pro*, *Ubuntu*, *User*, and *Tux*.

He has been involved with the MariaDB project since shortly after it began in early 2009. He currently works for SkySQL and splits his time between MariaDB documentation and maintaining the bits and pieces (including build, e-mail, web, and other servers), which keeps the MariaDB project running smoothly. In addition to his day-to-day responsibilities, he also serves as the MariaDB release coordinator and has been deeply involved with almost every MariaDB release.

He lives in Raleigh, North Carolina, U.S.A. with his lovely wife and awesome children.

I'd like to thank Amy, Ila, Lizzy, Anthon, and Rachel for their patience with me throughout the writing of this book. Also, thanks to the awesome team of MariaDB experts at SkySQL, who were very helpful at various points during the project. Lastly, I'd like to thank Monty and the rest of the MariaDB developers for the excellent database they've created.

About the Reviewers

Pradeesh Parameswaran started working on computers and programming right from the age of 10. He wrote the first program for PalmOS and published to Handango. He is a geek and loves explaining and helping people with their computer problems. Currently, he blogs about tech-related stuff and provides how-to information in his blog at prasys.info. He is also currently working for a telecommunications company in Malaysia. Also, he is a big fan of the open source stuff!

> I would like to thank my parents for the support and encouragement that they have given me over the years to enable me to grow.

Sergei Petrunia has been working on MariaDB since 2009. He has implemented features such as semijoin subquery optimizations, SHOW EXPLAIN, Cassandra storage engine, table elimination, and numerous smaller improvements. Prior to MariaDB, he was a member of the MySQL development team at MySQL AB and Sun Microsystems.

> I would like to thank my girlfriend, Yulia, for being patient while I was spending time to provide input for this book.

www.PacktPub.com

Support files, eBooks, discount offers, and more

You might want to visit www.PacktPub.com for support files and downloads related to your book.

Did you know that Packt offers eBook versions of every book published, with PDF and ePub files available? You can upgrade to the eBook version at www.PacktPub.com and as a print book customer, you are entitled to a discount on the eBook copy. Get in touch with us at service@packtpub.com for more details.

At www.PacktPub.com, you can also read a collection of free technical articles, sign up for a range of free newsletters and receive exclusive discounts and offers on Packt books and eBooks.

http://PacktLib.PacktPub.com

Do you need instant solutions to your IT questions? PacktLib is Packt's online digital book library. Here, you can access, read and search across Packt's entire library of books.

Why subscribe?

- ▸ Fully searchable across every book published by Packt
- ▸ Copy and paste, print and bookmark content
- ▸ On demand and accessible via web browser

Free access for Packt account holders

If you have an account with Packt at www.PacktPub.com, you can use this to access PacktLib today and view nine entirely free books. Simply use your login credentials for immediate access.

Table of Contents

Preface

MariaDB is a mature, stable, open source relational database. From its beginning in 2009 as a branch or fork of the MySQL database, to its status today as the default version of that database in most Linux distributions, and the database of choice for many companies large and small, MariaDB has proven that communities of users and developers, working and collaborating together, can do more than a single company could ever do.

MariaDB shares many features and capabilities of its parent database, but like most children it has also surpassed its parent in many ways. The recipes in this book tread some common ground, but they are mostly about the features that are unique to or were introduced first in MariaDB.

The *why* of certain features is there, to a small degree, but the main emphasis in each recipe is on the *what* and the *how*. The information you need to know to actually do something always trumps the theory behind it.

As part of the growing library of MariaDB-specific books from Packt Publishing and other publishers, the goal of this book is to give you a practical, hands-on experience with this powerful, feature-rich database.

What this book covers

Chapter 1, *Getting Started with MariaDB*, covers installing MariaDB on Linux, Windows, and Mac OS along with making backups, enabling common plugins, and other common tasks.

Chapter 2, *Diving Deep into MariaDB*, covers importing data, customizing the output of queries, migrating the data, and other topics.

Chapter 3, *Optimizing and Tuning MariaDB*, covers various configuration and optimization tasks as well as creating and removing indexes, JOINs, and other topics.

Chapter 4, *The TokuDB Storage Engine*, speaks about the alternative storage engine including how to enable it, and how to use and configure it.

Chapter 5, *The CONNECT Storage Engine*, explores the CONNECT storage engine including how to enable and configure it, and how to use it to connect to several different filetypes.

Chapter 6, *Replication in MariaDB*, includes recipes on global transaction IDs, multisource replication, and the binary log.

Chapter 7, *Replication with MariaDB Galera Cluster*, includes recipes that cover how to install and use this new clustering solution.

Chapter 8, *Performance and Usage Statistics*, covers using MariaDB's extended statistics, the audit plugin, and the performance schema.

Chapter 9, *Searching Data Using Sphinx*, covers how to install and use this useful full-text database indexer and search engine.

Chapter 10, *Exploring Dynamic and Virtual Columns in MariaDB*, is all about the built-in NoSQL features of MariaDB including dynamic and virtual columns features in MariaDB.

Chapter 11, *NoSQL with HandlerSocket*, is a chapter devoted to the NoSQL HandlerSocket feature and how to use it with various languages.

Chapter 12, *NoSQL with the Cassandra Storage Engine*, contains several recipes covering the installation and usage of the Cassandra storage engine.

Chapter 13, *MariaDB Security*, contains several recipes relating to securing MariaDB.

What you need for this book

To get the most out of this book, you'll need a computer that is capable of running MariaDB. Fortunately, this is quite easy as MariaDB runs well on many different versions of Windows, Mac OS, and Linux. Due to the limitations of some storage engines and other MariaDB components, there are some recipes which are Linux-only or Windows-only. These are marked as such in the text.

This book assumes that the reader is familiar with either the Windows, Mac OS, or Linux command-line environments; is comfortable with using a plain text editor; and knows how to download and install software. It is also helpful if the reader is familiar with databases and database concepts.

Who this book is for

This book is for anyone who wants to explore and learn how to use features that make MariaDB different from other databases in its class in a practical, hands-on way.

Conventions

In this book, you will find a number of styles of text that distinguish between different kinds of information. Here are some examples of these styles, and an explanation of their meaning.

Code words in text, database table names, folder names, filenames, file extensions, pathnames, dummy URLs, user input, and Twitter handles are shown as follows: "Open our `my.cnf` or `my.ini` file in a text editor such as Vim, Emacs, TextWrangler, or Notepad."

A block of code is set as follows:

```
#
# * HandlerSocket
#
handlersocket_address="127.0.0.1"
handlersocket_port="9998"
handlersocket_port_wr="9999"
```

When we wish to draw your attention to a particular part of a code block, the relevant lines or items are set in bold:

```
ANALYZE TABLE table_name PERSISTENT FOR
    COLUMNS (column_1,column_2,...)
    INDEXES (index_1,index_2,...);
```

Any command-line input or output is written as follows:

```
GRANT REPLICATION SLAVE, REPLICATION CLIENT ON *.*
  TO replicant@'192.168.4.%'
  IDENTIFIED BY 'sup3rs3kr37p455w0rd';
```

New terms and **important words** are shown in bold. Words that you see on the screen, in menus or dialog boxes for example, appear in the text like this: "The **Feedback** plugin is turned off by default."

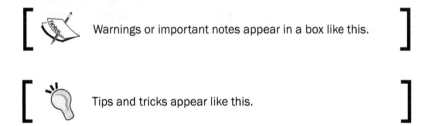

Warnings or important notes appear in a box like this.

Tips and tricks appear like this.

Reader feedback

Feedback from our readers is always welcome. Let us know what you think about this book—what you liked or may have disliked. Reader feedback is important for us to develop titles that you really get the most out of.

To send us general feedback, simply send an e-mail to feedback@packtpub.com, and mention the book title via the subject of your message.

If there is a topic that you have expertise in and you are interested in either writing or contributing to a book, see our author guide on www.packtpub.com/authors.

Customer support

Now that you are the proud owner of a Packt book, we have a number of things to help you to get the most from your purchase.

Downloading the example code

You can download the example code files for all Packt books you have purchased from your account at http://www.packtpub.com. If you purchased this book elsewhere, you can visit http://www.packtpub.com/support and register to have the files e-mailed directly to you.

Errata

Although we have taken every care to ensure the accuracy of our content, mistakes do happen. If you find a mistake in one of our books—maybe a mistake in the text or the code—we would be grateful if you would report this to us. By doing so, you can save other readers from frustration and help us improve subsequent versions of this book. If you find any errata, please report them by visiting http://www.packtpub.com/submit-errata, selecting your book, clicking on the **errata submission form** link, and entering the details of your errata. Once your errata are verified, your submission will be accepted and the errata will be uploaded on our website, or added to any list of existing errata, under the Errata section of that title. Any existing errata can be viewed by selecting your title from http://www.packtpub.com/support.

Piracy

Piracy of copyright material on the Internet is an ongoing problem across all media. At Packt, we take the protection of our copyright and licenses very seriously. If you come across any illegal copies of our works, in any form, on the Internet, please provide us with the location address or website name immediately so that we can pursue a remedy.

Please contact us at `copyright@packtpub.com` with a link to the suspected pirated material.

We appreciate your help in protecting our authors, and our ability to bring you valuable content.

Questions

You can contact us at `questions@packtpub.com` if you are having a problem with any aspect of the book, and we will do our best to address it.

1
Getting Started with MariaDB

In this chapter, we will cover the following recipes:

- ▶ Installing MariaDB on Windows
- ▶ Installing MariaDB on Linux
- ▶ Installing MariaDB on Mac OS X
- ▶ Enabling the Feedback plugin
- ▶ Switching between InnoDB and XtraDB
- ▶ Creating a backup user
- ▶ Making backups with XtraBackup
- ▶ Making backups with mysqldump
- ▶ Checking and optimizing tables automatically with mysqlcheck and cron
- ▶ Using progress reporting in the mysql client

Introduction

This chapter is all about getting us up and running with MariaDB using basic recipes, which provide the foundation for the other recipes in this book.

The first three recipes are the most basic of all the recipes and cover installing MariaDB on the Windows, Linux, and Mac OS X operating systems. We'll then cover a couple of common configuration options and some common maintenance tasks.

We'll finish the chapter with a recipe on the progress reporting feature of the `mysql` client application.

Installing MariaDB on Windows

There was a time when installing MariaDB on Windows meant downloading and unpacking a ZIP file. From then on, it was up to us to set up a system service, making sure that the paths were correct, and so on. Today, the process is completely automated with the MariaDB MSI package. The ZIP file is still available, but unless we know we want it (and we might!), there is no reason to use it.

How to do it...

Let's get started by following these steps:

1. Visit `http://mariadb.org/downloads` and select the version of MariaDB we are interested in. There will be a development version and a stable version. For most users, the stable version is recommended.

2. After choosing the version of MariaDB that we want, select either the 32-bit or 64-bit version of the MariaDB MSI package for Windows. For most computers, the 64-bit version will work fine; but if we are on an older computer, we may need to use the 32-bit version.

3. Once it is downloaded, the installer may launch automatically, or depending on our settings, we may need to manually launch it, as shown in the following screenshot:

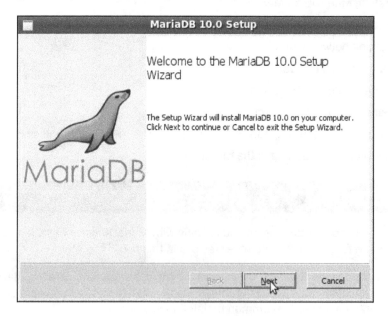

4. Once the installer starts, click through the defaults. We can change them if we want, but there is no need.

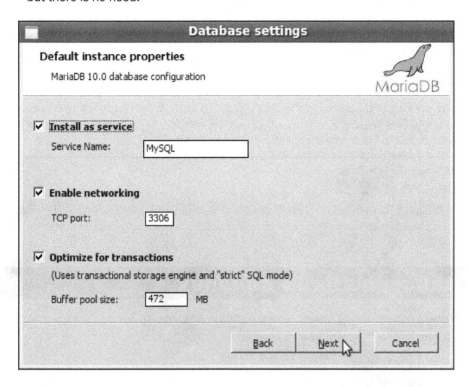

5. After the installation has finished, MariaDB will be up and running on our Windows computer.

How it works...

MSI stands for Microsoft installer. It's a standard package format for software installers on the Windows operating system. The MariaDB MSI package encapsulates all of the common manual steps for installing MariaDB. This includes steps such as setting up a Windows service so that MariaDB can be started automatically at boot time, creating the data directory, and so on.

There's more...

While clicking through the installer, there are some choices that we may wonder about. Two of them are HeidiSQL and the **Feedback** plugin.

HeidiSQL

In addition to installing MariaDB, the MSI package also, by default installs the HeidiSQL graphical client. This open source graphical client is a great way to interact with MariaDB, and the MariaDB and HeidiSQL developers have worked together to make sure that it supports all MariaDB features and options.

The Feedback plugin

One of the screens of the installer offers the option to turn on the **Feedback** plugin if we want to. Refer to the *Enabling the Feedback plugin* recipe later in this chapter for more information on this plugin and to know why it's a good idea to enable it.

See also

▶ The full documentation of the MariaDB MSI installer for Windows can be found at `https://mariadb.com/kb/en/installing-mariadb-msi-packages-on-windows/`

Installing MariaDB on Linux

Most of the installs of MariaDB are on various flavors of Linux. This recipe will get most Linux users up and running MariaDB quickly and easily.

Getting ready

First, determine which version of Linux we are running. In most cases, we will have installed Linux ourselves, so we will know this information. But on the off chance we do not know the information, the following command will give us the information we need:

`cat /etc/lsb-release`

On my desktop, the preceding command shows the following output:

```
daniel@gandalf:~$ cat /etc/lsb-release
DISTRIB_ID=Ubuntu
DISTRIB_RELEASE=10.04
DISTRIB_CODENAME=lucid
DISTRIB_DESCRIPTION="Ubuntu 10.04.4 LTS"
```

From this, I see that I am running Ubuntu 10.04 "lucid". This is all the information I need.

How to do it...

Let's get started by following the ensuing steps:

1. Visit http://mariadb.org/downloads/mariadb/repositories and select our distribution, release, version, and (for some distributions) the mirror that we would like to use, as shown in the following screenshot:

2. Once all of the choices have been made, instructions will appear at the bottom of the page.

3. On Fedora, CentOS, and Red Hat, the basic instructions are to copy the provided text into the MariaDB.repo file located at /etc/yum.repos.d/ and then to issue the following command in order to install MariaDB:

```
sudo yum install MariaDB-server MariaDB-client
```

4. During the initial installation with yum, we will be asked to accept the key used to sign MariaDB packages. This key has a fingerprint as follows:

```
1993 69e5 404b d5fc 7d2f e43b cbcb 082a 1bb9 43db
```

5. Assuming that the fingerprint shown by `yum` matches the key fingerprint shown in step 4, go ahead and answer `yes` to the question.

6. On Debian and Ubuntu, in addition to choosing the Linux distribution, release, and MariaDB version, we need to choose the mirror that we want to use. After selecting the items in all four boxes, customized instructions for installing MariaDB will appear at the bottom of the page. As an example, the commands to install MariaDB 10.0 on Ubuntu 12.04 LTS "Precise" are as follows:

```
sudo apt-get install python-software-properties
sudo apt-key adv --recv-keys --keyserver \
  keyserver.ubuntu.com 0xcbcb082a1bb943db
sudo add-apt-repository \
  'deb http://ftp.osuosl.org/pub/mariadb/repo/10.0/ubuntu
    precise main'
sudo apt-get update
sudo apt-get install mariadb-server
```

7. After the YUM or APT-based installation has finished, we can start and stop MariaDB with the following commands:

```
sudo /etc/init.d/mysql start
sudo /etc/init.d/mysql stop
```

How it works...

The repository configurator supports the following Linux distributions:

- Red Hat
- Ubuntu
- Debian
- Mint
- Mageia
- Fedora
- CentOS
- openSUSE

New Linux distributions are added from time to time, so it's possible that when we visit the website, another Linux distribution or two would have been added to the list.

The common feature of all of these distributions is that they use a package manager. Fedora, Red Hat, and CentOS use the **Yellowdog Updater Modified** (**YUM**) package manager. Debian, Ubuntu, and Mint use the **Advanced Package Tool** (**APT**) package manager. The MariaDB developers provide repositories for these distributions.

Other distributions such as Mageia and openSUSE are different. They use their own custom package managers. MariaDB packages for these Linux distributions are provided by the developers of those distributions. The repository configuration tool provides instructions for the commands that we need to run in order to install MariaDB.

See also

▸ The full documentation on installing MariaDB on Linux can be found at
  `https://mariadb.com/kb/en/mariadb-binary-packages/`

Installing MariaDB on Mac OS X

Installing MariaDB on Mac OS X is similar to installing it on Linux (refer to the previous recipe), with one important difference: the MariaDB developers do not provide the installer; instead, it is provided by the brew project.

Getting ready

In order to install MariaDB on Mac OS X, we must first install Xcode from the Mac App Store. Once that is installed, we need to install and configure `brew`. The complete set of instructions for how to do this are on the brew website, `http://brew.sh/`, but the basic command is:

```
ruby -e \
  "$(curl -fsSL https://raw.github.com/Homebrew/homebrew/go/install)"
```

After installing brew, we will run the following `doctor` command to make sure that everything is set up properly:

```
brew doctor
```

When the `doctor` command finds an issue, and it might find several, it will print out a suggested fix for each one. To ensure that `brew` is happy, we need to follow the instructions until the `doctor` command gives us the following message:

```
Your system is ready to brew.
```

How to do it...

Let's get started by following the ensuing steps:

1. Run the following commands in our terminal:

    ```
    brew update
    brew install mariadb
    ```

2. If there are any dependencies, they will be installed first, and then brew will download the latest stable MariaDB source code tarball, compile it, and then install it.

3. Once the installation has finished, link the MariaDB startup `plist` to the `LaunchAgents` directory as follows, so that MariaDB will start automatically:

    ```
    ln -sfv /usr/local/opt/mariadb/*.plist \
        ~/Library/LaunchAgents
    ```

4. To start MariaDB, use the following `launchctl` command to load the `plist` file:

    ```
    launchctl load \
        ~/Library/LaunchAgents/homebrew.mxcl.mariadb.plist
    ```

5. To stop MariaDB, unload the `plist` file:

    ```
    launchctl unload \
        ~/Library/LaunchAgents/homebrew.mxcl.mariadb.plist
    ```

How it works...

The brew installer works like a Linux package manager. Many open source software packages can be installed with it, including MariaDB.

The brew installer does not set a password for the root user, so the first thing that we should do after getting MariaDB running on Mac OS X is to run the `mysql_secure_installation` script. For more information, refer to the *Securing MariaDB with mysql_secure_installation* recipe in *Chapter 13, MariaDB Security*.

Enabling the Feedback plugin

The **Feedback** plugin gathers and submits anonymous usage information to the MariaDB developers. Enabling it is an easy way to help out the project.

Getting ready

We'll need a running install of MariaDB. Refer to the previous recipes for instructions on how to do this.

How to do it...

Let's get started by following the ensuing steps:

1. Stop MariaDB by following the directions in the recipe that we followed when installing MariaDB.

2. Open our `my.cnf` or `my.ini` file in a text editor such as Vim, Emacs, TextWrangler, or Notepad. On Windows, there is a helpful link under the MariaDB group that will automatically open the `my.ini` file in Notepad. On Linux, the `my.cnf` file is located at either `/etc/mysql/my.cnf` or `/etc/my.cnf` depending on the Linux distribution we are using.

3. Add the following line of code to the `[mysqld]` section of the system's `my.cnf` or `my.ini` file (if the section does not exist, create it):

   ```
   feedback=on
   ```

4. Save the file and then start MariaDB by following the instructions in the recipe we followed when installing MariaDB, and the plugin will be enabled.

How it works...

The **Feedback** plugin is turned off by default. Adding `feedback=on` to the configuration file lets MariaDB know that we want it enabled.

This plugin automatically sends anonymous usage data to the MariaDB developers, which helps them to prioritize development resources. Examples of the type of data it collects includes what operating system we're running, how much memory we have, what plugins we have enabled, and so on.

The collected data can be viewed at `http://mariadb.org/feedback_plugin`.

There's more...

The **Feedback** plugin can be customized in various ways. For example, we can choose the data that we want to send back. We can also configure the plugin to send the data to our own server instead of sending it to the MariaDB developers.

See also

▶ The full documentation of the **Feedback** plugin is available at `https://mariadb.com/kb/en/feedback-plugin/`

Switching between InnoDB and XtraDB

By default, MariaDB uses the XtraDB storage engine in place of InnoDB because it contains improvements to InnoDB that are useful for all users. If we want to use the InnoDB storage engine for some reason, it is easy to do so.

How to do it...

Let's get started by following the ensuing steps:

1. Stop MariaDB by following the directions in the recipe we followed when installing MariaDB.

2. Open our `my.cnf` or `my.ini` file in a text editor such as Vim, Emacs, TextWrangler, or Notepad. On Windows, there is a helpful link under the MariaDB group that will automatically open the `my.ini` file in Notepad. On Linux, the `my.cnf` file is located at either `/etc/mysql/my.cnf` or `/etc/my.cnf` depending on the Linux distribution we are using.

3. Add the following lines of code to the `[mysqld]` section of the system's `my.cnf` or `my.ini` file. If the section does not exist, add it.

   ```
   ignore_builtin_innodb
   plugin_load=innodb=ha_innodb.so
   ```

4. Save the file and then start MariaDB by following the instructions in the recipe we followed when installing MariaDB.

How it works...

To check if we are using InnoDB or XtraDB, we use the `SHOW ENGINES` command. If we are using XtraDB, the InnoDB line of the output will begin as shown in the following command line:

```
| InnoDB | DEFAULT | Percona-XtraDB,Supports...
```

And, if we are using the InnoDB plugin, the InnoDB line will begin as shown in the following command line:

```
| InnoDB | DEFAULT | Supports...
```

Only one of the storage engines can be loaded at one time. It is not possible to have both the InnoDB and XtraDB plugins loaded at the same time.

See also

- ▶ Refer to another InnoDB- and XtraDB-specific recipe, *Using extended keys with InnoDB and XtraDB*, in *Chapter 3, Optimizing and Tuning MariaDB*
- ▶ The InnoDB and XtraDB section of the MariaDB Knowledgebase has lots of great information on these storage engines, which is available at `https://mariadb.com/kb/en/xtradb-and-innodb/`

Creating a backup user

It is a bad idea to use a super user like root for making backups. One main reason is that backups often run automatically, and so the password has to be stored somewhere (for example, in the `my.cnf` file). If the user that is being used for backups has full access to the database, it could be abused, or an error in a backup script could cause all sorts of trouble.

In this recipe, we will create a backup user with the minimum permissions necessary to run both the `mysqldump` and `XtraBackup` programs.

How to do it...

Let's get started by following the ensuing steps:

1. Launch the `mysql` command-line client.
2. Create the backup user. For this recipe, we'll call the user `backupuser` and give the user the password `p455w0rd`. The user can be named anything we wish, and the password should definitely be changed to something unique:

   ```
   CREATE USER 'backupuser'@'localhost'
       IDENTIFIED BY 'p455w0rd';
   ```

3. Next, we will grant our new user a minimal set of permissions, just enough so that it can make backups as follows:

   ```
   GRANT SELECT, SHOW VIEW, LOCK TABLES, RELOAD,
       REPLICATION CLIENT
       ON *.* TO 'backupuser'@'localhost';
   ```

4. Lastly, we will use the `FLUSH PRIVILEGES` command to force MariaDB to reread the privileges table, which is always a good idea after granting new privileges to a user.

   ```
   FLUSH PRIVILEGES;
   ```

How it works...

There's no need for the user we use to make backups in order to have every privilege on our databases. They only need a specific subset. For example, they don't need the `INSERT` or `ALTER TABLE` privileges since backup users just need to read the tables in our databases. The set of privileges in this recipe are enough for both the `XtraBackup` and `mysqldump` programs, and will likely be sufficient for other backup programs as well.

Making backups with XtraBackup

XtraBackup is a backup tool from Percona.

Getting ready

The precompiled XtraBackup packages are only available for Linux. Percona provides both YUM and APT repositories.

You can follow the XtraBackup installation instructions on the Percona website available at `http://www.percona.com/doc/percona-xtrabackup/`. Also, create a backup user by following the instructions in the *Creating a backup user* recipe.

How to do it...

Let's get started by following the ensuing steps:

1. Run the following command by changing the `--user`, `--password`, and `/path/to/backups` parts to the correct values:

    ```
    sudo innobackupex --user=backupuser \
        --password=p455w0rd /path/to/backups
    ```

2. The `innobackupex` script will call `XtraBackup` and copy all of the files to a timestamped subdirectory of the specified backup directory. When it has finished, if everything went well, it will print a line similar to the following line of output:

    ```
    130729 12:05:12  innobackupex: completed OK!
    ```

How it works...

The `innobackupex` script is a wrapper around `XtraBackup`. By itself, the `XtraBackup` program only backs up InnoDB and XtraDB databases. When the `innobackupex` script is used, MyISAM, Aria, and other non-InnoDB tables are also backed up.

There's more...

Backups created by `XtraBackup` and the `innobackupex` scripts are not ready to be used to restore a database as is. Backups must be prepared prior to restoring. There are also some things that we need to be aware of when backing up to an NFS-mounted disk.

Restoring from a backup

In order to prepare an `XtraBackup` backup to be restored, we must first prepare it as follows:

```
sudo innobackupex --apply-log /path/to/backups
```

Then, we can restore it with the following command:

```
sudo innobackupex --copy-back /path/to/backup
```

As with running the script for the initial backup, look for the `completed OK!` message at the end of the preparing and restoring steps.

The `innobackupex` script will refuse to overwrite the files in the `data` directory, so it must be empty before a restore can happen.

As a final step, we will also likely need to fix permissions on the restored files with something similar to the following command:

```
sudo chown -R mysql:mysql /var/lib/mysql
```

XtraBackup and NFS

When backing up to an NFS-mounted volume, check to make sure that it is mounted with the `sync` option. Data may appear corrupt if our NFS volume is mounted with the `async` option. Refer to the XtraBackup documentation for more information.

Making backups with mysqldump

The `mysqldump` program is included with MariaDB and works well as a simple backup tool.

Getting ready

Create a backup user by following the instructions in the *Creating a backup user* recipe.

How to do it...

Let's get started by following the ensuing steps:

1. To make a complete backup of all the data to a file named `my-backup.sql`, run the following command:

   ```
   mysqldump --user=backupuser -p \
     --all-databases > my-backup.sql
   ```

2. If it completes successfully, `mysqldump` will place a line similar to the following command at the end of the output file:

   ```
   -- Dump completed on <date> <time>
   ```

3. If a dump fails, an error message will be printed to the screen and the data in the backup file will end right before the error took place. Checking both the error message and the end of the backup file can give us important clues to figure out the failure.

How it works...

The `mysqldump` program generates backups in SQL formatted text. These backups can then be restored to the same MariaDB install, to a different MariaDB server, or because they are in SQL format, to a different database altogether.

Depending on the sizes of the databases in our database server, and whether we choose to backup all of the databases or just one or two, the backup file created by `mysqldump` could potentially be very large. We need to keep this in mind when using this program.

There's more...

The `mysqldump` program has many options. We will discuss some of the most useful ones here.

--add-drop-database

The `--add-drop-database` option causes `mysqldump` to add SQL commands to the backup output to drop a given database and then recreate it prior to restoring the data. This helps us to prevent duplicate data from being written to the database.

--add-drop-table

Similar to the previous option, the `--add-drop-table` option causes `mysqldump` to add SQL commands to the backup output in order to drop the tables prior to recreating them and inserting data.

--add-locks

The `--add-locks` option surrounds the table output of the backup with `LOCK TABLES` and `UNLOCK TABLES` statements. When restoring from a backup, locking the tables speeds up the restore.

Checking and optimizing tables automatically with mysqlcheck and cron

The `mysqlcheck` command can check, repair, and optimize tables. When paired with cron, this bit of regular maintenance can be automated. This recipe is only for Linux operating systems.

How to do it...

Let's get started by following the ensuing steps:

1. Create a new user on the server or choose an existing user account. For this recipe, we'll say that we have a user called `sysuser` created just for this purpose.

2. Create a user in MariaDB that has `SELECT` and `INSERT` privileges on all the databases. Those are the privileges that are needed for `mysqlcheck`. For this recipe, we'll name this user `maint`.

3. Create a `.my.cnf` file at `/home/sysuser/.my.cnf` (or wherever sysuser's home is located) with the following contents:

```
[client]
user = maint
password=maintuserpassword
```

4. Next, change the mode of the `.my.cnf` file to only be readable by the sysuser:

```
sudo chmod 600 /home/sysuser/.my.cnf
```

5. Add the following lines of code to `/etc/cron.d/mariadb` (create the file if it doesn't exist):

```
# m h dom mon dow user command
15 23 * * 1   sysuser /usr/bin/mysqlcheck -A --auto-repair
15 23 * * 2-7 sysuser /usr/bin/mysqlcheck -A --optimize
```

How it works...

The `/etc/cron.d/` folder contains cron snippet files. The cron daemon looks in this folder and executes the commands just as it does for the user `crontab` files. The one key difference is that because this is a system folder and not a user folder, we need to tell cron which user to run the command as, which we do between the `datetime` command and the actual command.

When `mysqlcheck` is run, like other MariaDB utilities, it will automatically check for a `.my.cnf` file in the home directory of the user running it and will pick up options in the `[client]` section of that file. This is a perfect place to stick the login information as we can make the file readable only by that user. This way, we don't need to specify the username and password of our database maintenance user on the command line.

Two commands are run by the recipe. The first command runs only once a week, and it checks every database and autorepairs any problems it finds. The second command runs every other day of the week and optimizes the tables in every database.

There's more...

The `mysqlcheck` program has many options. Refer to `https://mariadb.com/kb/en/mysqlcheck/` or run the command with `--help` for a complete list.

One thing to note is that the `--analyze` (`-a`), `--check` (`-c`), `--optimize` (`-o`), and `--repair` (`-r`) options are exclusive. Only the last option on the command line will be used.

Security

Using a nonroot user to run `mysqlcheck` automatically is a good security precaution. To make the sysuser even more secure, lock the account so that it can't log in. Refer to our distribution documentation for how to do this.

Using progress reporting in the mysql client

One relatively unknown feature of MariaDB is the ability of the client to show progress reports for long commands.

How to do it...

Let's get started by following the ensuing steps:

1. There's nothing to configure as progress reporting is turned on by default and works with the ALTER TABLE, ADD INDEX, DROP INDEX, and LOAD DATA INFILE commands. It also works with the CHECK TABLE, REPAIR TABLE, ANALYZE TABLE, and OPTIMIZE TABLE commands when using the Aria storage engine. For example, if we needed to change a large table from using the MyISAM storage engine to the Aria storage engine, it might look similar to the following command:

```
MariaDB [test]> ALTER TABLE my_big_table engine=aria;
Stage: 1 of 2 'copy to tmp table'  29.26% of stage done
```

2. The progress report line will update every 5 seconds until the operation is complete.

How it works...

For the clients that support it, mysqld (the MariaDB server) sends progress report messages every 5 seconds. The mysql command-line client supports it, as does the mytop shell script included with MariaDB.

You can easily add support for progress messages on other clients by following the instructions at https://mariadb.com/kb/en/progress-reporting/. If our favorite client application does not support progress reporting, encourage the developers to add it!

There's more...

We can change the default 5 second update by setting the progress_report_time variable to a value greater than 5. Values ranging from 1 to 5 are ignored.

Disabling progress reporting

To disable progress reporting, set the progress_report_time variable to 0 or use the --disable-progress-reports option when launching the mysql client. Progress reporting is automatically disabled in batch mode.

Progress reporting in mytop

The mytop script included with MariaDB shows the progress of long running commands in the '%' column.

2
Diving Deep into MariaDB

In this chapter, we will cover the following recipes:

- ▶ Importing the data exported by mysqldump
- ▶ Using SHOW EXPLAIN with running queries
- ▶ Using LIMIT ROWS EXAMINED
- ▶ Using INSTALL SONAME
- ▶ Producing HTML output
- ▶ Producing XML output
- ▶ Migrating a table from MyISAM to Aria
- ▶ Migrating a table from MyISAM or Aria to InnoDB or XtraDB

Introduction

Now that we've got our feet wet with MariaDB, it's time to dive deeper and experiment with some of the useful features of MariaDB.

Importing the data exported by mysqldump

Importing data from a `mysqldump` backup is easy and quick. In this recipe, we'll import a backup of the **Internet Speculative Fiction Database** (**ISFDB**). This database is licensed under the Creative Commons Attribution license (CC BY) which allows us to use this database for this recipe and many of the other recipes in this book.

How to do it...

1. Go to `http://www.isfdb.org/wiki/index.php/ISFDB_Downloads` and download the latest MySQL 5.5 compatible file. The file will be almost 80 megabytes and will be named with the date the backup was made. In this recipe, we'll be using the `backup-MySQL-55-2014-02-22.zip` file. We can download that file or a more recent one. If we do use a more recent file, we'll need to update the names in the following steps.

2. After the download finishes, we unzip the file using the following command:

    ```
    unzip backup-MySQL-55-2014-02-22.zip
    ```

3. When unzipped, the file will be over 300 megabytes.

4. Our next step is to launch the `mysql` command-line client and create a database to import into:

    ```
    CREATE DATABASE isfdb;
    ```

5. After creating the database, quit the `mysql` command-line client.

6. Lastly, we import the file into MariaDB using the following command:

    ```
    mysql isfdb < backup-MySQL-55-2014-02-22
    ```

7. Depending on the speed of our computer processor, the size of the memory we have, and the speed of our hard drive, the file will be imported in a time span of a few seconds to a couple of minutes, and the `isfdb` database will be full of data tables. We can now go ahead and take a look at it if we're interested.

Downloading the example code

You can download the example code files for all Packt books you have purchased from your account at `http://www.packtpub.com`. If you purchased this book elsewhere, you can visit `http://www.packtpub.com/support` and register to have the files e-mailed directly to you.

How it works...

The special character < sends the contents of the `backup-2014-02-22` file to the `mysql` command. The `mysql` command, in turn, is set to connect to the `isfdb` database we just created, so that is where the data goes. In addition to the data, the backup file contains the necessary commands to create all of the necessary tables.

There's more...

To keep the recipe short, I didn't put down any of the usual options for the `mysql` command-line client. Depending on how we have things set up, we may need to specify the user (`-u`), password (`-p`), host (`-h`), or other options. We just need to be sure to put them before the name of the database (`isfdb` in the recipe).

See also

▶ The full documentation of the `mysqldump` command can be found at `https://kb.askmonty.org/en/mysqldump/`

Using SHOW EXPLAIN with running queries

The `SHOW EXPLAIN` feature was introduced in MariaDB 10.0. It enables us to get an `EXPLAIN` (that is, a description of the query plan) of the query running in a given thread.

Getting ready

Import the `ISFDB` database as described in the *Importing the data exported by mysqldump* recipe of this chapter.

How to do it...

1. Open a terminal window and launch the `mysql` command-line client and connect to the `isfdb` database.

   ```
   mysql isfdb
   ```

2. Next, we open another terminal window and launch another instance of the `mysql` command-line client.

3. Run the following command in the first window:

   ```
   ALTER TABLE title_relationships DROP KEY titles;
   ```

4. Next, in the first window, start the following example query:

   ```
   SELECT titles.title_id AS ID,
          titles.title_title AS Title,
          authors.author_legalname AS Name,
          (SELECT COUNT(DISTINCT title_relationships.review_id)
            FROM title_relationships
   ```

```
                        WHERE title_relationships.title_id = titles.title_id)
            AS reviews
        FROM   titles,authors,canonical_author
        WHERE
                (SELECT COUNT(DISTINCT title_relationships.review_id)
                    FROM title_relationships
                    WHERE title_relationships.title_id = titles.title_id)>=10
            AND canonical_author.author_id = authors.author_id
            AND canonical_author.title_id=titles.title_id
            AND titles.title_parent=0 ;
```

5. Wait for at least a minute and then run the following query to look for the details of the query that we executed in step 4 and QUERY_ID for that query:

```
SELECT INFO, TIME, ID, QUERY_ID
FROM INFORMATION_SCHEMA.PROCESSLIST
WHERE TIME > 60\G
```

6. Run SHOW EXPLAIN in the second window (replace id in the following command line with the numeric ID that we discovered in step 5):

```
SHOW EXPLAIN FOR id
```

7. Run the following command in the second window to kill the query running in the first window (replace query_id in the following command line with the numeric QUERY_ID number that we discovered in step 5):

```
KILL QUERY ID query_id;
```

8. In the first window, reverse the change we made in step 3 using the following command:

```
ALTER TABLE title_relationships ADD KEY titles (title_id);
```

How it works...

The SHOW EXPLAIN statement allows us to obtain information about how MariaDB executes a long-running statement. This is very useful for identifying bottlenecks in our database.

The query in this recipe will execute efficiently only if it touches the indexes in our data. So for demonstration purposes, we will first sabotage the title_relationships table by removing the titles index. This causes our query to unnecessarily iterate through hundreds of thousands of rows and generally take far too long to complete. The output of steps 3 and 4 will look similar to the following screenshot:

```
                              daniel@pippin ~
MariaDB [isfdb]> ALTER TABLE title_relationships DROP KEY titles;
Query OK, 83389 rows affected (0.30 sec)
Records: 83389  Duplicates: 0  Warnings: 0

MariaDB [isfdb]> SELECT titles.title_id AS ID,
    ->          titles.title_title AS Title,
    ->          authors.author_legalname AS Name,
    ->          (SELECT COUNT(DISTINCT title_relationships.review_id)
    ->            FROM title_relationships
    ->            WHERE title_relationships.title_id = titles.title_id)
    ->      AS reviews
    -> FROM   titles,authors,canonical_author
    -> WHERE
    ->          (SELECT COUNT(DISTINCT title_relationships.review_id)
    ->            FROM title_relationships
    ->            WHERE title_relationships.title_id = titles.title_id) >= 10
    ->       AND canonical_author.author_id = authors.author_id
    ->       AND canonical_author.title_id=titles.title_id
    ->       AND titles.title_parent=0 ;
```

While our sabotaged query is running, and after waiting for at least a minute, we switch to another window and look for all queries that have been running for longer than 60 seconds. Our sabotaged query will likely be the only one in the output. From this output, we get ID and QUERY_ID. The output of the command will look like the following with the ID and QUERY_ID as the last two items:

```
                              daniel@pippin ~
MariaDB [(none)]> SELECT INFO, TIME, ID, QUERY_ID
    ->    FROM INFORMATION_SCHEMA.PROCESSLIST
    ->    WHERE TIME > 60\G
*************************** 1. row ***************************
    INFO: SELECT titles.title_id AS ID,
       titles.title_title AS Title,
       authors.author_legalname AS Name,
       (SELECT COUNT(DISTINCT title_relationships.review_id)
         FROM title_relationships
         WHERE title_relationships.title_id = titles.title_id)
   AS reviews
FROM   titles,authors,canonical_author
WHERE
       (SELECT COUNT(DISTINCT title_relationships.review_id)
         FROM title_relationships
         WHERE title_relationships.title_id = titles.title_id) >= 10
     AND canonical_author.author_id = authors.author_id
     AND canonical_author.title_id=titles.title_id
     AND titles.title_parent=0
    TIME: 195
      ID: 94
QUERY_ID: 1016
1 row in set (0.00 sec)

MariaDB [(none)]>
```

Next, we use the ID number to execute SHOW EXPLAIN for our query. Incidentally, our query looks up all titles in the database that have 10 or more reviews and displays the title, author, and the number of reviews that the title has. The EXPLAIN for our query will look similar to the following:

An easy-to-read version of this EXPLAIN is available at
https://mariadb.org/ea/8v65g.

Looking at rows 4 and 5 of EXPLAIN, it's easy to see why our query runs for so long. These two rows are dependent subqueries of the primary query (the first row). In the first query, we see that 117044 rows will be searched, and then, for the two dependent subqueries, MariaDB searches through 83389 additional rows, twice. Ouch.

If we were analyzing a slow query in the real world at this point, we would fix the query to not have such an inefficient subquery, or we would add a KEY to our table to make the subquery efficient. If we're part of a larger development team, we could send the output of SHOW EXPLAIN and the query to the appropriate people to easily and accurately show them what the problem is with the query. In our case, we know exactly what to do; we will add back the KEY that we removed earlier.

For fun, after adding back the KEY, we could rerun the query and the SHOW EXPLAIN command to see the difference that having the KEY in place makes. We'll have to be quick though, as with the KEY there, the query will only take a few seconds to complete (depending on the speed of our computer).

There's more...

The output of SHOW EXPLAIN is always accompanied by a warning. The purpose of this warning is to show us the command that is being run. After running SHOW EXPLAIN on a process ID, we simply issue SHOW WARNINGS\G and we will see what SQL statement the process ID is running:

```
                       daniel@pippin ~
MariaDB [(none)]> SHOW WARNINGS\G
*************************** 1. row ***************************
   Level: Note
    Code: 1003
 Message: SELECT titles.title_id AS ID,
        titles.title_title AS Title,
        authors.author_legalname AS Name,
        (SELECT COUNT(DISTINCT title_relationships.review_id)
          FROM title_relationships
          WHERE title_relationships.title_id = titles.title_id)
   AS reviews
FROM   titles,authors,canonical_author
WHERE
        (SELECT COUNT(DISTINCT title_relationships.review_id)
          FROM title_relationships
          WHERE title_relationships.title_id = titles.title_id) >= 10
    AND canonical_author.author_id = authors.author_id
    AND canonical_author.title_id=titles.title_id
    AND titles.title_parent=0
1 row in set (0.00 sec)

MariaDB [(none)]>
```

This is useful for very long-running commands that after their start, takes a long time to execute, and then returns back at a time where we might not remember the command we started.

 In the examples of this recipe, we're using "\G" as the delimiter instead of the more common ";" so that the data fits the page better. We can use either one.

See also

- Some long-running queries can consume more resources than they are worth, and in those cases, the *Using LIMIT ROWS EXAMINED* recipe is helpful

- The full documentation of the KILL QUERY ID command can be found at https://mariadb.com/kb/en/data-manipulation-kill-connection-query/

- The full documentation of the SHOW EXPLAIN command can be found at https://mariadb.com/kb/en/show-explain/

Using LIMIT ROWS EXAMINED

The LIMIT ROWS EXAMINED clause is a good way to minimize the overhead of a very large or otherwise expensive query if we don't necessarily want or need to search every row in a large table or set of tables.

Getting ready

Import the ISFDB database as described in the *Importing the data exported by mysqldump* recipe, earlier in this chapter.

How to do it...

1. Open a terminal window and launch the mysql command-line client and connect to the isfdb database.

2. Run the following query from the *Using SHOW EXPLAIN with running queries* recipe, with one small addition at the end:

```
SELECT titles.title_id AS ID,
       titles.title_title AS Title,
       authors.author_legalname AS Name,
       (SELECT COUNT(DISTINCT title_relationships.review_id)
         FROM title_relationships
         WHERE title_relationships.title_id = titles.title_id)
                                           AS reviews
FROM   titles,authors,canonical_author
WHERE
       (SELECT COUNT(DISTINCT title_relationships.review_id)
         FROM title_relationships
         WHERE title_relationships.title_id = titles.title_id)
                                           >= 10
    AND canonical_author.author_id = authors.author_id
    AND canonical_author.title_id=titles.title_id
    AND titles.title_parent=0
LIMIT ROWS EXAMINED 10000;
```

How it works...

The `LIMIT` clause allows us to reduce the output of a `SELECT` query, but the full query is still run. On very large tables, because the full query is still being run, it may consume more resources than we would like. In MariaDB, we can use `LIMIT ROWS EXAMINED` to specify the number of rows we want the server to examine when executing our statement, thus minimizing the resources the query needs to use during execution.

This feature was designed to benefit queries running in something like a production web application where speed is critically important, possibly more so than having a complete answer.

`LIMIT ROWS EXAMINED` is also useful when testing a new query that we suspect will take a long time to run and consume a lot of resources. It's like testing on a subset of our full data without having to actually export and set up such a set. Instead, we can test on a full copy of our data, but with limits so that our testing is faster.

There's more...

Just because we are limiting the number of rows examined doesn't mean we can't also limit the output. We also need to be aware of the warnings this command gives.

Using LIMIT with LIMIT ROWS EXAMINED

When using `LIMIT ROWS EXAMINED`, we can still `LIMIT` the output to a specific number of rows. For example, we can examine 10000 rows and limit the output to the first 100 using the following command line:

```
LIMIT 100 ROWS EXAMINED 10000
```

Warning of incomplete results

With the limit set to 10000 rows, the query in this recipe completes quickly, but it comes with the following warning:

```
Query execution was interrupted. The query examined at least 10002
rows, which exceeds LIMIT ROWS EXAMINED (10000). The query result
may be incomplete.
```

This warning is understandable. We told the server we only wanted it to examine 10000 rows, and so it did, and then quit. But the full query needs to examine many more rows than that, and so the results we received are incomplete, and the server is letting us know.

Using INSTALL SONAME

The `INSTALL SONAME` command is used to install plugins in MariaDB. In this recipe, we'll install the Cassandra storage engine.

How to do it...

1. Connect to MariaDB using the `mysql` command-line client with a user that has the `INSERT` privilege on the `mysql.plugins` table. The root user has this privilege, but other users might as well.

2. Install the Cassandra storage engine plugin using the following command line:

   ```
   INSTALL SONAME 'ha_cassandra';
   ```

3. Issue the `SHOW plugins;` command and look for the following text:

   ```
   | CASSANDRA | ACTIVE | STORAGE ENGINE | ha_cassandra.so | GPL |
   ```

4. Next, issue the `SHOW STORAGE ENGINES;` command and look for the following text:

   ```
   | CASSANDRA | YES | Cassandra storage engine| NO | NO | NO |
   ```

5. The preceding output indicates that the Cassandra storage engine is installed and ready to go. The three `NO` columns are about transactions, distributed `XA` transactions, and `savepoints`, respectively. All three are features that the Cassandra storage engine does not support.

How it works...

When this command is run, the server looks in the configured plugin directory and loads the plugin with that name. We do not need to specify the file extension. The actual name of the `ha_cassandra` file will either be `ha_cassandra.dll` or `ha_cassandra.so` on Windows and Linux respectively.

There's more...

Installing plugins is not very difficult in MariaDB but there are some things that can trip us up if we're not careful.

Plugin names versus filenames

The name of a given plugin is defined in the data structures inside the plugin. The filename is the name of the file that contains the plugin. The two are similar, but they are not the same. For example, the name of the Cassandra storage engine plugin is CASSANDRA and the filename is `ha_cassandra.so`. The name is case insensitive, so when referring to it we can use CASSANDRA, Cassandra, cassandra, or even CaSsAnDrA if we want. The filename, on the other hand, is case sensitive if our underlying filesystem is case sensitive.

INSTALL SONAME versus INSTALL PLUGIN

The `INSTALL SONAME` command is just a variation of the `INSTALL PLUGIN` command. The main difference is that `INSTALL PLUGIN` requires two sets of information, the name and the filename, and `INSTALL SONAME` just needs the filename. The filename must be quoted. Here is the recipe using `INSTALL PLUGIN`:

```
INSTALL PLUGIN Cassandra SONAME 'ha_cassandra';
```

Apart from being shorter, `INSTALL SONAME` is no different from `INSTALL PLUGIN`, functionality-wise.

See also

▸ The complete documentation of the `INSTALL SONAME` command can be found at `https://mariadb.com/kb/en/install-soname/`

▸ The complete documentation of the Cassandra storage engine can be found at `https://kb.askmonty.org/en/cassandra/`

Producing HTML output

The `mysql` command-line client has several different output options. One of these is HTML.

Getting ready

Import the `ISFDB` database as described in the *Importing the data exported by mysqldump* recipe in this chapter. Create a file called `isfdb-001.sql` using the following command line:

```
SELECT * FROM authors LIMIT 100;
```

We could put whatever commands we want in this file, or give it a different name, but this works for the purposes of this recipe.

How to do it...

1. Open a terminal and navigate to where we saved the `isfdb-001.sql` file.

2. Issue the following command on the command line (not from within the `mysql` command-line client, but by calling the client with some special options):

   ```
   mysql --html isfdb < isfdb-001.sql > isfdb-001.html
   ```

3. Execute either a `dir` or `ls` command and we'll see that now there is a file named `isfdb-001.html` in the directory.

4. We can now either open the newly created `isfdb-001.html` file in our favorite text editor, or view it in a web browser, such as Firefox, Chrome, or Opera.

How it works...

When the `--html` flag is passed on the command line, the `mysql` command-line client will spit out an HTML table instead of a regular output; no headers, footers, or DOCTYPE, just a table with the results as one long string.

On the command line, we use the `<` and `>` redirectors to read in the `isfdb-001.sql` file and then to direct the output to the `isfdb-001.html` file, respectively.

There's more...

The HTML output that the `mysql` command-line client produces is not pretty. What's more, it's not a completely valid HTML file as there's no `DOCTYPE`, no `<head>` section, no `<body>` section, no `<title>`, and so on. The file we created begins with a `<TABLE>` tag and ends with a closing `</TABLE>` tag. And yes, all the tags use the old uppercase style of writing HTML code.

In Linux, there is an easy way to remedy this using the Tidy program. If it is not already installed, it is easy to do so using our package manager. To clean up our HTML, add spaces and indentation, change the case of the tags to lowercase, and add a DOCTYPE and all the necessary sections. We will simply modify our recipe to the following command line:

```
mysql --html isfdb < isfdb-001.sql | tidy -q -i -o isfdb-001.html
```

Tidy will detect the appropriate DOCTYPE, change the case of the tags, indent the code, and add in the missing sections.

Of course, even tidied up, HTML output is of limited use. It is, however, something the `mysql` command-line client can do.

See also

▸   The full documentation of the `mysql` command-line client can be found at https://kb.askmonty.org/en/mysql-command-line-client/

Producing XML output

The `mysql` command-line client has several different output options. One of these is XML.

Getting ready

Import the `ISFDB` database as described in the *Importing the data exported by mysqldump* recipe in this chapter. Create a file called `isfdb-001.sql` using the following command line:

```
SELECT * FROM authors LIMIT 100;
```

We could put whatever commands we want in this file, or give it a different name, but this works for the purposes of this recipe. This file has the same name and contents as the file used in the previous recipe. If we've already completed that recipe, we can just reuse the same file.

How to do it...

1. Open a terminal and navigate to where we saved the `isfdb-001.sql` file.

2. Issue the following command on the command line (not from within the `mysql` command-line client, but by calling the client with some special options):

   ```
   mysql --xml isfdb < isfdb-001.sql > isfdb-001.xml
   ```

3. Execute either a `dir` or `ls` command and we'll see that there is now a file named `isfdb-001.xml` in the directory.

4. To see the contents of the file, open it with our favorite text editor or an XML viewer.

How it works...

When the `--xml` flag is passed on the command line, the `mysql` command-line client will output a well-formed XML file, instead of a regular output.

On the command line we use the < and > redirectors to read in the `isfdb-001.sql` file and then to direct the output to the `isfdb-001.xml` file, respectively.

See also

▶ The full documentation of the `mysql` command-line client can be found at `https://kb.askmonty.org/en/mysql-command-line-client/`

Migrating a table from MyISAM to Aria

MariaDB ships with the MyISAM and Aria storage engines, among many others. The main difference between these two is that Aria is *crash safe*, whereas MyISAM is not. Being crash safe means that an Aria table can recover from catastrophic power loss or other unexpected failures in a much better way than a MyISAM table can. If we use MyISAM tables, an easy upgrade is to convert them to Aria tables.

Getting ready

Import the `ISFDB` database as described in the *Importing the data exported by mysqldump* recipe in this chapter.

How to do it...

1. Open the `mysql` command-line client and connect to the `isfdb` database.

2. Run the following command line:

    ```
    ALTER TABLE authors ENGINE=Aria;
    ```

3. The `ALTER` command will then change the table so that it uses the Aria storage engine.

4. After it has finished, a message similar to the following will be displayed:

    ```
    Query OK, 110829 rows affected (3.14 sec)

    Records: 110829  Duplicates: 0  Warnings: 0
    ```

5. If our system is older or is under heavy load and it takes longer than 5 seconds for `ALTER TABLE` to complete, we'll see a progress message letting us know how much of the task has been completed, updated every 5 seconds, until the task is finished.

How it works...

The `ALTER TABLE` command changes a table in two stages. First, it creates a new table identical in every way to the old table, except that the new table has the changes specified by the command. In our case, the only change is to use the Aria storage engine instead of the MyISAM storage engine. Then, the command copies all of the data to the new table.

In the second stage, `ALTER TABLE` removes the old table and renames the new table with the name of the old table.

On a table like `authors` that only has around a hundred thousand rows, the conversion is quick and easy; however, on a table with several billion rows, the conversion process will take significantly longer.

See also

▶   The full documentation of the `ALTER TABLE` command can be found at `https://kb.askmonty.org/en/alter-table/`

Migrating a table from MyISAM or Aria to InnoDB or XtraDB

The default storage engine of MariaDB is XtraDB, which is an enhanced version of InnoDB.

Getting ready

Import the ISFDB database as described in the *Importing the data exported by mysqldump* recipe in this chapter.

How to do it...

1. Open the mysql command-line client and connect to the isfdb database.

2. Run the following command line:

    ```
    ALTER TABLE awards ENGINE=InnoDB;
    ```

3. After the command line gets executed, a message similar to the following will be displayed:

    ```
    Query OK, 33102 rows affected (5.37 sec)

    Records: 33102  Duplicates: 0  Warnings: 0
    ```

4. If our system is older or is under heavy load and it takes longer than 5 seconds for the ALTER TABLE command line execution to complete, we'll see a progress message letting us know how much of the task has been completed. The message gets updated every 5 seconds, until the task is finished.

How it works...

The ALTER TABLE command converts the table over in two stages. First, it creates a new table, identical in every way to the old table, except that the new table uses the InnoDB or XtraDB storage engine (whichever we have configured as the active one) and copies all of the data to the new table.

In the second stage, ALTER TABLE removes the old table and renames the new table with the name of the old table.

On a table like awards that only has thirty thousand or more rows, the conversion is quick and easy; however, on a table with several billion rows, the conversion process will take significantly longer.

There's more...

Before converting all of the tables in a database from MyISAM or Aria to InnoDB/XtraDB, be aware that InnoDB/XtraDB uses more memory when running for the same amount of activity. Make sure our server has the memory capacity to handle it.

See also

 ▶ The full documentation for InnoDB and XtraDB can be found at
   `https://kb.askmonty.org/en/xtradb-and-innodb/`

 ▶ Full documentation of the ALTER TABLE command can be found at
   `https://kb.askmonty.org/en/alter-table/`

3
Optimizing and Tuning MariaDB

In this chapter, we will cover the following recipes:

- Using SHOW STATUS to check whether a feature is being used
- Controlling MariaDB optimizer strategies
- Using extended Keys with InnoDB and XtraDB
- Configuring the Aria two-step deadlock detection
- Configuring the MyISAM segmented key cache
- Configuring threadpool
- Configuring the Aria pagecache
- Optimizing queries with the subquery cache
- Optimizing semijoin subqueries
- Creating an index
- Creating a full-text index
- Removing an index
- Using JOINs
- Using microseconds in DATETIME columns
- Updating the DATETIME and TIMESTAMP columns automatically

Introduction

This chapter contains recipes for configuring and using various optimization and tuning-related features of MariaDB. This chapter is not meant as a complete or even a partial MariaDB optimization and tuning guide; it only contains recipes related to the topic.

Using SHOW STATUS to check if a feature is being used

The SHOW STATUS command shows information about the server. This includes things such as the number of bytes of data received and sent by the server, the number of connections served, the number of rows read, and so on. The command can also be used to check whether a feature has been enabled or is being used.

How to do it...

1. Launch the mysql command-line client and connect to our MariaDB database server.

2. Uninstall the Cassandra storage engine with:

   UNINSTALL SONAME 'ha_cassandra.so';

3. MariaDB will either respond with a Query OK message (if the Cassandra storage engine was installed and has now been uninstalled) or it will give the SONAME ha_cassandra.so does not exist error (if the Cassandra storage engine was not installed). Either of the messages is ok.

4. Issue the following SHOW STATUS command to see if the Cassandra storage engine is installed. The result will be an Empty set, which means that it is not installed:

   SHOW STATUS LIKE 'Cassandra%';

5. Install the Cassandra storage engine with the following command, and the result will be Query OK:

   INSTALL SONAME 'ha_cassandra.so';

6. Issue the SHOW STATUS command from step 3 again. This time, an output similar to the following screenshot will be displayed:

```
daniel@pippin ~
MariaDB [(none)]> SHOW STATUS LIKE 'Cassandra%';
Empty set (0.00 sec)

MariaDB [(none)]> INSTALL SONAME 'ha_cassandra.so';
Query OK, 0 rows affected (0.01 sec)

MariaDB [(none)]> SHOW STATUS LIKE 'Cassandra%';
+--------------------------------------+-------+
| Variable_name                        | Value |
+--------------------------------------+-------+
| Cassandra_row_inserts                | 0     |
| Cassandra_row_insert_batches         | 0     |
| Cassandra_multiget_keys_scanned      | 0     |
| Cassandra_multiget_reads             | 0     |
| Cassandra_multiget_rows_read         | 0     |
| Cassandra_network_exceptions         | 0     |
| Cassandra_timeout_exceptions         | 0     |
| Cassandra_unavailable_exceptions     | 0     |
+--------------------------------------+-------+
8 rows in set (0.00 sec)

MariaDB [(none)]>
```

How it works...

The SHOW STATUS output gives us two different sets of information in this recipe. Firstly, the actual presence of the Cassandra% variables tells us that the Cassandra storage engine is installed. Secondly, it shows us some useful information about our usage of the Cassandra storage engine since it was installed (or the server was last restarted) and if there have been any exceptions. Since we just installed the plugin, all the values will likely be zeroes unless we have an active application that used the plugin between the time when we ran the INSTALL and SHOW STATUS commands.

There's more...

In the recipe, we modified the full SHOW STATUS output to restrict it just to the information on the Cassandra storage engine by adding LIKE 'Cassandra%' to the end of the command. We could also just add the following line of command to get the complete output:

```
SHOW STATUS;
```

There is a lot of output, so it is often better to use LIKE and some text with the wildcard character (%) to shorten the output to just what we want to know.

Many plugins and storage engines in MariaDB provide the STATUS variables that are useful when we want to know how the engine or plugin is operating. However, not all do; the preferred method to check whether a given plugin or storage engine is installed is to use the SHOW PLUGINS; command.

See also

▶ The full documentation of the SHOW STATUS command is available at https://mariadb.com/kb/en/show-status/

▶ The full documentation of the SHOW PLUGINS command is available at https://mariadb.com/kb/en/show-plugins/

Controlling MariaDB optimizer strategies

Starting with MariaDB 5.3 and continuing with all major releases since, various optimizations have been introduced that improve the core performance of MariaDB. To keep upgrades as compatible and as trouble-free as possible or because it is only useful in certain limited instances, many of these optimizations are turned off by default. This recipe is about enabling optimizations which are turned off by default.

In this recipe, we will enable the **Multi-Range Read** optimizations, but the basic concepts apply to control any of the optimizer_switch flags.

How to do it...

1. Launch the mysql command-line client application and connect to our MariaDB server as the root user or as a user with the SUPER privilege.

2. Show the current status of all optimizer_switch flags with the following command:

   SELECT @@optimizer_switch\G

3. The output of the previous command will be similar to the following screenshot. There may be some differences depending on our local server settings.

```
daniel@pippin ~
MariaDB [(none)]> SELECT @@optimizer_switch\G
*************************** 1. row ***************************
@@optimizer_switch: index_merge=on,index_merge_union=on,index_merge_sort_union=o
n,index_merge_intersection=on,index_merge_sort_intersection=off,engine_condition
_pushdown=off,index_condition_pushdown=on,derived_merge=on,derived_with_keys=on,
firstmatch=on,loosescan=on,materialization=on,in_to_exists=on,semijoin=on,partia
l_match_rowid_merge=on,partial_match_table_scan=on,subquery_cache=on,mrr=off,mrr
_cost_based=off,mrr_sort_keys=off,outer_join_with_cache=on,semijoin_with_cache=o
n,join_cache_incremental=on,join_cache_hashed=on,join_cache_bka=on,optimize_join
_buffer_size=off,table_elimination=on,extended_keys=off,exists_to_in=off
1 row in set (0.00 sec)

MariaDB [(none)]>
```

4. In the output, the `mrr`, `mrr_cost_based`, and `mrr_sort_keys` flags are all set to `off`. Enable them with the following command:

```
SET optimizer_switch="mrr=on";

SET optimizer_switch="mrr_cost_based=on";

SET optimizer_switch="mrr_sort_keys=on";
```

5. Run the `SELECT` command from step 2 and confirm that the three `mrr` flags are now set to `on`.

How it works...

The `optimizer_switch` variable is basically a list of flags, which shows the status of the various available optimization strategies. When we use the `SET` command, we can turn various individual flags `off` and `on`. Any flags that we do not name in the `SET` command remain as they are.

There's more...

By default, the `SET` command only sets the variables for our current session. If we quit the client or we are disconnected for some reason and then we reconnect, the flags will be set to what they were before the changes were made.

To make our changes until MariaDB is shut down or restarted, add `GLOBAL` to the command as follows:

```
SET GLOBAL optimizer_switch="mrr=on";
```

If we want to make the change permanent, so that an optimization is either on or off permanently, we need to add it to our `my.cnf` or `my.ini` file. For example, to turn on all the `mrr` optimizations, add the following lines of code to the end of the file (or to an existing `[mysqld]` section):

```
[mysqld]
optimizer_switch = "mrr=on, mrr_cost_based=on,mrr_sort_keys=on"
```

Restart MariaDB to activate the changes.

See also

▶ The full documentation of the `optimizer_switch` is found at `https://mariadb.com/kb/en/optimizer-switch/` and `https://mariadb.com/kb/en/server-system-variables/#optimizer_switch`

▶ The documentation of the Multi-Range Read optimizations is available at `https://mariadb.com/kb/en/multi-range-read-optimization/`

Using extended keys with InnoDB and XtraDB

When creating an execution plan for a query, the MariaDB optimizer makes a cost-based decision about whether or not to use one or more indexes instead of reading through a table row-by-row. Indexes are often, but not always the faster choice. The extended key's optimization improves the index lookups for InnoDB and XtraDB tables.

How to do it...

1. Launch the `mysql` command-line client application and connect it to our MariaDB server as the root user or as a user with the `SUPER` privilege.

2. Enable the extended keys optimization with the following command:

   ```
   SET GLOBAL optimizer_switch='extended_keys=on';
   ```

3. Add the following code to our `my.cnf` or `my.ini` file (or to an existing [mysqld] section):

   ```
   [mysqld]
   ```

4. `optimizer_switch = 'extended_keys=on'` verifies that `extended_keys` is set to `on` with the following command:

   ```
   SHOW VARIABLES LIKE 'optimizer_switch'\G
   ```

How it works...

In this recipe, we turn on the `extended_keys` optimization globally for the running server and we then make the change permanent by adding it to our `my.cnf` config file. In this way, we turn the feature on, and then ensure that it stays on, without having to restart MariaDB.

There's more...

Many InnoDB or XtraDB tables have more than one key, for example, a primary key on the id column and a secondary key on the `username` column. Using the `extended_keys` optimization, MariaDB is able to create execution plans for some queries, which only touch the indexes of those keys. It does this by looking at the keys, and if all of the information that we are looking for is present, MariaDB uses that information instead of looking through tables row by row.

See also

▸ The full documentation of the extended keys optimization is available at
`https://mariadb.com/kb/en/extended-keys/`

▸ A blog post about the development of this feature is available at
`http://igors-notes.blogspot.com/2011/12/3-way-join-that-touches-only-indexes.html`

Configuring the Aria two-step deadlock detection

A deadlock is when there are two competing actions and both are waiting for the other to finish and so neither of them ever finish. The Aria storage engine is able to automatically detect and deal with deadlocks. To make effective use of this feature, we should configure it with the settings that work well for our needs.

How to do it...

1. Run the following command to show the current settings for Aria's two-step deadlock detection:

```
SHOW VARIABLES LIKE 'deadlock_%'\G
```

2. If our settings are set to the default values, the output of the previous command will be as shown in the following screenshot:

```
MariaDB [(none)]> SHOW VARIABLES LIKE 'deadlock_%'\G
*************************** 1. row ***************************
Variable_name: deadlock_search_depth_long
        Value: 15
*************************** 2. row ***************************
Variable_name: deadlock_search_depth_short
        Value: 4
*************************** 3. row ***************************
Variable_name: deadlock_timeout_long
        Value: 50000000
*************************** 4. row ***************************
Variable_name: deadlock_timeout_short
        Value: 10000
4 rows in set (0.00 sec)

MariaDB [(none)]>
```

3. Change the variables to our desired values, as follows:

```
SET GLOBAL deadlock_search_depth_short = 3;
SET GLOBAL deadlock_search_depth_long = 10;
SET GLOBAL deadlock_timeout_long = 10000000;
SET GLOBAL deadlock_timeout_short = 5000;
```

4. Make the changes permanent by adding the following lines of code to the bottom of our `my.cnf` or `my.ini` file (or to an existing `[mysqld]` section):

```
[mysqld]
deadlock_search_depth_short = 3
deadlock_search_depth_long = 10
deadlock_timeout_long = 10000000
deadlock_timeout_short = 5000
```

How it works...

If the Aria storage engine attempts to create a lock and is unable to do so, the possibility of having a deadlock exists. We only want to kill actual deadlocks and not a situation that will resolve itself in an amount of time for which we are comfortable waiting.

To detect deadlocks, whenever Aria cannot create a lock on a table, it first creates a wait-for graph of the possible deadlock with a search depth equal to `deadlock_search_depth_short`. If, after the search, the lock on the table still exists and Aria cannot determine if it is a deadlock, it will wait for the number of microseconds defined by the value of `deadlock_timeout_short` and then try again. If it is still unsuccessful, Aria will create a wait-for graph with a search depth equal to the value of `deadlock_search_depth_long`, and if a deadlock has still not been identified, Aria will wait for the number of microseconds defined by the value of `deadlock_timeout_long` and then time out with an error.

If a deadlock is detected at any point during the previous steps, Aria will determine the thread responsible for it and kill it, thereby releasing the deadlock and allowing a lock to be made and released as normal.

There's more...

It's important to remember that the `deadlock_timeout_short` and `deadlock_timeout_long` variables are defined in microseconds, not milliseconds or seconds. So a value of `10000000` is equal to ten seconds and a value of `5000` is equal to five-thousandths of a second.

For many users, the default timeout values of `50000000` (50 seconds) for the long timeout and `10000` (one-hundredth of a second) for the short timeout are perfectly adequate. The same is also true for the default values of the search depth variables. That said, it might be useful to experiment with different values if we're experiencing a lot of timeouts.

See also

▶ The full documentation of Aria two-step deadlock detection is available at
`https://mariadb.com/kb/en/aria-two-step-deadlock-detection/`

▶ The syntax documentation of the various deadlock options is available at
`https://mariadb.com/kb/en/aria-server-system-variables/`

▶ For more information on wait-for graphs and deadlocks, refer to
`http://en.wikipedia.org/wiki/Wait-for_graph` and
`http://en.wikipedia.org/wiki/Deadlock`

Configuring the MyISAM segmented key cache

We can dramatically improve the performance of our MyISAM tables by splitting the key cache into multiple segments. This is useful if we have high concurrency in our database usage (meaning there are lots of threads trying to access the key cache).

How to do it...

1. Launch the `mysql` command-line client application and connect to our MariaDB server as the root user or as a user with the `SUPER` privilege.

2. View the current number of segments with the following command:

   ```
   SHOW VARIABLES LIKE 'key_cache_segments'\G
   ```

3. Set the number of segments to `64` with the following command:

   ```
   SET GLOBAL key_cache_segments = 64;
   ```

4. Make the setting permanent by adding the following lines of code to the end of our `my.cnf` or `my.ini` file (or to an existing `[mysqld]` section):

   ```
   [mysqld]
   key_cache_segments = 64
   ```

How it works...

Whenever a MyISAM thread accesses the key cache, it needs to first acquire a lock. Lots of threads trying to get a lock on a single, monolithic key cache is a big choke point for large, busy MyISAM tables. Splitting the key cache into multiple segments reduces lock contention as a given thread only needs to lock the specific segment of the key cache that it needs, and not the entire key cache.

The `key_cache_segments` variable controls both the number of segments and checks whether or not the feature is turned on. A value of 0 (zero) turns off the feature and values of 1 or more turn on the feature and set the number of segments to use. To prevent upgrade issues with the old versions of MariaDB that don't have this feature, it is turned off by default.

There's more...

There are a few things we need to be aware of when configuring the segmented key cache.

Setting the number of segments to 1

It is possible to set the number of key cache segments to 1, which we might assume would be equal to turning the feature off, but it is not. Setting the number of segments to 1 tells MariaDB to activate and use the segmented key cache code, but with only one segment, which is actually more inefficient than the old, non-segmented code that is used when the number of segments is set to 0. So, while it is possible to set the `key_cache_segments` variable to 1, we never want to do so in practice.

Determining the optimal number of segments

The only way to determine the optimal number of segments is through testing and benchmarking with the `key_cache_segments` variable set to various values. Benchmarks run by the MariaDB developers suggest that 64 is a good number of segments to use, but this may not be true for our specific workload.

Other key cache variables

The other variables related to MyISAM key caches are `key_buffer_size`, `key_cache_age_threshold`, `key_cache_block_size`, and `key_cache_division_limit` that have all been updated to work equally well with both segmented and non-segmented key caches. There is no need to change or alter them when turning on or adjusting the segmented key cache.

See also

- The full documentation of the MyISAM segmented key cache is available at `https://mariadb.com/kb/en/segmented-key-cache/`

- The results from some segmented key cache benchmarks are available at `https://mariadb.com/kb/en/segmented-key-cache-performance/`

Configuring threadpool

Pool-of-threads, or **threadpool**, is a MariaDB feature that improves performance by pooling active threads together instead of the old **one thread per client connection** method, which does not scale well for typical web-based workloads with many short-running queries.

How to do it...

1. To enable threadpool on Linux, add the following line of code to our `my.cnf` file (or to an existing `[mysqld]` section) and then restart MariaDB:

   ```
   [mysqld]
   thread_handling = pool-of-threads
   ```

2. To enable threadpool on Windows, we don't have to do anything as it is set by default and uses the native Windows thread pooling.

3. To disable threadpool on Windows, add the following to our main `my.ini` file and then restart MariaDB:

   [mysqld]

   thread_handling = one-thread-per-connection

4. To disable threadpool on Linux, either change the `thread_handling` line to one-thread-per-connection, as on Windows, or remove the `thread_handling` line from our system's `my.cnf` file, and then restart MariaDB.

How it works...

When threadpool is enabled, MariaDB pools the threads together and automatically grows and shrinks the size of the pool as required. It also makes the best use of the underlying operating system's low-level thread pooling functionality. Threadpool is ideal if our workload includes many relatively short queries and the load is CPU-bound, as in **Online Transaction Processing** (**OLTP**) and other common website-style workloads. Threadpool is not ideal if our workload has long periods of quiet punctuated by short periods of high traffic. This can be mitigated somewhat through the use of the `thread_pool_min_threads` variable on Windows and the `thread_pool_idle_timeout` variable on Linux.

We may also run into issues with threadpool if we need our queries to always finish quickly no matter what because with threadpool, even short queries may be queued for later execution. Issues may also arise if we have many long, unyielding, and concurrent queries, such as in a data warehouse and we bump up against the limits defined by the `thread_pool_stall_limit` and `thread_pool_max_threads` variables.

There's more...

The goal for MariaDB's threadpool implementation is for it to have a good performance out of the box, with no need to tweak the settings in most cases. However, there are several settings that can be tweaked to get even better performance in some cases and with certain workloads. There are also some differences between the threadpool on Windows and Linux because of the functionality in which the underlying operating system's thread pooling works.

The thread_pool_stall_limit, thread_pool_max_threads, and extra_port variables

We can potentially run into an issue if our workload includes many long-running queries. The `thread_pool_stall_limit` variable defines, in milliseconds, how long until a running thread is considered to be stalled. The default is `500`. If there is a stalled query, MariaDB will create a new running thread, up to the value of the `thread_pool_max_threads` variable. The default value for this variable is also `500`.

If the maximum number of threads reach the `thread_pool_max_threads` limit, no new threads will be created, even if the threads are stalled. This could prevent an administrator from connecting to the server to resolve an issue with many stuck threads.

One solution to this is to set the `extra_port` variable. When this variable is defined, an additional port is opened and can be used by an administrator to connect to the server in situations where connecting using the default port is impossible. The `extra_port` variable must be set to a value different from the `port` variable.

The thread_pool_idle_timeout variable

The `thread_pool_idle_timeout` variable defines how long, in seconds, a thread should wait before it is retired. The default value is `60`. If we find that we're regularly creating new threads soon after others have been retired, it might be a good idea to increase this variable.

Pool-of-threads differences on Windows and Linux

Pool-of-threads tries to be as efficient as possibly it can be. One way it does this is by using the native thread pooling of the underlying operating system. This leads to a couple of differences between the Linux and Windows versions.

MariaDB on Windows has a variable, `threadpool_min_threads`, which allows us to specify the minimum number of threadpool threads that should be always kept alive. The default value is one. Windows will retire unused threads down to the minimum number and if our database has a sudden burst of traffic, which requires several new pools to be created, it could take a few seconds for MariaDB to create them. If we expect such *bursty* traffic, we can specify a number of threads to always be kept alive. This variable is not available on Linux.

Linux versions of MariaDB have their own variable, `thread_pool_size`, which is not available on Windows. This variable controls the number of thread groups. By default, this is the number of processors on our server. Clients connecting to Linux-based systems are grouped together into a thread group. There is a reason to lower the default value if, for example, we are using the `taskset` utility to run MariaDB on a set of dedicated processors. There may also be causes to increase this value if, for example, our CPU-bound workload is not fully utilizing our CPUs.

See also

▸ The full documentation of pool-of-threads is found at `https://mariadb.com/kb/en/thread-pool/`

▸ The comparison of threadpool versus thread-per-connection performance can be found at `http://blog.mariadb.org/mariadb-5-5-thread-pool-performance/`

▸ Additional pool-of-threads benchmarks can be found at `https://mariadb.com/kb/en/threadpool-benchmarks/`

Configuring the Aria pagecache

One difference between the Aria and MyISAM storage engines is Aria's `PAGE` row format. This is the default row format for Aria tables and must be used to take advantage of the crash-safe features of this storage engine.

A primary advantage of this row format is that rows are efficiently cached, which gives better performance. They also do not fragment as easily as the alternative `DYNAMIC` row format, and updates to them are quicker. The Aria pagecache is controlled by three variables.

How to do it...

1. Launch the `mysql` command-line client application and connect to our MariaDB server as the root user or as a user with the `SUPER` privilege.

2. View the current Aria pagecache settings with the following command:

   ```
   SHOW VARIABLES LIKE 'aria_pagecache%';
   ```

3. The output will look like the following screenshot:

4. Add the following lines of code to the end of our system's `my.cnf` or `my.ini` file (or to an existing `[mysqld]` section in the file), and then restart MariaDB:

```
[mysqld]
aria_pagecache_buffer_size = 536870912
aria_pagecache_age_threshold = 400
aria_pagecache_division_limit = 90
```

5. Check on the status of the Aria pagecache with the following command:

```
SHOW STATUS LIKE '%aria_pagecache%';
```

How it works...

The `aria_pagecache_buffer_size` variable should be set as large as we can afford. It is specified in bytes. In our recipe, we increased it from the default value of 128 MB to 512 MB. This variable may not be altered dynamically. It must be set in the server configuration file. Determining how much we can afford is tricky and will vary wildly from server to server. In general, if we make extensive use of Aria tables in our databases and we have RAM that is just sitting idle, we should increase `aria_pagecache_buffer_size` to use some of it.

The `aria_pagecache_age_threshold` variable controls how long a block in the pagecache will remain there without being accessed. The value is a ratio of the number of times the pagecache is accessed to the number of blocks in the pagecache. In our recipe, we increased this value from the default `300` to `400`, which has the effect of keeping pagecache blocks last longer. This variable can also be altered dynamically using the `mysql` command-line client, for example, with the following command:

```
SET GLOBAL aria_pagecache_age_threshold = 400;
```

The `aria_pagecache_division_limit` variable specifies the minimum percentage of the pagecache that must be *warm*. In our recipe, we changed it from 100 percent to 90 percent. This variable can also be altered dynamically by using the `mysql` command-line client, with the following command:

```
SET GLOBAL aria_pagecache_division_limit = 90;
```

There's more...

It's worth experimenting with these variables to see how they affect performance on our server's workload. In the case of the `aria_pagecache_buffer_size` variable, larger value is almost always better, unless we specify a value too high for our available RAM.

▶ The full documentation of the Aria storage engine is available at `https://mariadb.com/kb/en/aria/`

▶ Some Aria benchmark results are available at `https://mariadb.com/kb/en/benchmarking-aria/`

▶ More information on Aria's three storage formats (`FIXED`, `DYNAMIC`, and `PAGE`) is available at `https://mariadb.com/kb/en/aria-storage-formats/`

Optimizing queries with the subquery cache

The subquery cache is one of the several methods utilized by MariaDB to improve the performance of statements with subqueries. This is a feature unique to MariaDB and makes subqueries in MariaDB much faster than competing databases.

Getting ready

Import the ISFDB database as described in the *Importing the data exported by mysqldump* recipe in *Chapter 2, Diving Deep into MariaDB*.

How to do it...

1. Restart MariaDB to clear the subquery cache.

2. Launch the `mysql` command-line client application and connect to the `isfdb` database on our MariaDB server.

3. Run the following command to show our usage of the subquery cache:

   ```
   SHOW STATUS LIKE 'subquery%';
   ```

4. Because we just restarted MariaDB and cleared the subquery cache, the output will look like the following screenshot:

5. Run the following query:

```
SELECT titles.title_id AS ID,
   titles.title_title AS Title,
   authors.author_legalname AS Name,
   (SELECT COUNT(DISTINCT title_relationships.review_id)
     FROM title_relationships
     WHERE title_relationships.title_id = titles.title_id)
     AS reviews
FROM  titles INNER JOIN authors INNER JOIN canonical_author
ON
   (SELECT COUNT(DISTINCT title_relationships.review_id)
     FROM title_relationships
     WHERE title_relationships.title_id = titles.title_id)
     >= 12
   AND canonical_author.author_id = authors.author_id
   AND canonical_author.title_id=titles.title_id
   AND titles.title_parent=0;
```

6. Run the SHOW STATUS command from step 2 again. This time the output will look similar to the following screenshot:

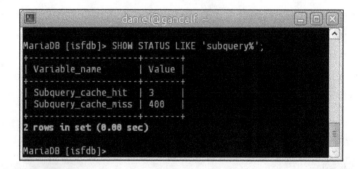

How it works...

The subquery cache is enabled by default in MariaDB. So there's nothing we have to do to start using it other than to run some queries with subqueries in them, which is what this recipe does. The two subquery-related STATUS variables show us how many times a subquery was able to make use of the cache (subquery_cache_hit) and how many times a subquery was not able to make use of the cache (subquery_cache_miss).

There's more...

To check if a query will be able to make use of the subquery cache before we actually run it, we can preface our query with EXPLAIN EXTENDED. The explanation will be accompanied by at least one warning. We will then run SHOW WARNINGS and the warning note containing our query will have the <expr_cache> text in it, if the subquery cache is used.

See also

- ▶ The full documentation of the subquery cache is available at https://mariadb.com/kb/en/subquery-cache/
- ▶ Some benchmarks demonstrating the benefit of the subquery cache are available at http://mysqlmaniac.com/2012/what-about-the-subqueries/

Optimizing semijoin subqueries

MariaDB includes several optimizations specifically targeted at semijoin subqueries. Semijoin subqueries are primarily the ones in which the subquery is an IN subquery located in the WHERE clause of our SQL statement. An example will be something like the following from the popular DBT3 benchmarking dataset:

```
SELECT * FROM part
WHERE p_partkey IN
    (SELECT l_partkey FROM lineitem
    WHERE l_shipdate between '1997-01-01' and '1997-02-01')
ORDER BY p_retailprice DESC LIMIT 10;
```

How to do it...

1. Launch the mysql command-line client application and connect to our MariaDB server as the root user or as a user with the SUPER privilege.

2. Run the following command to enable the exists_to_in optimization:

   SET GLOBAL optimizer_switch='exists_to_in=on';

3. Make the change permanent by adding the following lines of code to the end of our my.cnf or my.ini file (or by adding it to an existing [mysqld] section):

   ```
   [mysqld]
   optimizer_switch = 'exists_to_in=on';
   ```

How it works...

MariaDB has several subquery optimization strategies. Most of these are enabled by default. MariaDB evaluates the enabled strategies and chooses the best one for the subquery we are running. There is one that is not enabled by default, and that is the `exists_to_in` strategy; in this recipe, we will enable it.

In older versions of MariaDB, the main optimization for the `IN` subqueries was to turn them into an `EXISTS` subquery. This optimization, `in_to_exists`, is still present in MariaDB and is used where and when it is the best available choice; however, other better optimizations are now available for most `IN` subqueries.

In fact, MariaDB is so good at optimizing the `IN` subqueries that it made sense to create an optimization that was the reverse of the `in_to_exists` optimization. Naturally, it is called `exists_to_in`. This optimization does exactly what the name implies. It turns an `EXISTS` subquery into an `IN` subquery. MariaDB then takes the new query and uses its powerful set of optimizations to execute it in the optimal way.

There's more...

We can temporarily turn off MariaDB's subquery optimizations (only really recommended for benchmarking or other testing purposes) by running the following command:

```
SET optimizer_switch='semijoin=off';
```

To make the change permanent (again, this is not recommended), we can add the following code to the end of our `my.cnf` or `my.ini` file (or add it to an existing `[mysqld]` section):

```
[mysqld]
optimizer_switch = 'semijoin=off'
```

See also

- The *Subquery Optimizations* section of the MariaDB Knowledgebase contains several articles on the various optimizations available in MariaDB to improve the performance of subqueries. These articles can be found at `https://mariadb.com/kb/en/subquery-optimizations/`
- The full documentation of semijoin subquery optimizations in MariaDB is available at `https://mariadb.com/kb/en/semi-join-subquery-optimizations/`
- The full documentation of the `exists_to_in` subquery optimization strategy is found at `https://mariadb.com/kb/en/exists-to-in-optimization/`

Creating an index

An index helps MariaDB (or any database, really) to quickly locate often looked-for data that it will otherwise have to search for by reading through our tables row by row. Creating indexes of often-queried columns in large tables is a basic, but very useful optimization.

Getting ready

Import the ISFDB database as described in the *Importing the data exported by mysqldump* recipe in *Chapter 2, Diving Deep into MariaDB*.

How to do it...

1. Launch the `mysql` command-line client application and connect to the `isfdb` database on our MariaDB server.

2. Create an index on the `email_address` column of the `emails` table:

```
CREATE INDEX email ON emails(email_address(50));
```

3. Show the indexes on the `emails` table with the following command:

```
SHOW INDEX FROM emails\G
```

4. The output will look similar to the following screenshot:

How it works...

The `emails` table already has an index, the primary key. This is the most common type of index, but if we rarely search in a large table for a record matching a primary key, it does not do us much good. It is better to create indexes for the columns we are actually searching on.

An index on the `email_address` table contains a presorted list of the e-mail addresses, which makes looking them up much faster.

There's more...

If we are dealing with columns that are guaranteed to be unique, such as a primary key, we can create a unique index with the following command:

```
CREATE UNIQUE INDEX index_name ON table_name(column_name (length));
```

However, we can't do this for actual primary key columns; just columns that are unique. To create a primary key index, we must use an `ALTER TABLE` command. As an example, we'll create a new table that just contains author names copied from the `authors` table, and then add a primary key to it using the following commands:

```
CREATE TABLE authors2 (author mediumtext);
INSERT authors2 SELECT author_canonical FROM authors;
ALTER TABLE authors2 ADD author_id int NOT NULL
    PRIMARY KEY auto_increment FIRST;
```

The `ALTER TABLE` statement takes care of creating the missing primary key IDs. We can view a subsection of them with the following command:

```
SELECT * FROM authors2 WHERE author LIKE "%Bartholomew";
```

See also

- ▸ More information on indexes is available at
  `https://mariadb.com/kb/en/optimization-and-indexes/`
- ▸ The full documentation of the `CREATE INDEX` command is available at
  `https://mariadb.com/kb/en/create-index/`
- ▸ The full documentation of the `SHOW INDEX` command is available at
  `https://mariadb.com/kb/en/show-index/`

Creating a full-text index

A full-text index is a special type of index optimized to search through the text-based columns. They can only be created for columns of the type `CHAR`, `VARCHAR`, and `TEXT`.

Getting ready

Import the ISFDB database as described in the *Importing the data exported by mysqldump* recipe from *Chapter 2, Diving Deep into MariaDB*.

How to do it...

1. Launch the `mysql` command-line client application and connect to the `isfdb` database on our MariaDB server.

2. Create a `FULLTEXT` index on the `note_note` column of the `notes` table using the following command:

   ```
   CREATE FULLTEXT INDEX note ON notes(note_note);
   ```

3. When MariaDB has finished creating the index, we will get an output similar to the following:

   ```
   Query OK, 246719 rows affected (11.08 sec)
   Records: 246719  Duplicates: 0  Warnings: 0
   ```

4. Show the indexes on the `notes` table with the following command:

   ```
   SHOW INDEX FROM notes\G
   ```

5. The output of the `SHOW` command will look like the following screenshot:

How it works...

A FULLTEXT index enables us to search data using the MATCH() ... AGAINST syntax. The MATCH part of the syntax contains a comma-separated list of the columns to be searched. The AGAINST part of the syntax contains the string to search for and may also contain an optional modifier to indicate the type of search to be performed. The search types are IN NATURAL LANGUAGE MODE, IN BOOLEAN MODE, and WITH QUERY EXPANSION. The default type is IN NATURAL LANGUAGE MODE and doesn't need to be explicitly specified. An example using the index we just created is as follows:

```
SELECT * FROM notes
  WHERE MATCH(note_note)
  AGAINST('artificial','intelligence');
```

This query matches all the rows that either have the words artificial or intelligence in them, not necessarily both. To ensure that both words appear in the note, we can search for IN BOOLEAN MODE as follows:

```
SELECT * FROM notes
  WHERE MATCH(note_note)
  AGAINST('+artificial,+intelligence' IN BOOLEAN MODE);
```

There's more...

There are several limitations to the full-text indexes that we need to be aware of. Words that are three characters in length (or less) or words longer than 84 characters are excluded from the index. Partial words are also excluded. Lastly, if a word is a stopword, which is a list of common words such as there, done, then, and always, or if the word appears in more than half of the rows, it is excluded from the results unless we use IN BOOLEAN MODE.

See also

- ▶ The full documentation of full-text indexes is available at
  https://mariadb.com/kb/en/full-text-indexes/
- ▶ The full documentation of the CREATE INDEX command is available at
  https://mariadb.com/kb/en/create-index/
- ▶ The full documentation of the SHOW INDEX command is available at
  https://mariadb.com/kb/en/show-index/
- ▶ The full list of stopwords is available at
  https://mariadb.com/kb/en/stopwords/

Removing an index

If an index is not used, the only thing it is doing is wasting space and slowing down our INSERT and UPDATE statements. So if an index is not being used, we should remove it.

Getting ready

Import the ISFDB database as described in the *Importing the data exported by mysqldump* recipe from *Chapter 2*, *Diving Deep into MariaDB*.

How to do it...

1. Launch the mysql command-line client application and connect to the isfdb database on our MariaDB server.

2. Drop the full-text index on the note_note column of the notes table, which we created in the previous recipe using the following command:

    ```
    DROP INDEX note ON notes;
    ```

3. After the command's execution is complete, verify that the full-text index is removed with the following command:

    ```
    SHOW INDEX FROM notes;
    ```

How it works...

The DROP INDEX command actually creates and runs an ALTER TABLE statement to remove an index. So when removing an index on a large table, we'll see the standard ALTER TABLE progress messages.

There's more...

The last thing we want to do is to remove an index that we use regularly. To figure out what indexes we are actually using, we need to enable **user statistics**. To do so, we need to add the following code to the end of our main my.cnf or my.ini file (or add it to an existing [mysqld] section) and then restart MariaDB:

```
[mysqld]
userstat = 1
```

Once it is enabled, we will need to let the server run for a while to gather statistics. Once we feel that enough time has passed for the statistics to represent our typical usage, we can show the index statistics with the following command:

```
SHOW INDEX_STATISTICS;
```

See also

▸ More information on indexes can be found at
   `https://mariadb.com/kb/en/optimization-and-indexes/`

▸ The full documentation of the `DROP INDEX` command is available at
   `https://mariadb.com/kb/en/drop-index/`

▸ More information on user statistics can be found at
   `https://mariadb.com/kb/en/user-statistics/`

Using JOINs

Joining data from two or more tables is how we unlock the power of a relational database such as MariaDB. There are three basic `JOIN` types: `INNER`, `CROSS`, and `LEFT` (or `OUTER`).

Getting ready

Import the ISFDB database as described in the *Importing the data exported by mysqldump* recipe from *Chapter 2, Diving Deep into MariaDB*.

How to do it...

1. Launch the `mysql` command-line client application and connect to the `isfdb` database on our MariaDB server.

2. Perform an `INNER JOIN` of the `authors` and `emails` tables to show us a list of authors and their corresponding e-mail addresses using the following command:

```
SELECT author_canonical, email_address
  FROM authors INNER JOIN emails
    ON authors.author_id = emails.author_id;
```

3. Perform a `LEFT JOIN` of the `emails` and `authors` tables to show us a list of authors and their corresponding e-mail addresses using the following command:

```
SELECT author_canonical, email_address
  FROM emails LEFT JOIN authors
    ON authors.author_id = emails.author_id;
```

4. Perform a `CROSS JOIN` of awards and award types using the following command:

```
SELECT * FROM awards CROSS JOIN award_types LIMIT 10;
```

How it works...

The results of an INNER JOIN are the rows that match in both the tables for the specified join conditions. So, for example, all rows in the emails table that match the row in the authors table based on the join conditions will be shown. But any results in the authors table that don't exist will not be shown in the results.

The LEFT JOIN is similar to the INNER JOIN except that it produces results from all rows from the table on the left, even if they don't match anything in the table on the right. The emails table I'm using has 782 rows, so the result set of the LEFT JOIN example also has 782 rows. Columns from the emails table that do not match up with the columns from the authors table are set to NULL for that row of the results.

A CROSS JOIN is the product of the two tables. Every row in each table is joined to every other row in the other table. Think of it as multiplying the two tables together. For example, a cross join of a table with 15 rows and a table with 10 rows is a table of 150 rows. This makes this kind of JOIN potentially dangerous if we accidentally cross join two very large tables. In our example, we add a LIMIT clause to cut it off after 10 rows of output.

There's more...

The utility of INNER JOIN and LEFT JOIN is easy to see. They let us combine the data from multiple tables into a single result. The CROSS JOIN, on the other hand, may not seem to be quite as useful at first glance. However, they do have an important, if limited, set of use. For example, a CROSS JOIN can be used with a table of colors and a table of materials to give us all possible material and color combinations. That said, it's best to be careful with them to avoid unintended consequences.

See also

▶ Refer to https://mariadb.com/kb/en/joins/ for full documentation of JOIN in MariaDB

Using microseconds in the DATETIME columns

There was a time when measuring dates and times accurately to within a single second were as precise as we needed it to be. However, those days are gone. Users expect their apps to have response times of well under a second, and so our databases must be able to track those times as well.

How to do it...

1. Launch the `mysql` command-line client application and connect it to our MariaDB server.

2. Create a test database if it doesn't already exist and switch to it using the following command:

   ```
   CREATE DATABASE IF NOT EXISTS test;
   USE test;
   ```

3. Create a simple two-column table named `times` using the following command:

   ```
   CREATE TABLE times (
       id int NOT NULL AUTO_INCREMENT,
       dt datetime(6),
       PRIMARY KEY (id)
   );
   ```

4. Run the following `INSERT` statements at least four times and add some sample data to our table using the following command:

   ```
   INSERT INTO times (dt) VALUES (NOW()), (NOW(6));
   ```

5. Select all of the data from our table with the following `SELECT` command:

   ```
   SELECT * FROM times;
   ```

   On running the `SELECT` command, we get an output similar to the following screenshot:

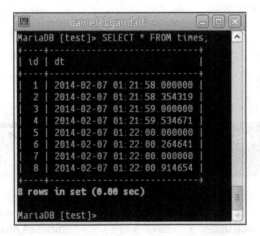

How it works...

When creating the `times` table, in order for our `dt` column to support `datetime` values with microseconds, we need to specify the precision. If we don't, it will default to a precision of one second. In this recipe, we set it to the highest precision, `6`. If we try to use a higher value, we will get an error.

When inserting data into our tables, we put in two rows at a time. First, a row with the default precision of the `NOW()` function (1 second), and then with the highest precision (`6`). When we use the default precision of `NOW()` the microseconds part of the `datetime` gets entered as all zeroes. This is useful to keep in mind if we are migrating an application to use microseconds, both the table itself and the functions we use to enter our `datetime` data need to use microseconds.

There's more...

The `CURRENT_TIMESTAMP` function is a synonym for the `NOW()` function and the two can be used interchangeably.

See also

▶ Refer to `https://mariadb.com/kb/en/microseconds-in-mariadb/` for more information on using microseconds

▶ The full documentation of the `NOW()` and `CURRENT_TIMESTAMP()` functions is at `https://mariadb.com/kb/en/now/` and `https://mariadb.com/kb/en/current_timestamp/`

Updating DATETIME and TIMESTAMP columns automatically

If our database has a `DATETIME` or `TIMESTAMP` column that we want to be updated whenever the record is updated, there is no need for us to put that logic in our application. MariaDB can take care of it for us.

How to do it...

1. Launch the `mysql` command-line client application and connect to our MariaDB server.

2. Create a `test` database if it doesn't already exist and switch to it using the following command:

```
CREATE DATABASE IF NOT EXISTS test;

USE test;
```

3. Create a simple table named `dtts` using the following commands:

```
CREATE TABLE dtts (
    id int(11) NOT NULL AUTO_INCREMENT,
    name varchar(25),
    dt datetime(6) NOT NULL DEFAULT CURRENT_TIMESTAMP(6),
    ts timestamp(3) NOT NULL DEFAULT CURRENT_TIMESTAMP(3)
      ON UPDATE CURRENT_TIMESTAMP(3),
    PRIMARY KEY (id)
);
```

4. Insert some data into our new table using the INSERT command:

```
INSERT INTO dtts (name) VALUES
    ('Thomass'),('Gordon'),('Howard'),('Ezra');
```

5. Fix the misspelling of `Thomas`:

```
UPDATE dtts SET name = 'Thomas'
   WHERE name = 'Thomass';
```

6. View our table using the following command:

```
SELECT * FROM dtts;
```

7. The output will look similar to the following screenshot (but with today's date):

```
                          daniel@gandalf ~
MariaDB [test]> INSERT INTO dtts (name) VALUES
    ->     ('Thomass'),('Gordon'),('Howard'),('Ezra');
Query OK, 4 rows affected (0.05 sec)
Records: 4  Duplicates: 0  Warnings: 0

MariaDB [test]> UPDATE dtts SET name = 'Thomas'
    ->     WHERE name = 'Thomass';
Query OK, 1 row affected (0.05 sec)
Rows matched: 1  Changed: 1  Warnings: 0

MariaDB [test]> SELECT * FROM dtts;
+----+--------+----------------------------+-------------------------+
| id | name   | dt                         | ts                      |
+----+--------+----------------------------+-------------------------+
|  1 | Thomas | 2014-02-07 01:28:18.214747 | 2014-02-07 01:28:24.874 |
|  2 | Gordon | 2014-02-07 01:28:18.214747 | 2014-02-07 01:28:18.214 |
|  3 | Howard | 2014-02-07 01:28:18.214747 | 2014-02-07 01:28:18.214 |
|  4 | Ezra   | 2014-02-07 01:28:18.214747 | 2014-02-07 01:28:18.214 |
+----+--------+----------------------------+-------------------------+
4 rows in set (0.00 sec)

MariaDB [test]>
```

How it works...

In this recipe, we created a table with four columns. An `id` column, a `name` column, a `dt` column of the type `datetime(6)`, and a `ts` column of the type `timestamp(3)`.

The `dt` column has a type of `datetime(6)`, which means it has full microsecond precision, and it has a default value of `CURRENT_TIMESTAMP(6)`. The `ts` column has a type of `timestamp(3)`, which gives it only millisecond precision, and it has the addition of `ON UPDATE CURRENT_TIMESTAMP(3)`, which automatically updates the stored time value whenever the row is updated. With the update we made to the first row, we can see that the code is working as the `dt` and `ts` columns are different.

There's more...

Both `datetime` and `timestamp` columns can have their `DEFAULT` and `ON UPDATE` values set to the output of the `CURRENT_TIMESTAMP` function. We just need to take care to match the precision to avoid needless warnings about truncated data (if we specify a higher precision than the column is configured for) or avoid having data added with less precision than we wanted (if we input values with a lower precision than the column is configured for).

It is also worth noting that the `CURRENT_TIMESTAMP()` function is a synonym for the `NOW()` function.

See also

- For more on `DATETIME` columns, refer to https://mariadb.com/kb/en/datetime/
- For more on `TIMESTAMP` columns, refer to https://mariadb.com/kb/en/timestamp/
- The full documentation of the `NOW()` and `CURRENT_TIMESTAMP()` functions is available at https://mariadb.com/kb/en/now/ and https://mariadb.com/kb/en/current_timestamp/
- Notes related to the implementation of this feature in MariaDB are available at https://mariadb.atlassian.net/browse/MDEV-452

4
The TokuDB Storage Engine

In this chapter, we will cover the following recipes:

- ▶ Installing TokuDB
- ▶ Configuring TokuDB
- ▶ Creating TokuDB tables
- ▶ Migrating to TokuDB
- ▶ Adding indexes to TokuDB tables
- ▶ Modifying the compression of a TokuDB table

Introduction

TokuDB is a high-performance storage engine for MariaDB, optimized for write-intensive workloads. It is highly scalable and uses a storage technology that the developer, **Tokutek**, calls **Fractal Tree Indexes**. It can be used with no application or code changes instead of (and alongside) MyISAM, Aria, and InnoDB/XtraDB tables. It is ACID and MVCC compliant.

ACID compliance means that TokuDB transactions have atomicity, consistency, isolation, and durability. More information on ACID is available at http://en.wikipedia.org/wiki/ACID.

MVCC compliance means that TokuDB has multiversion concurrency control for database transactions. More information on MVCC is available at http://en.wikipedia.org/wiki/Multiversion_concurrency_control.

Fractal trees are a modification of B-trees, which is what InnoDB uses to store data (to be more accurate, InnoDB uses a balanced B+ tree). Whereas InnoDB has a single small cache for an entire data tree, TokuDB implements several large caches at multiple levels in a tree. It then buffers inserts, updates, deletes, and other operations until it has a large batch of them that it can apply as a single operation, greatly reducing the number of input/output (I/O) operations and thus increasing performance.

The video presentation at `http://youtu.be/c-n2LGPpQEw` is a good introduction to Fractal Tree Indexes.

TokuDB is only supported on 64-bit Linux systems, so the recipes in this chapter will not work on Windows or Mac OS X.

Installing TokuDB

Before we can start using TokuDB, we must first install it. TokuDB is included in MariaDB, but it is not activated by default.

How to do it...

Follow the ensuing steps:

1. Launch the `mysql` command-line client application with a user that has the `SUPER` privilege (like the `Root` user).

2. Run the following command:

   INSTALL SONAME 'ha_tokudb.so';

3. Run the `SHOW PLUGINS;` command and verify that the TokuDB plugins are `ACTIVE`. The output will be similar to the following screenshot (it has been edited to show just the TokuDB entries):

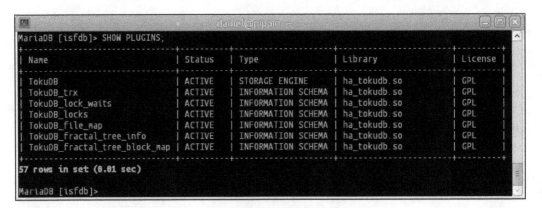

4. Run the SHOW ENGINES; command and verify that the TokuDB storage engine is listed and enabled (the **Support** column). The output of the TokuDB line will be similar to the following:

Engine	Support	Comment
TokuDB	YES	Tokutek TokuDB Storage Engine

How it works...

Like some of the other plugins and alternative storage engines that ship with MariaDB, TokuDB is disabled by default. To enable it, we use the INSTALL SONAME command. There are several parts to the TokuDB storage engine, which is why one command appears to enable several plugins.

There's more...

Some additional steps we may want to perform when installing TokuDB are to make it the default storage engine and to create a TokuDB-specific configuration file.

Making TokuDB the default storage engine

We can make TokuDB the default storage engine by running the following command:

```
SET GLOBAL default_storage_engine=TokuDB;
```

To make it permanent, we then add the following to the end of our system's my.cnf or my.ini file (or to an existing [mysqld] section) and restart MariaDB:

```
[mysqld]
default-storage-engine=TokuDB
```

Creating a TokuDB-specific configuration file

On Linux systems, such as Fedora, Debian, CentOS, Ubuntu, and others, MariaDB comes configured with support for modular configuration files. At the bottom of the default configuration file is a line beginning with an exclamation mark (!). This command includes all the files that end in .cnf in the directory named on the line.

Using multiple files for our configuration allows us to enable and disable features by just moving files around. We can also make changes without having to edit an increasingly long configuration file.

The directory will be located in one of two places. On Red Hat, CentOS, and Fedora, the location is /etc/my.cnf.d/. On Debian, Ubuntu, and Linux Mint, the location is /etc/mysql/conf.d/.

When creating our own custom configuration file, it's best to give it a descriptive name. Something like `tokudb.cnf` is perfect. The file needs a `[mysqld]` section at the very least, but we could put other sections in the file if we needed or wanted to.

See also

▸ The MariaDB knowledge base has a section devoted to TokuDB, which is available at `https://mariadb.com/kb/en/tokudb/`

▸ The TokuDB section of the Tokutek website also contains lots of good information and is available at `http://www.tokutek.com/products/tokudb-for-mysql/`

Configuring TokuDB

Like other storage engines, TokuDB has many custom settings and options. Thankfully, there are only a few that we really need to know about up front, and the default settings are fairly optimized.

Getting ready

This recipe is going to assume a few things; firstly, that our server has 16 GB of RAM, and secondly that we have two SSD drives, `/dev/sdb1` and `/dev/sdc1`, mounted under the `/mnt/` directory.

How to do it...

Follow the ensuing steps:

1. Open the `my.cnf` file and add the following lines to an existing `[mysqld]` section:

   ```
   # TokuDB Cache should be set to at least half of available RAM
   tokudb-cache-size = 9GB

   # TokuDB File Locations
   tokudb-data-dir = /mnt/sdb1
   tokudb-log-dir  = /mnt/sdb1
   tokudb-tmp-dir  = /mnt/sdc1
   ```

2. Disable the write cache on our disks with the following:

   ```
   hdparm -W0 /dev/sdb1
   hdparm -W0 /dev/sdc2
   ```

3. Show the status of TokuDB with the following command:

   ```
   SHOW ENGINE TokuDB STATUS;
   ```

How it works...

There are many settings for TokuDB that we can tweak, enable, and disable; but for many users, the defaults work well. One such default is that TokuDB will automatically set the `tokudb-cache-size` option to be equal to half of our system RAM. In our recipe, we set it manually to be a bit more than half, but we will need to test to see if it helps with our databases and workloads. The TokuDB developers recommend that this setting should never be set to lower than half.

Like with InnoDB, we can set the location of TokuDB's log, data, and temporary files to be different from the configured default for other tables. In our example, we configure them to live on our fast solid-state drives (SSDs). For simplicity, we configure the data and logs to go to the same place. However, we set the temporary files to go to a completely different drive, so that they don't impact the performance of our data drive. We could just set the MariaDB default locations to these and TokuDB would write there by default, but sometimes it's better for performance if we stick certain table types in one location and other table types in another.

Next, we turn off the write cache on our drives. The write cache is problematic because during a power failure or other catastrophic event, we don't want any unwritten data to be in a drive's onboard cache. When the operating system tells us it has written the data to disk, we want it to have actually been written, not temporarily sitting in a cache somewhere. Many servers have battery-backed RAID cards and other protections, but they are not 100 percent foolproof.

Incidentally, the `SHOW ENGINE TokuDB STATUS;` command is case insensitive. We can use `TokuDB`, `TOKUDB`, `tokudb`, or any other case variant we can think of.

There's more...

There are many additional options for TokuDB that are not covered here. The TokuDB section of the MariaDB knowledge base at `https://mariadb.com/kb/en/tokudb/` contains links to many useful resources for getting the most out of this powerful storage engine.

See also

- In addition to the TokuDB section of the MariaDB knowledge base mentioned in the previous section, another good resource for learning about the various TokuDB configuration options is the Tokutek website at `http://tokutek.com`.

Creating TokuDB tables

Creating a TokuDB table is much like creating a MyISAM, Aria, or InnoDB/XtraDB table. There are some more options and abilities we should know about.

Getting ready

Import the ISFDB database as described in the *Importing the data exported by mysqldump* recipe from *Chapter 2, Diving Deep into MariaDB*.

How to do it...

Follow the ensuing steps:

1. Launch the `mysql` command-line client and connect to the `isfdb` database.

2. Use the following `CREATE` statement to create our TokuDB table:

```
CREATE TABLE authors_tokudb (
    author_id int NOT NULL AUTO_INCREMENT,
    author_canonical mediumtext,
    author_lastname varchar(128),
    author_birthplace mediumtext,
    author_birthdate date DEFAULT NULL,
    author_deathdate date DEFAULT NULL,
    PRIMARY KEY (author_id),
    KEY (author_lastname),
    KEY (author_birthdate),
    KEY (author_deathdate)
) ENGINE=TokuDB;
```

3. Import some data from the `authors` table into our new table:

```
INSERT authors_tokudb
    SELECT
        author_id, author_canonical,
        author_lastname, author_birthplace,
        author_birthdate, author_deathdate
    FROM authors;
```

4. Verify that the indexes are working with the following command:

```
SHOW INDEXES FROM authors_tokudb;
```

5. The output of the preceding steps will have four rows with information on each of the indexes we created.

6. Optimize the table with the following command:

```
OPTIMIZE TABLE authors_tokudb;
```

7. The output of the `OPTIMIZE` command will be similar to the following screenshot:

How it works...

At first glance, the `CREATE TABLE` statement in this recipe looks similar to other `CREATE TABLE` statements we have seen earlier, but there are a few differences. The obvious one is that we specify `ENGINE=TokuDB` after the data definition. This is necessary if we have not set TokuDB to be the default storage engine.

Next, in the data definition, we have defined three `KEY` indexes in addition to our `PRIMARY KEY` index.

After creating our table, we populate it using the data selected from the `isfdb.authors` table. Then, we take a look at our indexes to make sure they are there and then we optimize our new table. The optimization step basically applies pending additions and deletions to our indexes. The optimization step is not needed for performance reasons in TokuDB like it is with other storage engines.

See also

▶ The *Adding indexes to TokuDB tables* recipe for more information on indexes in TokuDB

▶ The *Modifying the compression of a TokuDB table* recipe for more information on TokuDB's `ROW_FORMAT` compression settings

Migrating to TokuDB

TokuDB doesn't do us any good if we don't use it. Migrating existing tables to TokuDB, whether they are MyISAM, Aria, or InnoDB/XtraDB, is fairly painless.

Getting ready

Import the ISFDB database as described in the *Importing the data exported by mysqldump* recipe in *Chapter 2, Diving Deep into MariaDB.*

How to do it...

Follow the ensuing steps:

1. Launch the `mysql` command-line client and connect to the `isfdb` database.

2. Alter the `pub%` tables to be TokuDB tables:

   ```
   ALTER TABLE pub_authors ENGINE=TokuDB;

   ALTER TABLE pub_content ENGINE=TokuDB;

   ALTER TABLE pub_series ENGINE=TokuDB;

   ALTER TABLE publishers ENGINE=TokuDB;
   ```

3. Run `SHOW CREATE TABLE` on each of the tables to verify that they now have `ENGINE=TokuDB` after the data definition section. Using the `publishers` table as an example, we get the following output:

   ```
   MariaDB [isfdb]> ALTER TABLE publishers ENGINE=TokuDB;
   Query OK, 16382 rows affected (0.56 sec)
   Records: 16382  Duplicates: 0  Warnings: 0

   MariaDB [isfdb]> SHOW CREATE TABLE publishers\G
   *************************** 1. row ***************************
           Table: publishers
   Create Table: CREATE TABLE `publishers` (
     `publisher_id` int(11) NOT NULL AUTO_INCREMENT,
     `publisher_name` mediumtext,
     `publisher_wikipedia` mediumtext,
     `note_id` int(11) DEFAULT NULL,
     PRIMARY KEY (`publisher_id`),
     KEY `publisher_name` (`publisher_name`(50))
   ) ENGINE=TokuDB AUTO_INCREMENT=47660 DEFAULT CHARSET=latin1
   1 row in set (0.00 sec)

   MariaDB [isfdb]>
   ```

4. Convert additional tables in the `isfdb` database to TokuDB format if required.

How it works...

The `ALTER TABLE` statement works in three stages. It first creates a new table using the new table definition. It then copies data from the old table to the new table. The last step is to rename the new table to the same name as the old table.

There's more...

The `ALTER TABLE` method of migrating to TokuDB is probably the best way, but there are others. For example, if we have a backup made with `mysqldump`, we could do a search and replace on the schema definitions in our backup file and change the `CREATE TABLE` statements to create TokuDB tables instead of what they were configured to create. Then, when we import the file, the restored tables will be TokuDB tables.

Another method is to create a table based on an existing table, alter it, and then backup the existing table and import the backup into the new table, as follows:

```
CREATE TABLE notes_tokudb LIKE notes;
ALTER TABLE notes_tokudb ENGINE=TokuDB;
SELECT * FROM notes INTO OUTFILE '/tmp/notes.tmp';
LOAD DATA INFILE '/tmp/notes.tmp' INTO TABLE notes_tokudb;
```

That said, for most cases, if not all, the `ALTER TABLE` method is preferred.

See also

 ▸ The *How to quickly insert data into MariaDB* page of the MariaDB knowledge base goes into more detail about large data import operations, and the instructions can be adapted for TokuDB easily. This is available at `https://mariadb.com/kb/en/how-to-quickly-insert-data-into-mariadb/`.

Adding indexes to TokuDB tables

TokuDB has advanced indexing capabilities compared to other storage engines, but we can't use them if we don't add them to our tables.

Getting ready

Import the ISFDB database as described in the *Importing the data exported by mysqldump* recipe in *Chapter 2, Diving Deep into MariaDB*.

How to do it...

Follow the ensuing steps:

1. Launch the `mysql` command-line client and connect to the `isfdb` database.

2. View the current indexes on the `authors` table with the following command:

   ```
   SHOW INDEXES FROM authors;
   ```

3. Alter the `authors` table to use the TokuDB storage engine and change the index on the `author_canonical` column to `CLUSTERING`, as shown in the following commands:

   ```
   ALTER TABLE authors
     DROP KEY canonical,
     ADD CLUSTERING KEY canonical (author_canonical(50)),
     ENGINE=TokuDB;
   ```

4. Create another index, this time on the `author_birthdate` column, as shown in the following commands:

   ```
   CREATE CLUSTERING INDEX birthdate
     ON authors (author_birthdate);
   ```

5. View the indexes again as we did in step 2.

How it works...

Clustered indexes include all the columns of a table and can be used as covering indexes. They also have performance advantages compared to other indexes because of the way TokuDB works. We can define clustered indexes in some other storage engines, but only one of them. TokuDB lets us define multiple clustered indexes. Being able to define more than one gives TokuDB tables a great performance boost over a wide range of queries.

In our recipe, we defined clustered indexes in two ways, first using an `ALTER TABLE` statement to replace an existing index with a clustered index, and then to add a new index using the `CREATE INDEX` statement.

There's more...

Some of the other advantages of TokuDB's indexing capabilities include being able to use an `auto_increment` column in any index and within any position in that index. Also, TokuDB indexes can have up to 32 columns.

See also

▸ More information on TokuDB's clustering indexes is available at `http://tokutek.com/2009/05/introducing_multiple_clustering_indexes/`.

Modifying the compression of a TokuDB table

TokuDB has several compression options to help us strike the perfect balance between disk space and performance.

Getting ready

Import the ISFDB database as described in the *Importing the data exported by mysqldump* recipe in *Chapter 2, Diving Deep into MariaDB*.

How to do it...

Follow the ensuing steps:

1. Launch the `mysql` command-line client and connect to the `isfdb` database.

2. Alter the `titles` table to use default compression, as shown in the following command:

   ```
   ALTER TABLE titles ENGINE=TokuDB
     ROW_FORMAT=default ;
   ```

3. Alter the `pub_content` table to use high compression, as shown in the following command:

   ```
   ALTER TABLE pub_content ENGINE=TokuDB
     ROW_FORMAT=tokudb_small;
   ```

4. Alter the `canonical_author` table to have fast compression, as shown in the following command:

   ```
   ALTER TABLE canonical_author ENGINE=TokuDB
     ROW_FORMAT=tokudb_fast;
   ```

5. Alter the `notes` table to use the `lzma` compressor, as shown in the following command:

   ```
   ALTER TABLE notes ENGINE=TokuDB
     ROW_FORMAT=tokudb_lzma;
   ```

6. Alter the `pubs` table to not use any compression, as shown in the following command:

    ```
    ALTER TABLE pubs ENGINE=TokuDB
      ROW_FORMAT=tokudb_uncompressed;
    ```

7. Optimize all the tables we just altered, as shown in the following command:

    ```
    OPTIMIZE TABLE
      titles, pub_content, canonical_author, notes, pubs;
    ```

How it works...

Apart from being able to switch the compression of tables to whatever works best in our situation, a big advantage of TokuDB compared to other storage engines is its ability to highly compress data and still have great performance. The amount and type of compression we use is controlled by the `ROW_FORMAT` option. If we do not specify row format when creating a table, it will default to the `default` row format.

The official recommendation from Tokutek, the developers of TokuDB, is to use standard compression (`default`) on machines with six or fewer cores and high compression (`tokudb_small`) only on machines with more than six cores.

There's more...

The `tokudb_fast` and `tokudb_small` compression options are actually just aliases to `tokudb_quicklz` and `tokudb_lzma`, respectively. They may be changed in the future if other compression options are added to TokuDB. Likewise, the default compression is currently also `tokudb_quicklz`.

There are two other compression options: the deprecated `tokudb_zlib` compression option, which is what TokuDB used as its default until `tokudb_quicklz` debuted in TokuDB Version 5.2, and `tokudb_uncompressed`, which disables compression (useful for uncompressable data).

5
The CONNECT Storage Engine

In this chapter, we will cover the following recipes:

- ▶ Installing the CONNECT storage engine
- ▶ Creating and dropping CONNECT tables
- ▶ Reading and writing CSV data using CONNECT
- ▶ Reading and writing XML data using CONNECT
- ▶ Accessing MariaDB tables using CONNECT
- ▶ Using the XCOL table type
- ▶ Using the PIVOT table type
- ▶ Using the OCCUR table type
- ▶ Using the WMI table type
- ▶ Using the MAC address table type

Introduction

In this chapter, we will explore some of the features of the CONNECT storage engine. This storage engine allows us to access data in various file formats such as XML, CSV, and other types of files stored on our host system. Its purpose is to connect MariaDB to these various data types. It's a very handy tool for bringing various pieces of an infrastructure together. So, the CONNECT storage engine tables are not exactly tables in the traditional sense (they may not even physically exist). With that in mind, there are some things we need to realize when working with this storage engine.

First, `DROP TABLE` does not delete content the way MyISAM, InnoDB, and other tables do. CONNECT tables are definitions of where the data we want to access is and what format it is in. For example, an XML file stored in a user's home directory. When we drop a CONNECT table using `DROP`, we are dropping the *where-and-what* definition stored in the CONNECT table and not the data itself.

Secondly, indexing behaves differently for CONNECT tables. Most (but not all) of the CONNECT data types that connect to files support indexing but only as long as there are no NULL values. Virtual CONNECT tables, which connect to a source of information such as another database, the filesystem, or the operating system, cannot be indexed because data from these sources is unknown until we access it.

More about indexing CONNECT tables can be found at `https://mariadb.com/kb/en/using-connect-indexing/` and the full documentation of the CONNECT storage engine can be found at `https://mariadb.com/kb/en/connect/`.

Installing the CONNECT storage engine

The CONNECT storage engine is not installed by default. So, the first thing that we have to do is to install and enable it.

How to do it...

1. On Fedora, CentOS, or Red Hat systems, we can run the following command line:

    ```
    sudo yum install MariaDB-connect-engine
    ```

    On Debian, Ubuntu, or Linux Mint systems, we can run the following command line:

    ```
    sudo apt-get install mariadb-connect-engine-10.0
    ```

2. On all systems, launch the `mysql` command-line client and connect it to our MariaDB server with a user that has the `SUPER` privilege.

3. Enable the CONNECT storage engine by running the following command line:

    ```
    INSTALL SONAME 'ha_connect';
    ```

4. Verify the installation by running the following two commands and look for `CONNECT` in the output:

    ```
    SHOW ENGINES;
    ```
    ```
    SHOW PLUGINS;
    ```

How it works...

On Windows and MacOS, the CONNECT storage engine is included but not active. On Linux, we need to install the CONNECT package before we can enable it using the `mysql` command-line client.

See also

▸ The full documentation of the CONNECT storage engine can be found at `https://mariadb.com/kb/en/connect/`

Creating and dropping CONNECT tables

CONNECT tables are only superficially similar to other tables. In this recipe, we'll create a CONNECT DIR table.

Getting ready

Enable the CONNECT engine as specified in the *Installing the CONNECT storage engine* recipe at the beginning of this chapter.

How to do it...

1. Connect to MariaDB with the `mysql` command-line client and to the `test` database with a user that has the CREATE privilege. If the `test` database is absent, create one.

2. Run the following CREATE statement to create a table that lists the files in the data directory of the test database:

```
CREATE TABLE test_data (
    path varchar(256) NOT NULL flag=1,
    filename varchar(256) NOT NULL flag=2,
    filesize double(12,0) NOT NULL flag=5
) ENGINE=CONNECT DEFAULT CHARSET=latin1
    TABLE_TYPE=DIR FILE_NAME='*.frm'
    OPTION_LIST='subdir=1';
```

Select everything in the table. The output will vary depending on the tables in the test database and their location and size. Though the columns will be similar to the following screenshot, the contents will not match:

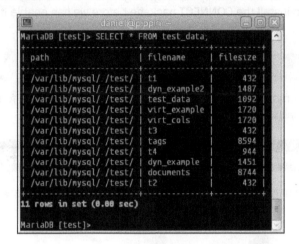

Use the SUM() and COUNT() functions to summarize the output, as shown in the following code. As with step 3, the columns in your output will match but the results will not:

```
SELECT path, COUNT(*), SUM(filesize)
    FROM test_data GROUP BY path;
```

3. The output will be similar to the following screenshot:

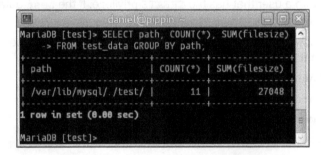

4. Drop the test_data table using the following statement:

```
DROP TABLE test_data;
```

How it works...

When we define a table using `ENGINE=CONNECT`, we are assigning the CONNECT storage engine to look at the data that is stored somewhere outside our MariaDB database. This data could be in a file, in another database, or as in this recipe, in the filesystem itself. The whole purpose of this storage engine is to, for lack of a better term, connect us to different sources of data.

As it connects to so many different forms of data, the CONNECT engine adds over two dozen table options and five column options to the standard `CREATE TABLE` syntax. These options enable us to correctly describe the data we want MariaDB to connect to.

The most important of these is the `TABLE_TYPE` option. We use this to inform CONNECT about the several supported table types that we are creating. These include `CSV`, `XML`, `INI`, `ODBC`, `MYSQL`, `DIR`, and others. For this recipe, we used the `DIR` type, which is one of the simpler ones to define in a `CREATE TABLE` statement.

The `FILE_NAME` option is the other one we will use on all CONNECT tables. It defines the file that we will be reading and writing data to. In this recipe, it simply defines a `*.frm` wildcard pattern to list every file in the directory housing our `test` database that ends with that extension.

Another important table option is `OPTION_LIST`. CONNECT provides over two dozen options but they aren't enough for some of the supported data types that CONNECT can connect to. The `OPTION_LIST` option is a catchall for all supplemental options. The documentation for each table type lists these supplemental options and what they do. For our recipe, we set the supplemental option `subdir=1`. It means that we want our directory listing to recursively descend up to one directory below our default directory.

When CONNECT accesses a directory to gather data for us for the DIR table type, it collects the predefined pieces of information, such as path, file name, and file size. It flags each type of data with a number. Our column definition maps these flags to our columns. The following is a table of the flag numbers for the DIR table type and the information they contain:

Flag Number	Information
1	Path
2	File name
3	File type
4	File attributes
5	File size
6	Last write-access date
7	Last read-access date
8	File creation date

Keep in mind that flags for other table types are not the same because they are dealing with different types of data. When defining a new CONNECT table, we should always consult the CONNECT documentation for the list of flags.

There's more...

The `CREATE TABLE` statements for CONNECT tables can be tricky to define properly. A table definition may be accepted by the server, but it may not do anything or connect to our file the wrong way.

OPTION_LIST options

The `OPTION_LIST` option is specified in the following pattern:

```
OPTION_LIST='option1=optvalue1,option2=optvalue2,...'
```

No spaces or other blanks are allowed between the equal signs or commas; it must be one long space-free string.

Another thing to note is that option values cannot contain commas, but they can contain equal signs. For example, the following is valid for connecting to an HTML table in an XML document:

```
OPTION_LIST='name=table,coltype=HTML,attribute=border=3;cellspacing=2;cel
lpadding=5,headattr=title=mytable;bgcolor=gray'
```

It can be a little tricky to parse, but we just need to remember that semicolons (`;`) are fine to separate parts of complex options in an option list. However, commas (`,`) can only be used as option separators.

Dropping CONNECT tables

The standard `DROP` statement is used to remove a CONNECT table from our database, but unlike what happens with a normal table, the corresponding data and index files are not removed. To really remove a dropped CONNECT table, we need to first drop it and then navigate to wherever the data is (as defined by the `FILE_NAME` option) and remove the data file or files. In this recipe, this isn't necessary because we're actually connecting to the output of a directory listing from our filesystem and not to an actual file. However, it is something to remember when we connect to actual files in other recipes in this chapter.

Files and CONNECT

When we define a connection to an actual file, say with the XML table type, the file we specify with the `FILE_NAME` option does not need to actually exist. If it does, great; however, if it doesn't, CONNECT will not create it until we actually `INSERT` some data into the table.

When CONNECT does create a file, it will either use the value we defined in the FILE_NAME option or use the TABLENAME.TABLETYPE pattern for the name, for example, myfile.xml for a table of the XML type and a name of myfile.

See also

▶ The full documentation of how to CREATE and DROP CONNECT tables, including tables of all the various options can be found at https://mariadb.com/kb/en/creating-and-dropping-connect-tables/

▶ DIR and other Special Virtual Tables are documented at https://mariadb.com/kb/en/connect-table-types-special-virtual-tables/

Reading and writing CSV data using CONNECT

CSV (**comma separated values**) is a very common data-interchange format. MariaDB can easily import CSV formatted files using the LOAD DATA INFILE command, and there is a CSV storage engine that stores data in the CSV format. However, neither of these handles cases where we need to be capable of querying CSV files that are updated outside of MariaDB and CSV files that we don't have to import before we can query them. The CONNECT storage engine's CSV data type allows us to do this easily.

Getting ready

We need to have some CSV data to work with for this recipe. We'll use data from the ISFDB database for this. To start with, perform the following steps:

1. Import the ISFDB database as described in the *Importing the data exported by mysqldump* recipe from *Chapter 2, Diving Deep into MariaDB.*

2. Install and enable the CONNECT storage engine as described in the *Installing the CONNECT storage engine* recipe at the beginning of this chapter.

3. Launch the mysql command-line client application and connect to the isfdb database on our MariaDB server. Then create a /tmp/authors.csv file with the following statement:

```
SELECT author_id, author_canonical, author_legalname,
       author_birthplace, author_birthdate, author_deathdate
    INTO OUTFILE '/tmp/authors.csv'
    FIELDS TERMINATED BY ',' ENCLOSED BY '"'
FROM authors ORDER BY author_id LIMIT 100;
```

How to do it...

1. Launch the `mysql` command-line client application and connect to the `isfdb` database on our MariaDB server.

2. Create a table named `authors_csv`, which uses the CONNECT storage engine's CSV data type and is connected to the `authors_csv.CSV` file we created in preparation for this recipe (change the `FILE_NAME` value to wherever the file is actually located):

```
CREATE TABLE authors_csv (
    author_id int(11) NOT NULL,
    author_canonical varchar(1024) NOT NULL,
    author_legalname varchar(1024) NOT NULL,
    author_birthplace varchar(1024) NOT NULL,
    author_birthdate varchar(10),
    author_deathdate varchar(10)
) ENGINE=CONNECT TABLE_TYPE='CSV'
FILE_NAME='/tmp/authors.csv'
SEP_CHAR=',' QCHAR='"' QUOTED=1;
```

3. Run the following `SELECT` statement to verify that we are reading from the CSV file:

```
SELECT * FROM authors_csv;
```

4. Run the following `INSERT` statement to add a couple of rows to the CSV file:

```
INSERT authors_csv VALUES (
    101,"Fake Author",
    "Author, Fake",
    "Charlotte, North Carolina, USA",
    "1970-01-01",""), (
    102,"Really Fake Author",
    "Author, Really Fake",
    "St. Paul, Minnesota, USA",
    "1969-12-31","");
```

5. Open the CSV file in a text editor and add the following row to the bottom of the file, then save and close the file:

```
103,"Fake","Fake","Fake, USA","1970-04-01",
```

6. Run the SELECT statement from step 3 and verify the three rows we added with author_id numbers greater than 100 in the output, which is shown in the following screenshot:

How it works...

When we create a table that uses the CONNECT storage engine's CSV data type, we're not actually creating a table in the traditional sense. Instead, we are telling CONNECT how to read the file. Most of the statement we use to create the table is the standard CREATE TABLE syntax, but there are several bits at the end that are specific to the CONNECT storage engine and the CSV data type; the primary ones being TABLE_TYPE and the FILE_NAME parts.

The other three are more specific to the CSV table type. SEP_CHAR defines the separator character, a comma (,), in our recipe, and QCHAR defines the character used to quote values, double quotes (") for this CSV file.

The QUOTED option is special. This option sets how CONNECT should handle quoting. There are four settings that it recognizes. They are as follows:

▸ A setting of 0 means fields will only be quoted if they contain the separator character or if they begin with the quoting character (in which case the quoting character will be doubled)

▸ A setting of 1 means all text fields will be quoted unless they are NULL (numeric fields will not be quoted)

▸ A setting of 2 means all fields will be quoted unless they are NULL

▸ A setting of 3 means all fields will be quoted, including NULL fields

Inserting using the mysql command-line client works like we would expect, and the new rows are added to the bottom of the file. We can also make insertions outside of MariaDB by editing the CSV file directly.

There's more...

There are a few more things to be aware of when working with CSV files using the CONNECT storage engine.

CSV header lines

Some CSV files have a header line that contains the names of the columns. We can instruct CONNECT to ignore this line with a `HEADER=1` option when defining the table. A common place to define this is after the `FILE_NAME` option.

Changing the number and order of columns read using flags

For some CSV files, if we plan on just reading the data, we may only care about a subset of the columns in the file, or we may want them to be read in a different order. For both of these situations, we use the `FLAG` option as part of the column definition when creating the table. For example, the following code is a modified version that only contains a reordered subset of the information in our example CSV file:

```
CREATE TABLE authors_csv2 (
    author_id int(11) NOT NULL,
    author_birthdate varchar(10) NOT NULL FLAG=5,
    author_birthplace varchar(1024) NOT NULL FLAG=4,
    author_canonical varchar(1024) NOT NULL FLAG=2
) ENGINE=CONNECT DEFAULT CHARSET=utf8
TABLE_TYPE='CSV'
FILE_NAME='/tmp/authors_csv.CSV'
SEP_CHAR=',' QCHAR='"' QUOTED=1;
```

We will run into trouble if we write to this table, so if we do decide to do this, we should treat the table as read-only and possibly set `READONLY=1` when defining the table so that CONNECT will not even attempt to perform an `INSERT` query.

See also

- ▶ The full documentation on connecting to CSV data files can be found at `https://mariadb.com/kb/en/connect-table-types-data-files/`
- ▶ More information on data types in the CONNECT storage engine can be found at `https://mariadb.com/kb/en/connect-data-types/`

Reading and writing XML data using CONNECT

There is a lot of data stored in XML format. MariaDB can easily export data as XML, but before the CONNECT engine, it did not have a way to easily read from and write to external XML documents.

Getting ready

Import the ISFDB database as described in the *Importing the data exported by mysqldump* recipe from *Chapter 2, Diving Deep into MariaDB*. Then, install and enable the CONNECT storage engine as described in the *Installing the CONNECT storage engine* recipe at the beginning of this chapter. Then, export the isfdb-001.xml file as described in the *Producing XML output* recipe from *Chapter 2, Diving Deep into MariaDB*. For this recipe, it is assumed that the XML file is located in /tmp/isfdb-001.xml, but it will be wherever we were when we exported it from MariaDB. We'll need to alter the FILE_NAME option in the recipe to point at it.

How to do it...

1. Launch the mysql command-line client application and connect to the isfdb database on our MariaDB server.

2. Run the following CREATE TABLE statement:

```
CREATE TABLE authors_xml (
    author_id int,
    author_canonical varchar(1024),
    author_legalname varchar(1024),
    author_birthplace varchar(1024),
    author_birthdate char(10),
    author_deathdate char(10),
    note_id int,
    author_wikipedia varchar(1024),
    author_views int,
    author_imdb varchar(1024),
    author_marque int,
    author_image varchar(1024),
    author_annualviews int,
    author_lastname varchar(1024),
```

```
        author_language int
) ENGINE=CONNECT TABLE_TYPE=XML FILE_NAME='/tmp/isfdb-001.xml'
        TABNAME='resultset'
        OPTION_LIST='rownode=row,colnode=field,coltype=HTML'
;
```

3. Run the following SELECT statement to get a list of authors born in the United Kingdom (may be empty):

```
SELECT
    author_id, author_canonical
FROM authors_xml
WHERE author_birthplace LIKE '%UK';
```

4. Run the following INSERT statement to add a row to our XML file:

```
INSERT authors_xml VALUES (
    101,"Terry Pratchett","Pratchett, Terry",
    "Beaconsfield, Buckinghamshire, UK",
    "0000-00-00","0000-00-00",101,
    "",101,"",101,"",101,"Terry",101 );
```

5. Run the SELECT statement from step 3 to see that the row was added.

How it works...

For this recipe, we're using the XML output produced by MariaDB. The file has the following format:

```
<resultset>
  <row>
    <field name="first_column"></field>
    <field name="second_column"></field>
    ...
    <field name="last_column"></field>
  </row>
</resultset>
```

This style of XML is actually quite similar to an HTML table, except with different tag names (resultset instead of table, row instead of tr, and field instead of td).

Defining the columns for this table so that we can read the XML data is similar to the process of creating columns in a regular MyISAM or InnoDB table. However, after the ENGINE=CONNECT part, we add options to tell the CONNECT storage engine how to read the file.

The data we are interested in is between the `<resultset>` tags, so we specify
`TABNAME='resultset'`. We then inform CONNECT about the data using the `OPTION_LIST`
option. In this option, we first specify `coltype=HTML`, which means that the column tags
are all going to be named the same, so we should read them by their position and not by
their names. Next, we give the names of the tags that specify the rows and the columns,
`rownode=row` and `colnode=field` respectively.

Once the table is defined, we can query it much like a regular table. We can also insert data
with some things to be aware of as described in the next section.

There's more...

XML data can be tricky to work with mainly because it is such a flexible data storage format.
The CONNECT storage engine tries to accommodate as much variation as it can, but there
will always be some XML files that it simply cannot read from or write to properly.

Inserting XML data

In this recipe, we inserted some data. From within MariaDB, it appeared that the data was
inserted properly; however, if we view the XML file, it's plain to see that CONNECT did not put it
in the way the other entries were inserted. For this reason, it's often best to stick to inserting
into simple XML documents or just treating them as read-only data.

Tree versus HTML-like data structures

Some XML data is like the data in our recipe; it is similar in structure to an HTML table.
Other XML data is more like a tree. For example, our data may have had the following format:

```
<resultset>
  <row>
    <first_column></first_column>
    <second_column></second_column>
    ...
    <last_column></last_column>
  </row>
</resultset>
```

If our data had been defined as shown in the preceding code lines, we would have defined our
table as follows:

```
CREATE TABLE table_name (
  first_column data_definition,
  second_column data_definition,
  ...,
  last_column data_definition)
```

```
ENGINE=CONNECT TABLE_TYPE=XML TABNAME='resultset'

FILE_NAME='/tmp/isfdb-001.xml'

OPTION_LIST'rownode=row';
```

This simplified definition is possible because CONNECT is smart enough to figure out that, as we didn't say otherwise, the tags in between the `<row>` and `</row>` tags must be the names of the columns.

Tags and tag attributes

For some XML files, we may want to query and update both tag names and attributes within tags. For this, the CONNECT storage engine provides us with the `FIELD_FORMAT` option.

Suppose our XML data had the following format:

```
<resultset attribute1="value" attribute2="value">
  <row>
    <first_col>
      <sub1></sub1>
      <sub2></sub2>
    </first_col>
    <second_col attribute="value" />
    <last_col>
      <sub1></sub1>
      <sub2></sub2>
    </last_col>
  </row>
</resultset>
```

We could create our table as follows:

```
CREATE TABLE table_name (
  attribute1 data_def FIELD_FORMAT='@attribute1',
  attribute2 data_def FIELD_FORMAT='@attribute2',
  subitem1 data_def FIELD_FORMAT='first_col/sub1',
  subitem2 data_def FIELD_FORMAT='first_col/sub2',
  attribute data_def FIELD_FORMAT='second_col/@attribute',
  last_col data_def FIELD_FORMAT='last_col'
) ENGINE=CONNECT TABLE_TYPE=XML TABNAME='resultset'
  FILE_NAME='/tmp/isfdb-001.xml'
```

The `FIELD_FORMAT` option allows us to specify which tag we want to read from and which attribute inside a tag uses the @ sign. We don't need to specify the top-level tag; so, for those attributes, we just name them.

See also

▶ The full documentation for the CONNECT storage engine's XML data type is at: `https://mariadb.com/kb/en/connect-table-types-data-files/`

Accessing MariaDB tables using CONNECT

Using the CONNECT storage engine, we can set up connections to local or remote MariaDB database tables and have them appear as if they are part of our MariaDB database.

Getting ready

Import the ISFDB database as described in the *Importing the data exported by mysqldump* recipe from *Chapter 2, Diving Deep into MariaDB*. Then, install and enable the CONNECT storage engine as described in the *Installing the CONNECT storage engine* recipe at the beginning of this chapter.

How to do it...

1. Launch the `mysql` command-line client application and connect to the `isfdb` database on our MariaDB server.

2. Run the following CREATE TABLE statement by altering the `user:pass` part of the CONNECTION option with a username and password that has rights to the `isfdb` database:

```
CREATE TABLE websites_2 (
    site_id int(11),
    site_name varchar(255),
    site_url varchar(1024),
    PRIMARY KEY (site_id)
) ENGINE=CONNECT TABLE_TYPE=MYSQL
CONNECTION='mysql://user:pass@localhost/isfdb/websites';
```

3. Run the following two SELECT statements to test that our connection is working and that the output is the same for both tables (we're using the LENGTH part to limit the output to just the shorter URLs; feel free to omit it):

```
SELECT * FROM websites WHERE LENGTH(site_url)<40;
SELECT * FROM websites_2 WHERE LENGTH(site_url)<40;
```

4. Add some data to the table using the following INSERT statement:

```
INSERT websites_2 VALUES
    ("","MariaDB.com","https://mariadb.com"),
    ("","MariaDB.org","https://mariadb.org");
```

5. Run the SELECT statements from step 3 again to verify whether the new entries have appeared in both the tables.

How it works...

It may seem silly to set up a connection from our local isfdb database to our local isfdb database, but it serves as a good demonstration of the ability of the CONNECT storage engine to connect us to other MariaDB databases. This functionality is similar to that of the **FEDERATEDX** storage engine which also ships with MariaDB.

The usefulness of this feature becomes obvious when we are able to connect to remote database tables on other servers. They can be anywhere in the world, but we can connect and interact with them as if they are local. We'll be limited by the speed of our network connection between our local and remote MariaDB servers, but the utility and flexibility are hard to beat.

The key to configuring this data type is the CONNECTION option. It has the following format:

mysql://username:password@host/database_name/table_name

This format is basically a MariaDB URL. The host parameter can be any valid IP address, domain name, or the localhost key word.

If we connect with a user that doesn't require a password, we can skip :password of the username:password part of the URL.

The definitions of the original websites table and our new websites_2 table are slightly different. This is because the CONNECT storage engine does not support certain data types such as TINYTEXT or certain options such as AUTO INCREMENT. In practice, this mostly works out fine; we just exclude the options that aren't supported and modify the data type to be something close to what we need. Then, when we insert data, the original table's configuration will take care of making sure only the correct data is inserted. For example, in our recipe, the original table took care of inserting the correct auto-incremented values into the site_id column when we inserted our two rows of data.

There's more...

It probably goes without saying that this feature needs to be used with great care. Any time we open our database server to the Internet we're just asking for trouble. The best way to do this, if we need to connect two servers together that aren't in the same building (or even the same country), is to connect them via a VPN or another private, encrypted network connection.

We also need to ensure that permissions on our server are locked down good and tight as any user with the permission to issue a SHOW CREATE TABLE query can see the CONNECTION parameter, password, and other details.

See also

▶ The full documentation of the **CONNECT Table Type** is at https://mariadb. com/kb/en/connect-table-types-mysql-table-type-accessing-mysqlmariadb-tables/

Using the XCOL table type

In a perfect world, all data in a MariaDB database would be properly defined and normalized. We don't live in such a world, and sometimes, we have to work with tables that contain one or more catchall columns stuffed full of related values. The **XCOL** table type enables us to work with this data as if it was stored in a separate rather than a single column.

How to do it...

1. Launch the mysql command-line client application and connect to the test database on our MariaDB server. If the test database does not exist, create it first.

2. Run the following CREATE TABLE statement to create our example table:

```
CREATE TABLE superheroes (
    team varchar(50),
    heroes varchar(1024)
);
```

3. Add some data to our new table:

```
INSERT superheroes VALUES
    ("The Avengers","Thor, Iron Man, Black Widow, Hawkeye, Hulk,
Captain America"),
    ("The Justice League", "Superman, Batman, Aquaman, Flash, Wonder
Woman"),
    ("The X-Men", "Storm, Cyclops, Wolverine, Rogue, Iceman");
```

4. Create an XCOL table that references our superheroes table (change username to a user that has read access rights to the superheroes table without needing a password):

```
CREATE TABLE superheroes_xcol ENGINE=CONNECT
    TABLE_TYPE=XCOL TABNAME='superheroes'
    OPTION_LIST='user=username,colname=heroes';
```

5.   Run the following `SELECT` statements to test our `XCOL` table:

```
SELECT * FROM superheroes_xcol;

SELECT * FROM superheroes_xcol WHERE heroes LIKE "S%";

SELECT team, count(heroes) FROM superheroes_xcol GROUP BY team;
```

How it works...

An XCOL table is useful when we have a column in a table that is a list of values. The XCOL table gives us a view into this data and lets us query it as if it was separate.

There's more...

There are a few particulars of the XCOL table type that can cause unexpected issues. One is that an XCOL table is actually reconnecting to the server when it is being queried. If we're connected with a user that requires a password, we need to either supply a password to the option list when we create the table or supply the option list with a user that can read the table without a password.

Another thing to be aware of is that proxy tables are strictly read only. This is not obvious because the error message we get if we try to `INSERT` is a cryptic `COLBLK SetBuffer: undefined Access Method` instead of something more understandable.

Finally, XCOL and proxy tables are inefficient and consume more resources when accessed than a regular table. If we try to set up an XCOL table that connects to a large table, then we will run into serious performance issues. If we have a need to deal with lots of unstructured data, a better option is dynamic columns which are discussed in *Chapter 10, Exploring Dynamic and Virtual Columns in MariaDB*.

See also

▶   The full documentation of the XCOL data type can be found at
    `https://mariadb.com/kb/en/connect-table-types-xcol-table-type/`

▶   The full documentation of the Proxy table type can be found at
    `https://mariadb.com/kb/en/connect-table-types-proxy-table-type/`

Using the PIVOT table type

The **PIVOT** table type is very useful to sort and sum the columns in a table. It's similar to `GROUP BY` but with a more understandable layout. This sort of task is often used to sort and sum columns of data in a desktop spreadsheet program.

How to do it...

1. Launch the `mysql` command-line client application and connect to the `test` database on our MariaDB server. If the `test` database does not exist, create it first.

2. Run the following `CREATE TABLE` statement to create an `expenses` table:

```
CREATE TABLE expenses (
    who varchar(64),
    day varchar(10),
    what varchar(64),
    amount varchar(10)
);
```

3. Add some data to the table by executing the following command lines:

```
INSERT expenses VALUES
    ("Daniel","2013-09-01","Clothing",42.50),
    ("Amy","2013-09-02","Food",5.22),
    ("Daniel","2013-09-01","Clothing",27.75),
    ("Daniel","2013-09-03","Food",10.27),
    ("Amy","2013-09-03","Gas",42.84),
    ("Amy","2013-09-01","Food",15.01),
    ("Amy","2013-09-01","Clothing",11.00),
    ("Daniel","2013-09-01","Gas",34.10),
    ("Amy","2013-09-02","Food",15.00),
    ("Daniel","2013-09-01","Food",12.50),
    ("Daniel","2013-09-02","Gas",32.20),
    ("Daniel","2013-09-03","Clothing",82.80),
    ("Amy","2013-09-03","Food",8.72),
    ("Daniel","2013-09-03","Gas",15.08),
    ("Daniel","2013-09-02","Clothing",17.27),
    ("Amy","2013-09-03","Clothing",32.00) ;
```

4. Create a PIVOT table (change `username` to a user that has read access rights to the `expenses` table without needing a password):

```
CREATE TABLE expenses_pivot
    ENGINE=CONNECT TABLE_TYPE=PIVOT TABNAME=expenses
    OPTION_LIST='user=username';
```

5. Run the following SELECT statement to show our pivoted data. The result is shown in the following screenshot:

```
SELECT * FROM expenses_pivot;
```

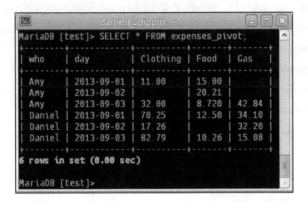

How it works...

When our expenses table is pivoted, the default pivot places the contents of the what column next to the who and day columns. We could get the same data with the following query, but the output is not that well-organized and easy to read:

```
SELECT who, day, what, SUM(amount)

FROM expenses

GROUP BY who, day, what;
```

What the CONNECT storage engine is doing when it pivots a table is to first find a facts column; in our sample table, this column is the prices column. It then determines the column to pivot on; in our sample table, it automatically chose the what column. It then aggregates the facts (the prices) by summing the prices together by day and what. It then gets the distinct values of the what column (the pivot column) and creates a column for each value. It constructs all this in memory, and after it has everything sorted, it outputs the table.

One potential issue with this table type is that the CONNECT engine reads in the values to pivot on only when a PIVOT table is created. If those values change, we may get odd results or an error, for example, if we delete all rows from the expenses table that match Gas or if we insert a row where the what column is Electricity. The only remedy in this case is to DROP and then recreate the PIVOT table.

There's more...

CONNECT tries to guess the column we want to pivot on, but we can also specify the column using `pivotcol=column_name` in the `OPTION_LIST` option. We can also change the default function from `SUM` to something else, such as `AVG`, to compute the average amount instead of the total amount spent on a day. For example, the following is a query creating a table that pivots on the `day` column and computes the average:

```
CREATE TABLE expenses_pivot2
  ENGINE=CONNECT TABLE_TYPE=PIVOT TABNAME=expenses
  OPTION_LIST='user=daniel,pivotcol=day,function=AVG';
SELECT * FROM expenses_pivot2;
```

We can also drop columns from our pivot tables; for example, we are interested in the grand totals for each day without regard to the `who` column. The following is an example that does this:

```
CREATE TABLE expenses_pivot3
  ENGINE=CONNECT TABLE_TYPE=PIVOT TABNAME=expenses
  OPTION_LIST='user=daniel';
ALTER TABLE expenses_pivot3 DROP COLUMN who;
SELECT * FROM expenses_pivot3;
```

See also

▸ The full documentation of the PIVOT data type is at
   https://mariadb.com/kb/en/connect-table-types-pivot-table-type/

Using the OCCUR table type

If a table contains many columns, all of which contain similar types of data, it can be difficult to answer questions which deal with comparing those values. This is where the **OCCUR** data type can prove useful.

How to do it...

1. Launch the `mysql` command-line client application and connect to the `test` database on our MariaDB server. If the `test` database does not exist, create it first.

2. Run the following `CREATE TABLE` statement to create a `gadgets` table:

```
CREATE TABLE gadgets (
  who varchar(64),
  phone int,
```

```
    tablet int,

    mp3player int,

    camera int


);
```

3. Add some data to our gadgets table using the following statement:

```
INSERT gadgets VALUES
    ("Jim",1,2,1,2),
    ("Bob",0,0,3,0),
    ("Tom",1,1,1,0),
    ("Joe",1,1,1,1),
    ("Rob",2,2,0,0),
    ("Tim",0,3,1,1)
;
```

4. Run the following statement to create our OCCUR table (replace `username` with a user that has read access rights to the gadget table without needing a password):

```
CREATE TABLE gadgets_occur (
    who varchar(64) NOT NULL,
    gadget varchar(16) NOT NULL,
    number int NOT NULL
) ENGINE=CONNECT TABLE_TYPE=OCCUR TABNAME=gadgets
OPTION_LIST='user=username,occurcol=number,rankcol=gadget'
COLIST='phone,tablet,mp3player,camera';
```

5. Run the following `SELECT` statements to view our OCCUR table in action:

```
SELECT * FROM gadgets_occur;
SELECT * FROM gadgets_occur
    WHERE gadget="tablet" and number > 1;
```

How it works...

When we create an OCCUR table, we are basically viewing the data in the source table in a different way. In our recipe, instead of columns with the number of gadgets each person owns being listed with one row per user, we flip it such that the number of each gadget is listed by itself.

When defining an OCCUR table, we first specify the tables we want our values stored in. The first column we defined, `name`, matches the same column in our source table. The other two are the columns we're mapping data to, so their names do not match. For this recipe, we use `gadget` and `number` since those names match the data being stored.

With our columns defined, we now need to tell the CONNECT storage engine how to map the data. After defining which table our OCCUR column is connecting to with the `TABNAME` option, the rest of the configuration happens in the `OPTION_LIST` and `COLIST` variables.

In the `OPTION_LIST` variable, we first define which column in our OCCUR table we want to use to hold the numbers we're tracking using the `occurcol` variable; for our recipe, we're using the `number` column. We then name the column using the `rankcol` variable that will hold the column names we're interested in. Lastly, with the `COLIST` option, we name those columns.

With the setup complete, we can easily ask questions that are much more difficult to ask our original table. For example, we can get a list of every person who owns multiples of the given gadget types using the following command line:

```
SELECT * FROM gadgets_occur
 WHERE number > 1;
```

We can approximate this query on the gadgets table only with difficulty. For example, the following four queries give us the same data as the previous single query, but it is separated:

```
SELECT who,phone FROM gadgets WHERE phone > 1;
SELECT who,tablet FROM gadgets WHERE tablet > 1;
SELECT who,mp3player FROM gadgets WHERE mp3player > 1;
SELECT who,camera FROM gadgets WHERE camera > 1;
```

Going further, we can add `UNION ALL` in between the queries to combine all of the numbers together, but while this gives us the numbers, it doesn't tell us what gadget each number represents:

```
SELECT who,phone AS gadget FROM gadgets WHERE phone > 1 UNION ALL
SELECT who,tablet FROM gadgets WHERE tablet > 1 UNION ALL
SELECT who,mp3player FROM gadgets WHERE mp3player > 1 UNION ALL
SELECT who,camera FROM gadgets WHERE camera > 1;
```

A better solution is to use an OCCUR table.

There's more...

In our example as some people did not own certain gadgets, the values in the original table were set to zero. We omitted those by specifying `NOT NULL` for the columns in our OCCUR table.

See also

▶ The full documentation of the OCCUR data type can be found at
   `https://mariadb.com/kb/en/connect-table-types-occur-table-type/`

Using the WMI table type

Windows includes an interface through which various components of the operating system can provide useful system information. This interface is called **Windows Management Instrumentation** (**WMI**). The WMI table type allows us to easily connect to and display information from this interface.

Getting ready

As WMI is specific to the Windows operating system, this recipe uses Windows.

How to do it...

1. Launch the `mysql` command-line client application and connect to the `test` database on our MariaDB server. If the test database does not exist, create it first.

2. Run the following `CREATE TABLE` statement to create a WMI table:

```
CREATE TABLE alias (
    friendlyname char(32) NOT NULL,
    target char(64) NOT NULL
) ENGINE=CONNECT TABLE_TYPE='WMI'
OPTION_LIST='Namespace=root\\cli,Class=Msft_CliAlias';
```

3. Run the following `SELECT` statement to query the table:

```
SELECT * FROM alias;
```

How it works...

The WMI table type maps rows to each instance of the related information. To accomplish this mapping, our column names must match the properties that we're interested in. This matching is case insensitive.

Apart from naming, when configuring a WMI table, we need to tell the CONNECT storage engine the `Namespace` and `Class` of the data that we are looking up. We define these as variables in the `OPTION_LIST`. Our recipe is actually a handy way to get a list of common classes.

There's more...

We don't always need to define tables when using the WMI data type as some namespaces have default values in the class specification that CONNECT can look up when creating the table. For example, we can create a table that queries the CSPROD class simply by naming it `csprod`:

```
CREATE TABLE csprod
  ENGINE=CONNECT TABLE_TYPE='WMI';
```

Performance

Some WMI providers are slow to respond. There's not a whole lot that can be done about it as it is due to the way WMI works. It is something to be aware of.

A related issue is that some WMI providers output a lot of information. So much so that for some, it can bog down our system or cause a query to take far too long to complete. To combat this, CONNECT has an `Estimate` option that has a default value of 100. This option limits the output to 100 rows. For instances where we need to increase this, we can do so when creating our WMI tables. For most providers, keeping it at 100 is preferred.

Other information

A couple of other bits of information that are useful to know about WMI tables are that they cannot be indexed and that they are read-only.

See also

▶ The full documentation of the WMI data type can be found at `https://mariadb.com/kb/en/connect-table-types-special-virtual-tables/`

Using the MAC address table type

The **MAC** table type allows us to look up and query various bits of information about the network connection and network setup of our local machine.

Getting ready

The MAC table type works only in Windows. So, this recipe requires the Windows OS.

How to do it...

1. Launch the `mysql` command-line client application and connect to the `test` database on our MariaDB server. If the `test` database does not exist, create it first.

2. Run the following `CREATE TABLE` statement to create a MAC table:

```
CREATE TABLE host (
    hostname varchar(132)  flag=1,
    domain   varchar(132)  flag=2,
    ipaddr   char(16)      flag=15,
    gateway  char(16)      flag=17,
    dhcp     char(16)      flag=18,
    leaseexp datetime      flag=23
) ENGINE=CONNECT TABLE_TYPE=MAC;
```

3. Run the following `SELECT` statement to query the information about our current network settings:

```
SELECT * FROM host;
```

How it works...

Information on our network cards and their current settings is actually pretty easy to get, so the MAC table type is more of a convenient feature compared to other CONNECT storage engine table types. That said, it can be a very useful way to inform our applications about their network connection as all of that data is now available right inside the database.

There are many network parameters that we can query, and the ones that we connect to in our table definition are set using the `flag=` option when defining a MAC table.

The following table lists all of the values, their flags, and their data definitions:

Flag	Value	Data type
1	Host Name	varchar(132)
2	Domain	varchar(132)
3	DNS address	varchar(24)
4	Node type	int(1)
5	Scope ID	varchar(256)
6	Routing	int(1)
7	Proxy	int(1)
8	DNS	int(1)
10	Name	varchar(260)
11	Description	varchar(132)
12	MAC address	char(24)
13	Type	int(3)
14	DHCP	int(1)
15	IP address	char(16)
16	SUBNET mask	char(16)
17	GATEWAY	char(16)
18	DHCP server	char(16)
19	Have WINS	int(1)
20	Primary WINS	char(16)
21	Secondary WINS	char(16)
22	Lease obtained	datetime
23	Lease expires	datetime

There's more...

Flag values of less than 10 are specific to the computer. Other flag values are specific to the network card or cards in the computer (which may or may not be removable).

See also

▸ The full documentation of the MAC table type is at: https://mariadb.com/kb/en/connect-table-types-special-virtual-tables/

6

Replication in MariaDB

In this chapter, we will cover the following recipes:

- ▶ Setting up replication
- ▶ Using global transaction IDs
- ▶ Using multisource replication
- ▶ Enhancing the binlog with row event annotations
- ▶ Configuring binlog event checksums
- ▶ Selectively skipping the replication of binlog events

Introduction

Replication is what allows MariaDB to scale to thousands of servers, millions of users, and petabytes of data. But let's not get ahead of ourselves. Replication on a small scale is a great way to grow the number of users our application can support with minimal effort. As we gain users, we can grow the number of replication servers to match.

There are many different ways to set up how we do replication. In this chapter, we'll only touch on a couple of basic ones: a single master to multiple slaves, and multiple masters to a single slave.

 Historically, replication source servers have been called *masters* and replication target servers have been called *slaves*. To avoid confusion, we'll be using these names.

Setting up replication

Setting up replication is not hard as long as all the various bits are in place. This recipe is all about the most basic concept of replication topologies; a single master server replicating to multiple slaves is shown in the following diagram:

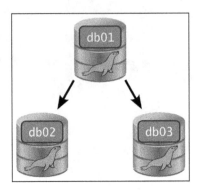

Getting ready

This recipe assumes that we have three servers. The servers are named db01, db02, and db03, and they reside on the 192.168.4.0 network with IP addresses 192.168.4.101.to 192.168.4.103. One server, db01, will be our replication master, and the other two will be our replication slaves.

For the purposes of this recipe, the servers are assumed to contain fresh installs of MariaDB, with just the default databases set up.

How to do it...

1. On all three hosts, launch the mysql command-line client and connect to the local MariaDB server with the root user (or another user with the GRANT privilege) and run the following command:

    ```
    GRANT REPLICATION SLAVE, REPLICATION CLIENT ON *.*

    TO replicant@'192.168.4.%'

    IDENTIFIED BY 'sup3rs3kr37p455w0rd';
    ```

2. Exit from the client and stop MariaDB.

3. Edit each system's my.cnf or my.ini file and add the following to the [mysqld] section (it may already exist, so look for it first, and feel free to adjust the path if desired):

    ```
    log_bin = /var/log/mysql/mariadb-bin
    ```

4. While editing the config file, change the bind address to the IP address of the server.

5. While editing the config file, on each server, set a unique `server_id` and `relay_log` filename in the `[mysqld]` section for the `db01` server as follows:

```
server_id = 101

relay_log = db01-relay-binlog
```

6. On both the replication slave servers, edit the system `my.cnf` or `my.ini` file and add the following to the `[mysqld]` section:

```
read_only
```

7. Launch the `mysql` command-line client on the replication master server and run the following command to discover the proper filename to use in the next step:

```
SHOW MASTER STATUS;
```

8. For this recipe, we'll get the following output:

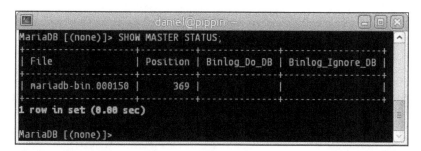

9. Launch the `mysql` command-line client on each replication slave server and run the following commands:

```
CHANGE MASTER TO MASTER_HOST='192.168.4.101',

MASTER_USER = 'replicant',

MASTER_PASSWORD = 'sup3rs3kr37p455w0rd',

MASTER_LOG_FILE = 'mariadb-bin.000150',

MASTER_LOG_POS = 0;

START SLAVE;
```

10. Run the following command and confirm that `Slave_IO_Running` and `Slave_SQL_Running` are both `Yes` and that there are no errors:

```
SHOW SLAVE STATUS;
```

11. On the replication master server, launch the `mysql` command-line client and run the following commands to create a database and insert some data:

```
CREATE DATABASE IF NOT EXISTS temp;

USE temp;


CREATE TABLE doctors (
    id int NOT NULL AUTO_INCREMENT PRIMARY KEY,
    given_names varchar(255),
    surname varchar(255),
    birthdate date);


INSERT INTO doctors VALUES (
    (1,'William','Hartnell','1908-01-08'),
    (2,'Patrick','Troughton','1920-03-25'),
    (3,'Jon','Pertwee','1919-07-07'),
    (4,'Tom','Baker','1934-01-20'));
```

12. On the replication slave servers, launch the `mysql` command-line client and run the following commands to verify that the data entered on the replication master server has been replicated to the replication slave servers:

```
USE temp;


SELECT * FROM doctors;
```

How it works...

The MariaDB binary log is at the heart of replicating from one machine to others. In basic terms, events are written to the log on the replication master server and then to the database. Replication slaves read the log on the replication master and apply them to their own copy of the database.

For simplicity, the `replicant` user we created for this recipe has the permissions needed on both the master and the slave servers. Strictly speaking, the REPLICATION SLAVE privilege is only needed on the user we created on the replication master server and the REPLICATION CLIENT privilege is only needed when we use the commands SHOW MASTER STATUS; and SHOW SLAVE STATUS;. By configuring our replication user with both of these privileges, we can use it for all of our replication tasks on any of our servers. And if we decide down the road to promote one of the slave servers to be the master server, the user is already set up and ready to go.

The CHANGE MASTER TO command with its various variables is what actually configures the replication. We could configure these variables in the my.cnf or my.ini config files, but this is not recommended because it hardcodes the settings, which can interfere with our other activities such as changing the master server on the fly.

The read_only variable is important because it prevents a rogue application or user from trying to INSERT on a replication slave. Doing so is a great way to corrupt our data when using a master-slave topology like we are using here.

For step 11, an alternative to typing out all of the commands to create the temp database, create the doctors table, and INSERT the data is to download the 4399OS_06_01.sql file from the book's website and to import it as follows:

```
mysql -u username -p < 4399OS_06_01.sql
```

Change username to a user that has rights to create a database and insert data. Also, because it's a file and we don't have to type it in, the file inserts more rows of data than are there in the recipe.

There's more...

There are many little things that are important to know about replication.

Common causes of replication failures

If the skip_networking variable is set in our my.cnf or my.ini file, MariaDB will limit connections to localhost only. This will break replication, as the whole point is for multiple servers to communicate with each other. This variable has been deprecated in favor of setting the bind_address variable to 127.0.0.1, which does the same thing.

If we see Can't connect or Connection refused errors when we run SHOW SLAVE STATUS;, then checking to see what both of these variables are set to is a good place to start. The bind_address variable must be set to the IP address we use to access the server remotely from other clients. If our server has one or more IP addresses assigned, such as a public and private IP address for example, we will almost always want to set it to the private IP address. Private IPv4 addresses are easy to recognize. They almost always take the form of either 192.168.x.x or 10.x.x.x. Private IPv6 addresses also exist but are rarely used. They begin with fd.

Another common failure is not setting the server_id variable. All servers in a replication group must have unique server IDs. The default value, if the server_id variable is not set, is 1. So, when setting it, choose a different number. Valid values are anything from 1 to 4,294,967,295.

Binary logs versus relay logs

In this recipe, the replication slaves are not configured to store a log of their own. They simply read the binary log of the replication master server and apply it. The slaves can be configured to store a log of their own by adding the following to the `[mysqld]` section of the `my.cnf` or `my.ini` file:

```
log_slave_updates
```

Doing so adds some overhead to a slave server, but by setting this variable it can act as a replication master with its own downstream slaves. In this way, multilevel replication topologies can be created.

The log on the replication slaves is called the relay log instead of binary log. Both of these logs have the same format. On replication slave servers, they are called relay logs simply to specify that the log is from a replication master as opposed to being a log of activity on the local server itself.

Safer replication

One good way to increase safety and crash protection for MariaDB is to set the following two options in the `[mysqld]` section of our `my.cnf` or `my.ini` file:

```
innodb_flush_logs_at_trx_commit = 1

sync_binlog = 1
```

Both of these options force an explicit write-to-disk (`fsync`) operation whenever writing to these files. This helps ensure that our data is written to the disk as soon as possible. This adds safety in case of system failures or power outages to our databases and replication, but it has the potential to really impact performance as extra `fsync` operations are relatively expensive, resource wise. To combat this, the MariaDB developers have created a group commit operation that groups `fsync` operations together whenever possible. The optimization works best with highly parallel workloads and is enabled automatically. Enabling the variables still results in slightly lower performance, but combined with the `fsync` grouping it is not so bad that it isn't worth doing.

See also

- A lot more information can be found in the replication section of the MariaDB Knowledge Base at `https://mariadb.com/kb/en/replication/`
- The full documentation of the group commit optimization can be found at `https://mariadb.com/kb/en/group-commit-for-the-binary-log/`

Using global transaction IDs

Global Transaction ID (**GTID**) is a new feature in MariaDB 10.0 and above. It helps us achieve greater reliability and flexibility with our replication.

Getting ready

This recipe builds upon the previous one, so to get ready for this recipe, simply set up a basic replication as described in the *Setting up replication* recipe.

How to do it...

1. On both our replication slave servers, launch the `mysql` command-line client and run the following commands:

   ```
   STOP SLAVE;

   CHANGE MASTER TO MASTER_USE_GTID = SLAVE_POS;

   START SLAVE;
   ```

2. Check on the status of our replication slave servers with the following command:

   ```
   SHOW ALL SLAVES STATUS\G
   ```

3. Look at the bottom of the output for the following lines (the `Gtid_Slave_Pos` value will likely be different and the lines are separated by several other lines in the output):

   ```
   Using_Gtid: Slave_Pos

   Gtid_Slave_Pos: 0-101-2320
   ```

4. Insert more data into our `temp.doctors` table on the replication master server, and then run the following `SELECT` statement on our replication slave servers to confirm that replication is still happening:

   ```
   SELECT * FROM temp.doctors;
   ```

How it works...

The GTID feature is enabled automatically, but when replication slaves connect to master servers, they can choose to use either the traditional filename and offset or GTID to determine where to start replicating from. To use GTID, we use the `MASTER_USE_GTID` variable instead of the `MASTER_LOG_FILE` and `MASTER_LOG_POS` variables.

Because we started with a server that was already set up and using a traditional filename and position replication, the only thing we had to do was temporarily stop replication, set the `MASTER_USE_GTID` variable, and then start replication up again.

There's more...

There are three possible values we can use for the `MASTER_USE_GTID` variable. The one we used in the recipe is `SLAVE_POS` as this variable starts replication at the position of the last GTID replicated to our slave server. This is a safe default value to use.

The other two possible values are `CURRENT_POS` and the actual GTID number we want to use. Using `CURRENT_POS` is usually fine, unless we are changing a server from being the master to being a slave. The value of `CURRENT_POS` is whatever `binlog` entry that server has in its local binary log. If the most recent entry is something that doesn't exist on the current master server, then replication to the slave will fail. If our slave server does not have binary logging turned on, then the value of `CURRENT_POS` will be the same as `SLAVE_POS`.

The third option, using a specific GTID, is useful if we know exactly what number to start from, but it's more of an expert option used only when we know it's the right thing to do. It's much safer to stick to the other two.

See also

▶ More about **Global Transaction ID** is available at
   https://mariadb.com/kb/en/global-transaction-id/

▶ The full documentation of the `CHANGE MASTER TO` command can be found at
   https://mariadb.com/kb/en/change-master-to/

Using multisource replication

A familiar replication topology is one where we have a single master server and several slave servers. Another alternative topology is where we have a single slave server connected to multiple master servers. This is called multisource replication.

Getting ready

For this recipe, we'll be working on the assumption that we have three servers, db01, db02, and db03, which are each running a fresh install of MariaDB. The first two will be our replication masters, and the last one will be our replication slave as shown in the following diagram:

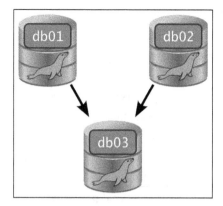

We'll further assume that all three servers are on the same subnet, `192.168.4.0`, with the final part of their individual IP addresses being `101`, `102`, and `103`, respectively.

How to do it...

1. On all three servers, launch the `mysql` command-line client and run the following command to add our replication user:

    ```
    GRANT REPLICATION SLAVE, REPLICATION CLIENT ON *.*
        TO replicant@'192.168.4.%' IDENTIFIED BY 'sup3rs3kr37p455w0rd';
    ```

2. Quit the `mysql` command-line client and then stop MariaDB.

3. Edit the system `my.cnf` or `my.ini` file on each server. Make sure the `log_bin` variable is set (it is by default).

4. On `db01`, add the following settings to the `[mysqld]` section:

    ```
    bind_address = 192.168.4.101
    relay_log = db01-relay-binlog
    server_id = 101
    ```

5. On `db02`, add the following settings to the `[mysqld]` section:

    ```
    bind_address = 192.168.4.102
    relay_log = db02-relay-binlog
    server_id = 102
    ```

6. On `db03`, add the following settings to the `[mysqld]` section:

    ```
    read_only
    replicate_ignore_db=mysql,information_schema,performance_schema
    bind_address = 192.168.4.103
    relay_log = db03-relay-binlog
    server_id = 103
    ```

7.   Start MariaDB on all three hosts.

8.   On db03, launch the mysql command-line client and run the following commands:

```
CHANGE MASTER 'db01' TO MASTER_HOST='db01',
   MASTER_USER = 'replicant',
   MASTER_PASSWORD = 'sup3rs3kr37p455w0rd',
   MASTER_USE_GTID = CURRENT_POS;


CHANGE MASTER 'db02' TO MASTER_HOST='db02',
   MASTER_USER = 'replicant',
   MASTER_PASSWORD = 'sup3rs3kr37p455w0rd',
   MASTER_USE_GTID = CURRENT_POS;


START ALL SLAVES;
```

9.   While on db03, in the mysql command-line client, run the following command to check the replication status:

```
SHOW ALL SLAVES STATUS;
```

10. On db01 and db02, create databases with uniquely named tables on each server and input data.

11. On db03, run queries to see that the data has been replicated.

How it works...

Multisource replication is a replication topology where there are many master servers replicating to a single slave. Setting it up is very similar to setting up traditional replication but with a few key differences.

One thing we need to do to prevent potential conflicts on the slave server is to list the tables we want to ignore. This is done with the replicate_ignore_db option. In our recipe, we set this option in the my.cnf or my.ini file, but it can also be set as a GLOBAL or SESSION variable using the mysql command-line client. The option takes a comma-separated list of the databases we want the slave server to not replicate. A good default is to set this to the system database, mysql, and the performance_schema and information_schema, but there may be other databases we don't want to replicate; if so, they should also be added to the list.

Because we are dealing with multiple master servers, we need to name them when running the CHANGE MASTER command. The name we choose is also used when running the SHOW ALL SLAVES STATUS; command so we can tell the master servers apart.

If we want to see the status of replication from an individual master server, we specify the name in the SHOW SLAVE STATUS; command as follows:

```
SHOW SLAVE 'db02' STATUS;
```

There's more...

There will always be warnings when starting replication but they are just informational. The number of warnings corresponds directly to the number of configured replication masters. For example, refer to the following screenshot:

Other ignore options

We are not restricted to just ignoring whole databases; we can also ignore specific tables using the replicate_ignore_table variable.

Instead of specifying the tables or databases to ignore, we also have the option of specifying only the tables and databases we want to replicate. We use the replicate_do_table and replicate_do_db options for this.

Additional files

After setting up multisource replication, a few new files will appear in our slave server's data directory. These include a multi-master.info file and relay and .info files for each master server we have configured. These files are used by MariaDB to keep track of replication, so leave them alone.

See also

▶   The full documentation of **Multi-source replication** can be found at
     https://mariadb.com/kb/en/multi-source-replication/

Enhancing the binlog with row event annotations

When using replication, it's popular to set `binlog_format` to `row`. The only issue with this is that when we look at the binlog, it is harder to read because the statements aren't included. We can see the changes but not the SQL statement that made the changes.

Getting ready

For this recipe, we'll assume that we've set up replication as described in either the *Setting up replication* or *Using multisource replication* recipes earlier in this chapter. Pick a master server and a slave server to use. In this recipe, we'll call the master server `db01` and the slave server `db03`.

How to do it...

1. On `db01`, edit the system `my.cnf` or `my.ini` file and add the following to the `[mysqld]` section:

   ```
   binlog_format = row
   binlog_annotate_row_events
   ```

2. On `db03`, edit the system `my.cnf` or `my.ini` file and add the following to the `[mysqld]` section:

   ```
   binlog_format = row
   replicate_annotate_row_events
   ```

3. Restart MariaDB on both servers.

4. On `db01`, launch the `mysql` command-line client and run the following commands:

   ```
   DROP DATABASE IF EXISTS test;
   CREATE DATABASE test;
   USE test;
   CREATE TABLE t1(a char(1));
   INSERT INTO t1 VALUES ('a'),('b'),('c'),('d');
   CREATE TABLE t2(a char(1));
   INSERT INTO t2 VALUES ('a'),('b'),('c'),('d');
   CREATE TABLE t3(a char(1));
   INSERT DELAYED INTO t3 VALUES ('a'),('b'),('c'),('d');
   DELETE t1, t2 FROM  t1 INNER JOIN t2 INNER JOIN t3
       WHERE t1.a=t2.a and t2.a=t3.a;
   ```

5. On db01, run the following command in the mysql command-line client:

    SHOW BINLOG EVENTS;

6. While still on db01, exit the mysql command-line client and look in the mysql directory under /var/log/ for the binlog file with the highest number. We'll assume it's 150. Run the following command to look at the events stored in the file:

    mysqlbinlog /var/log/mysql/mariadb-bin.000150

7. The result will have differences but will show annotations for binlog events similar to the following screenshot:

```
# at 1045
#140212 22:47:34 server id 101  end_log_pos 1083        GTID 0-101-5299
/*!100001 SET @@session.gtid_seq_no=5299*//*!*/;
BEGIN
/*!*/;
# at 1083
# at 1147
# at 1190
#140212 22:47:34 server id 101  end_log_pos 1147        Annotate_rows:
#Q> INSERT INTO t2 VALUES ('a'),('b'),('c'),('d')
#140212 22:47:34 server id 101  end_log_pos 1190        Table_map: `test`.`t2` mapped to number 126
#140212 22:47:34 server id 101  end_log_pos 1231        Write_rows: table id 126 flags: STMT_END_F

BINLOG '
VkD8UhNlAAAAKwAAAKYEAAAAAH4AAAAAAAEABHRlc3QAAnQyAAH+Av4BAQ==
VkD8UhdlAAAAKQAAAM8EAAAAAH4AAAAAAAEAAf/+AWH+AWL+AWP+AWQ=
'/*!*/;
# at 1231
#140212 22:47:34 server id 101  end_log_pos 1258        Xid = 192
COMMIT/*!*/;
# at 1258
#140212 22:47:34 server id 101  end_log_pos 1296        GTID 0-101-5300
/*!100001 SET @@session.gtid_seq_no=5300*//*!*/;
# at 1296
#140212 22:47:34 server id 101  end_log_pos 1385        Query    thread_id=64    exec_time=0    error_code=0
SET TIMESTAMP=1392263254/*!*/;
CREATE TABLE t3(a char(1))
/*!*/;
DELIMITER ;
# End of log file
ROLLBACK /* added by mysqlbinlog */;
/*!50003 SET COMPLETION_TYPE=@OLD_COMPLETION_TYPE*/;
/*!50530 SET @@SESSION.PSEUDO_SLAVE_MODE=0*/;
daniel@pippin:~$
```

How it works...

When binary logging is enabled, we can look through the log and see when changes were made, but we don't see the statements that made those changes. Adding binlog_annotate_row_events to our configuration tells MariaDB to annotate our binary log with the statements that changed data. This makes it much easier to search through the binary log to find the statement or event we are looking for.

There's more...

There are situations where we may want to output data from our binary logs without the annotations. To do this, we simply add `--skip-annotate-row-events` to the `mysqlbinlog` command when we run it. By default, `mysqlbinlog` will print annotations if they are in the log.

See also

▶ The full documentation of the annotate row events feature can be found at https://mariadb.com/kb/en/annotate_rows_log_event/

▶ The full documentation of the `mysqlbinlog` command can be found at https://mariadb.com/kb/en/mysqlbinlog/

Configuring binlog event checksums

A rare, but still possible, problem can occur if the filesystem where we store our binary and relay logs gets corrupted. It can be especially damaging if we don't detect it early on. Event checksums are a way to detect this quickly.

Getting ready

For this recipe, we'll assume that we've set up replication as described in either the *Setting up replication* or the *Using multisource replication* recipes earlier in this chapter. Pick a master server and a slave server to use. In this recipe, we'll call db01 as the master server and db03 as the slave server.

How to do it...

1. On db01, launch the `mysql` command-line client and run the following commands:

   ```
   SET GLOBAL BINLOG_CHECKSUM = 1;
   SET GLOBAL MASTER_VERIFY_CHECKSUM = 1;
   ```

2. On db03, launch the `mysql` command-line client and run the following command:

   ```
   SET GLOBAL SLAVE_SQL_VERIFY_CHECKSUM = 1;
   ```

How it works...

When checksums are enabled on our master and slave servers, it adds an extra layer of checking as events are copied over and applied. This helps us better to detect filesystem corruption of our binary and relay log files.

When first enabled, the binary log file is immediately rotated so that we don't have a situation where a part of a log file has checksums and the other part doesn't.

There's more...

In the recipe, we set the options dynamically so that we don't have to restart the server. To make the settings permanent, we need to add them to the `[mysqld]` section of the `my.cnf` or `my.ini` file.

The `mysqlbinlog` utility doesn't verify checksums by default. To have it do so, run it with the `--verify-binlog-checksum` option.

See also

▸ The full documentation of **Binlog Event Checksums** can be found at
  `https://mariadb.com/kb/en/binlog-event-checksums/`

▸ Also, refer to the **Binlog Event Checksums interoperability** page at `https://mariadb.com/kb/en/binlog-event-checksum-interoperability/`

Selectively skipping the replication of binlog events

Sometimes, we want to skip replicating certain events to our replication slave servers. MariaDB lets us do this dynamically.

Getting ready

For this recipe, we'll assume that we've set up replication as described in either the *Setting up replication* or *Using multisource replication* recipes earlier in this chapter. Pick a master server and a slave server to use. In this recipe, we'll call db01 as the master server and db03 as the slave server.

How to do it...

1. On db01, launch the `mysql` command-line client and run the following command to turn on replication skipping:

   ```
   SET @@skip_replication=1;
   ```

2. On db01, create an empty database:

   ```
   CREATE DATABASE w;
   ```

3. On db03, run the following commands to turn off replication of skipped events:
    ```
    STOP SLAVE;
    SET GLOBAL REPLICATE_EVENTS_MARKED_FOR_SKIP = FILTER_ON_MASTER;
    START SLAVE;
    ```

4. On db01, create another empty database:
    ```
    CREATE DATABASE wx;
    ```

5. On db03, switch to filtering on the slave:
    ```
    STOP SLAVE;
    SET GLOBAL REPLICATE_EVENTS_MARKED_FOR_SKIP = FILTER_ON_SLAVE;
    START SLAVE;
    ```

6. On db01, create another empty database:
    ```
    CREATE DATABASE wxy;
    ```

7. On db03, switch off filtering:
    ```
    STOP SLAVE;
    SET GLOBAL REPLICATE_EVENTS_MARKED_FOR_SKIP = REPLICATE;
    START SLAVE;
    ```

8. On db01, create a fourth empty database:
    ```
    CREATE DATABASE wxyz;
    ```

9. On db03, check to see whether only the first and last databases (w and wxyz) exist (filtering was turned on when we created the wx and wxy databases).
    ```
    SHOW DATABASES;
    ```

10. On db01, turn off @@skip_replication by using the following command line:
    ```
    SET @@skip_replication=0;
    ```

How it works...

The @@skip_replication session variable, when set to true (that is, 1), causes all events logged to the binary log on the master server to be flagged for skipping. Actual skipping only happens if the slave servers have the REPLICATE_EVENTS_MARKED_FOR_SKIP variable set to either FILTER_ON_MASTER or FILTER_ON_SLAVE. The default value for that variable is REPLICATE, which means that events are replicated even though there's a skip flag set.

One possible way this feature can be used is if we have a situation where we need to create a temporary database, give it some data, run some analytics or reports on it, and then drop it. If it's just a temporary thing, we might not want it replicated to the slave servers.

The actual filtering can take place either on the master server, by setting `REPLICATE_EVENTS_MARKED_FOR_SKIP` to `FILTER_ON_MASTER`, or on the slave server by setting the option to `FILTER_ON_SLAVE`. The end result is the same; the only difference is that with `FILTER_ON_SLAVE`, the events are transferred over the network before they are filtered.

MariaDB does not have to be stopped to change the `REPLICATE_EVENTS_MARKED_FOR_SKIP` variable, but replication does. So, in this recipe, we bracketed each change with `STOP SLAVE;` and `START SLAVE;` commands. Trying to change it without stopping replication first gives an error.

There's more...

While handy, this feature should be used with great caution. When events are not replicated, the data on the master server will be different from the data on the slave. Many problems could arise if this is handled badly. It is up to the application or user to properly handle this by either replicating the data some other way or by thoroughly cleaning up when finished.

Another way to stop replication is to set `@@sql_log_bin=0`, but this stops all replication to all slaves. By using the `@@skip_replication` variable instead, we can selectively stop replication to specific slaves while continuing to replicate to other slaves.

See also

▶ The full documentation of this is available at `https://mariadb.com/kb/en/selectively-skipping-replication-of-binlog-events/`

7
Replication with MariaDB Galera Cluster

In this chapter, we will cover the following recipes:

- Installing MariaDB Galera Cluster
- Dropping a node from MariaDB Galera Cluster
- Shutting down MariaDB Galera Cluster

Introduction

Two of the primary reasons for replicating data between MariaDB servers are to provide greater performance and more redundancy. The traditional master-slave replication covered in *Chapter 6, Replication in MariaDB*, provides for great read performance by having several read-only slave servers. However, it only solves the redundancy issue partially. In classic replication, there is only one master server node, and if it fails, then one of the slave server nodes must be promoted to become a master server node for the others. Getting this to work correctly in an automated way is difficult.

An easier way to configure replication will be if every node was a master server node. Reads and writes can happen to any of the nodes and the replication component will make sure that everything just works.

MariaDB Galera Cluster makes this sort of replication easy to set up and use. Every node in a Galera Cluster is equal, so if any single node fails it is alright. The cluster will continue running and we can repair or replace the faulty node without worrying about whether it is a master or a slave server.

MariaDB Galera Cluster is only available on Linux-based operating systems, so all the recipes in this chapter are Linux-only.

Installing MariaDB Galera Cluster

MariaDB Galera Cluster is a separate product from MariaDB. So, installing it is similar, but not quite the same as installing MariaDB. In particular, the package names for MariaDB's server components are different and there is an extra `galera` package that needs to be installed.

Getting ready

For this recipe, we'll assume that we have three servers named db01, db02, and db03, with IP addresses `192.168.1.101`, `192.168.1.102`, and `192.168.1.103`, respectively. We'll further assume that they are all running fresh installs of Ubuntu 12.04 LTS.

How to do it...

1. On all the three hosts, install MariaDB Galera Cluster using the following commands:

   ```
   sudo apt-key adv --recv-keys --keyserver keyserver.ubuntu.com
     0xcbcb082a1bb943db
   ```

   ```
   sudo add-apt-repository 'deb
     http://ftp.osuosl.org/pub/mariadb/repo/10.0/ubuntu precise main'
   ```

   ```
   sudo apt-get update
   ```

   ```
   sudo apt-get install mariadb-galera-server
   ```

2. On all the three hosts, stop MariaDB using the following command so that we can add modify the configuration:

   ```
   sudo service mysql stop
   ```

3. On all the three hosts, create a `galera_common.cnf` file at /etc/mysql/conf.d/ with the following content:

   ```
   # Galera-common configuration
   [mysqld]
   wsrep-cluster-name = "test_cluster"
   wsrep-provider = /usr/lib/galera/libgalera_smm.so
   wsrep-provider-options = "gcache.size=256M;
   gcache.page_size=128M"
   wsrep-sst-auth = "galera:mypassword"
   binlog-format = row
   default-storage-engine = InnoDB
   innodb-doublewrite = 1
   ```

```
innodb-autoinc-lock-mode = 2
innodb-flush-log-at-trx-commit = 2
innodb-locks-unsafe-for-binlog = 1
```

4. On db01, create a galera_db01.cnf file at /etc/mysql/conf.d/ with the following content:

```
# Galera-specific configuration
[mysqld]
wsrep-node-name = "db01"
wsrep-new-cluster
wsrep-sst-receive-address = 192.168.1.101
wsrep-node-incoming-address = 192.168.1.101
```

5. On db01, start MariaDB using the following command:

```
sudo service mysql start
```

6. On db01, launch the mysql command-line client and run the following commands to create a galera user:

```
GRANT ALL ON *.* TO 'galera'@'192.168.1.%' IDENTIFIED BY
   'mypassword';

FLUSH PRIVILEGES;
```

7. On db02 and db03, back up the /etc/mysql/debian.cnf file:

```
sudo cp -avi /etc/mysql/debian.cnf /etc/mysql/debian.cnf.dist
```

8. On db02 and db03, edit the /etc/mysql/debian.cnf file so that the passwords match those in that file on db01.

9. On db02, create a galera_db02.cnf file at /etc/mysql/conf.d/ with the following content:

```
# Galera-specific configuration
[mysqld]
wsrep-node-name = "db02"
wsrep-cluster-address = gcomm://192.168.1.101
wsrep-sst-receive-address = 192.168.1.102
wsrep-node-incoming-address = 192.168.1.102
```

10. On db03, create a galera_db03.cnf file at /etc/mysql/conf.d/ with the following content:

```
# Galera-specific configuration
[mysqld]
wsrep-node-name = "db03"
wsrep-cluster-address = gcomm://192.168.1.101
wsrep-sst-receive-address = 192.168.1.103
wsrep-node-incoming-address = 192.168.1.103
```

11. Start MariaDB on db02 and db03 using the following command:

    ```
    sudo service mysql start
    ```

12. On all the three hosts, launch the mysql command-line client and run the following command:

    ```
    SHOW STATUS LIKE 'wsrep%';
    ```

13. In the output, the wsrep_incoming_addresses variable should have the IP addresses of all the three servers, the wsrep_cluster_size variable should be 3, and the wsrep_connected and wsrep_ready variables should both be ON.

14. On db01, edit the /etc/mysql/conf.d/galera_db01.cnf file. Remove the wsrep-new-cluster line and replace it with the following line of code:

    ```
    wsrep-cluster-address =
       gcomm://192.168.1.101,192.168.1.102,192.168.1.103
    ```

15. On db02 and db03, edit the /etc/mysql/conf.d/galera_db*.cnf files and change the wsrep-cluster-address line to match the line we added to db01 in the previous step.

16. Test out the cluster by creating databases and tables on one server, inserting data on a different server, and reading the data on the third server. All changes will be replicated to all the three servers regardless of which server the change is made on.

How it works...

As mentioned previously, MariaDB Galera Cluster is a separate product from MariaDB; when installing it on Ubuntu and Debian, we specify the mariadb-galera-server package instead of mariadb-server. The mariadb-galera-server package will pull in all of the correct packages, including the important galera package, which contains the external program that handles the replication between the hosts.

> The minimum size of MariaDB Galera Cluster is three, so it is used in this recipe. However, more nodes are recommended so that if a node (or two) fail, the total number of nodes in the cluster never dips below three.

There are only a few settings that are unique to each individual cluster node; so in this recipe, we put the common settings in one configuration file and the unique ones into a separate file. All of these files are available to download from the book's website.

Whenever a cluster node starts, it needs to know whether it should join an existing cluster or start a new cluster. This is controlled via the `wsrep-new-cluster` and `wsrep-cluster-address` variables. When the `wsrep-new-cluster` variable exists in our configuration, MariaDB Galera Cluster knows to bootstrap a new cluster. When that line doesn't exist and `wsrep-cluster-address` is set to `gcomm://192.168.1.101`, the node will try to connect to that server and join the cluster that it is a part of. As nodes join, their addresses are shared among all the cluster members so that every node knows where every other node is.

> Older versions of MariaDB Galera Cluster used an empty `gcomm://` value to indicate that a new cluster should be created. This behavior has been deprecated. Now, we should always use the `wsrep-new-cluster` variable to indicate when we want to create a new cluster. Also, to avoid problems, we should only have `wsrep-new-cluster` or `wsrep-cluster-address` defined, never both and we should never use an empty `gcomm://` value.

After the initial bootstrapping, it is a good idea to update our configuration to have the entire cluster addresses listed in case we need to restart any of the nodes. We want our initial node to connect to the running cluster instead of creating a new cluster, and we want our existing nodes to have more connection options than just the first node (on the chance that it is down when new nodes are trying to start up).

There's more...

The instructions in this recipe are specific to Ubuntu Linux, but they can easily be adapted to Debian, CentOS, Red Hat, and Fedora. For Debian, the only difference is to change the `add-apt-repository` line to point at a Debian repository instead of an Ubuntu repository. The installation and configuration steps are the same.

For CentOS, Red Hat, and Fedora, apart from configuring the MariaDB Yum repository, the major change is that the configuration files are placed under `/etc/my.cnf.d/` instead of `/etc/mysql/conf.d/`. Also, the packages to install on them are `MariaDB-Galera-server` and `MariaDB-client`.

Additional nodes can be easily added by repeating the steps for `db02` and `db03`, and updating the configuration files with the appropriate IP addresses.

Use the repository configuration tool available at `https://downloads.mariadb.org/mariadb/repositories/` to generate the appropriate repository configurations.

Configuring MariaDB Galera Cluster

To make things simple, Galera-specific status and configuration variables are all prefaced with `wsrep`, so you can view them with the following commands:

```
SHOW STATUS LIKE 'wsrep%';
SHOW VARIABLES LIKE 'wsrep%'\G
```

There are also a few non-Galera-specific variables that should be set for MariaDB Galera Cluster to run properly. The `binlog-format`, `default-storage-engine`, and `innodb-%` variables from the recipe are the most important ones.

See also

- The documentation of the various configuration and `STATUS` variables is available at `https://mariadb.com/kb/en/mariadb-galera-cluster-configuration-variables/` and `https://mariadb.com/kb/en/mariadb-galera-cluster-status-variables/`
- The full documentation of MariaDB Galera Cluster is available at `https://mariadb.com/kb/en/galera/`
- The Codership group at `https://groups.google.com/forum/?fromgroups#!forum/codership-team` is a great place to talk with other Galera cluster users
- The Galera wiki available at `http://www.codership.com/wiki/` also contains lots of information

Dropping a node from MariaDB Galera Cluster

MariaDB Galera Cluster exists so that we can eliminate single points of failure in our infrastructure. Once set up, a single node can be taken out of the cluster for maintenance without impacting the rest of the cluster or causing downtime for our applications.

Getting ready

Create MariaDB Galera Cluster as described in the *Installing MariaDB Galera Cluster* recipe earlier in this chapter. In this recipe, we'll be shutting down `db03`.

How to do it...

1. On `db03`, run the following command to check whether the node is up to date:

    ```
    mysql -e "SHOW STATUS LIKE 'wsrep_local_state_comment'"
    ```

2. If the value is *synced*, then the node is up to date and we can safely shut down the node with the following command:

    ```
    sudo service mysql stop
    ```

3. On the other cluster nodes, run the following command to check whether the node has been destroyed:

    ```
    mysql -e "SHOW STATUS LIKE 'wsrep_%'"
    ```

4. We'll know the node is destroyed if the number of nodes in `wsrep_cluster_size` is 2 and the IP address of `db03` is not listed in `wsrep_incoming_addresses`.

How it works...

All the nodes in MariaDB Galera Cluster are equal. We can read and write to any node we wish and the changes will be replicated to all nodes. Because of this, dropping a node is easier than with a traditional replication setup where we need to worry about which node is the master server that the slave server nodes read. All nodes in MariaDB Galera Cluster are primary master server nodes, so our only concern is that the node is up to date before shutting it off like we would any single non-clustered MariaDB server.

There's more...

Nodes are usually taken down for maintenance reasons. Adding the node back is as easy as starting it back up with the following command:

```
sudo service mysql start
```

There will be a period of time as it brings itself back up to date with the other nodes in the cluster, but after a few seconds or minutes (depending on how far behind it is), it will be good to go. We just check the value of the `wsrep_local_state_comment` variable on the joining node and when it is synced, we know that the node is up to date.

See also

> ▸ Information on various ways of monitoring our MariaDB Galera Cluster is available at `http://www.codership.com/wiki/doku.php?id=monitoring`

Shutting down MariaDB Galera Cluster

There can be a time when we want to shut down our entire cluster; maybe for a move to a different facility, or because we are replacing it completely. Whatever the reason, this recipe outlines the preferred way to do so.

Getting ready

Create MariaDB Galera Cluster as described in the *Installing MariaDB Galera Cluster* recipe earlier in this chapter.

How to do it...

1. Ensure that any applications using the cluster are shut down.
2. On db03, run the following command to check whether the node is up to date:

   ```
   mysql -e "SHOW STATUS LIKE 'wsrep_local_state_comment'"
   ```

3. If the value is synced, run the following command to shut down the node:

   ```
   sudo service mysql shutdown
   ```

4. On db02 and db01, repeat the same steps, first on db02, and then on db01.

How it works...

Shutting down MariaDB Galera Cluster is just like shutting down MariaDB. To be careful, we should make sure that the applications which use the cluster are shut down so that the cluster is idle.

Then, it is just a simple matter of shutting down the nodes one at a time.

The only thing left to do after all nodes are shut down is to make a note of which node was shut down last, as it will need to start up first if we want to restart the cluster. In our recipe, we shut down db01 last, as it was the first one we started when creating the cluster. In practice, it doesn't matter; we just need to know which one was shut down last as it will be the cluster node that is most up to date. It may also be a good idea to remove the `wsrep-cluster-address` line and add the `wsrep-new-cluster` line to the config on db01 (or whichever server we shut down last) so that we don't have to remember to do it prior to starting the cluster up again.

The danger with starting the cluster up again using a server that was not the last one to be turned off is that it will not have the modifications or additions to our data that were made in the time between when it was shut down and when the last node in the cluster was shut down.

See also

- ▸ The full documentation of MariaDB Galera Cluster is available at `https://mariadb.com/kb/en/galera/`

- ▸ The Codership group at `https://groups.google.com/forum/?fromgroups#!forum/codership-team` is a great place to talk with other Galera cluster users

- ▸ The Galera wiki available at `http://www.codership.com/wiki/` also contains lots of information

8

Performance and Usage Statistics

In this chapter, we will cover the following recipes:

- ▸ Installing the Audit Plugin
- ▸ Using the Audit Plugin
- ▸ Using engine-independent table statistics
- ▸ Using extended statistics
- ▸ Enabling the performance schema
- ▸ Using the performance schema

Introduction

There are several ways of tracking and measuring our usage of MariaDB. Some, such as the MariaDB Audit Plugin, come from third parties. Others, such as the performance schema, are built in. All of this helps us know what is happening on our server so that we can track our current usage better, analyze long term performance trends, and plan for our future needs.

The recipes in this chapter introduce several auditing and tracking features that we can enable in MariaDB.

Installing the Audit Plugin

There are many third-party tools that can enhance our MariaDB server. The Audit Plugin from SkySQL is one of them. This plugin is used by organizations to comply with government regulations that require the tracking and auditing of access to sensitive data.

Getting ready

Locate the plugin directory on your local machine. This can be done by connecting to MariaDB using the `mysql` command-line client and then running the following command:

```
SHOW GLOBAL VARIABLES LIKE 'plugin_dir';
```

The directory displayed is our local MariaDB plugin directory.

How to do it...

1. Download the appropriate version of the MariaDB Audit Plugin (either Windows or Linux) from the SkySQL downloads page available at `http://www.skysql.com/downloads/`.

2. On Windows, navigate to the location where we downloaded the plugin ZIP file and unpack it by right-clicking on the file in Windows Explorer and choosing **Extract all...**.

3. On Linux, navigate to the location where we downloaded the plugin TAR file and unpack it either by right-clicking on the file and choosing **Extract Here** in our file manager or by using the `tar` command in a terminal window using the following command:

   ```
   tar -zxvf server_audit-1.1.5.tar.gz
   ```

4. When the file is unpacked, there will be a directory corresponding to the name of the file. Inside the directory, there are subdirectories for 32-bit and 64-bit computers and for debug versions of the plugin. Navigate to the non-debug directory that corresponds to our machine. Most likely, this will be 64-bit. Inside the directory, there will be a file named `server_audit.so` or `server_audit.dll`. This is the plugin for Linux and Windows respectively.

5. Copy the plugin to our local MariaDB plugin directory. On Windows, we could select the file, copy it with *Ctrl + C*, navigate to the plugin directory, and paste it with *Ctrl + V*. On Linux, we can use the following command (altered to point at wherever our local plugin directory is):

   ```
   sudo cp -avi server_audit.so /usr/lib64/mysql/plugin/
   ```

6. With the plugin in place, we now open the `mysql` command-line client and run the following command to install and activate the plugin:

   ```
   INSTALL PLUGIN server_audit SONAME 'server_audit.so';
   ```

7. Run the `SHOW PLUGINS;` command to verify that the audit plugin is present in the list of installed plugins.

How it works...

The Audit Plugin is not included with MariaDB, so we need to download and install it manually. The procedure we use in this recipe also applies to installing other third-party plugins. Some plugins that we may choose to use will come as source code that we need to compile before we can install them. Other plugins, such as the Audit Plugin, come precompiled and are ready to use once we've copied them to the correct location.

After the plugin is in the `plugin` directory, we need to let MariaDB know that it exists and we want to use it. We do this with the `INSTALL PLUGIN` command, just as we would for plugins that ship with MariaDB and are not activated by default.

Finally, we verify that MariaDB has loaded the plugin by running the `SHOW PLUGINS;` command. If the plugin appears in the output, then we know that it has been installed.

There's more...

If we want to remove the `server_audit` plugin, we will use the following command:

```
UNINSTALL PLUGIN 'server_audit';
```

If we are using the Audit Plugin to comply with a regulation, we may want to restrict the ability to uninstall the plugin. To do this, we add the following code to the `[mysqld]` section of our `my.cnf` or `my.ini` file:

```
plugin-load=server_audit=server_audit.so
server_audit=FORCE_PLUS_PERMANENT
```

Once we have added the code, we need to restart MariaDB to activate the change. Once we do so, any attempt to uninstall the plugin will result in an error, and the plugin will remain installed.

See also

▶ The full documentation of the MariaDB Audit Plugin is available from SkySQL or in the MariaDB Knowledge Base at `https://mariadb.com/kb/en/mariadb-audit-plugin/`

▶ The following *Using the Audit Plugin* recipe covers configuring and using the plugin

Using the Audit Plugin

Installing the MariaDB Audit Plugin, as described in the previous recipe, doesn't do a whole lot for us. In order to get the most out of this plugin, we need to configure it. That is what this recipe is about.

Getting ready

Complete the *Installing the Audit Plugin* recipe described earlier in this chapter to install the Audit Plugin, prior to using the Audit Plugin.

How to do it...

1. Connect to MariaDB using the `mysql` command-line client with a user that has the `SUPER` privilege.

2. Show the Audit Plugin variables with the following command:

   `SHOW GLOBAL VARIABLES LIKE 'server_audit%';`

   The preceding command displays an output similar to the following screenshot:

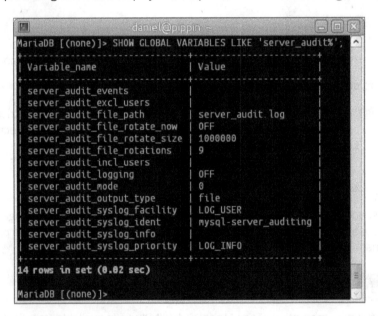

```
MariaDB [(none)]> SHOW GLOBAL VARIABLES LIKE 'server_audit%';
+-----------------------------+-----------------------+
| Variable_name               | Value                 |
+-----------------------------+-----------------------+
| server_audit_events         |                       |
| server_audit_excl_users     |                       |
| server_audit_file_path      | server_audit.log      |
| server_audit_file_rotate_now| OFF                   |
| server_audit_file_rotate_size| 1000000              |
| server_audit_file_rotations | 9                     |
| server_audit_incl_users     |                       |
| server_audit_logging        | OFF                   |
| server_audit_mode           | 0                     |
| server_audit_output_type    | file                  |
| server_audit_syslog_facility| LOG_USER              |
| server_audit_syslog_ident   | mysql-server_auditing |
| server_audit_syslog_info    |                       |
| server_audit_syslog_priority| LOG_INFO              |
+-----------------------------+-----------------------+
14 rows in set (0.02 sec)

MariaDB [(none)]>
```

3. Turn off the audit logging with the following command:

   `SET GLOBAL server_audit_logging=OFF;`

4. Turn on the audit logging with the following command:

```
SET GLOBAL server_audit_logging=ON;
```

5. Force the audit logfile to rotate immediately with the following command:

```
SET GLOBAL server_audit_file_rotate_now=ON;
```

6. Show the location of the current logfile, whether the plugin is active (ON), and whether there are any errors with the following command:

```
SHOW GLOBAL STATUS LIKE 'server_audit%';
```

The preceding command displays an output similar to the following screenshot:

7. Add the untrusted_user and untrusted_user2 users to the list of users to audit and then check that they were added with the following commands:

```
SET GLOBAL server_audit_incl_users = 'untrusted_user';
```

```
SET GLOBAL server_audit_incl_users =
  CONCAT(@@global.server_audit_incl_users,
    ',untrusted_user2');
```

```
SHOW GLOBAL VARIABLES LIKE 'server_audit_incl_users';
```

The preceding commands display an output similar to the following screenshot:

```
daniel@pippin: ~
MariaDB [test]> SET GLOBAL server_audit_incl_users = 'untrusted_user';
Query OK, 0 rows affected (0.00 sec)

MariaDB [test]> SET GLOBAL server_audit_incl_users =
    -> CONCAT(@@global.server_audit_incl_users, ',untrusted_user2');
Query OK, 0 rows affected (0.00 sec)

MariaDB [test]> SHOW GLOBAL VARIABLES LIKE 'server_audit_incl_users';
+-------------------------+--------------------------------+
| Variable_name           | Value                          |
+-------------------------+--------------------------------+
| server_audit_incl_users | untrusted_user,untrusted_user2 |
+-------------------------+--------------------------------+
1 row in set (0.00 sec)

MariaDB [test]>
```

8. Exclude the `trusted_user` and `trusted_user2` users from audit logging and then verify that they are excluded with the following commands:

```
SET GLOBAL server_audit_excl_users = 'trusted_user';
```

```
SET GLOBAL server_audit_excl_users =
  CONCAT(@@global.server_audit_excl_users, ',trusted_user2');
```

```
SHOW GLOBAL VARIABLES LIKE 'server_audit_excl_users';
```

The preceding commands display an output similar to the following screenshot:

```
daniel@pippin: ~
MariaDB [test]> SET GLOBAL server_audit_excl_users = 'trusted_user';
Query OK, 0 rows affected (0.00 sec)

MariaDB [test]> SET GLOBAL server_audit_excl_users =
    -> CONCAT(@@global.server_audit_excl_users, ',trusted_user2');
Query OK, 0 rows affected (0.00 sec)

MariaDB [test]> SHOW GLOBAL VARIABLES LIKE 'server_audit_excl_users';
+-------------------------+----------------------------+
| Variable_name           | Value                      |
+-------------------------+----------------------------+
| server_audit_excl_users | trusted_user,trusted_user2 |
+-------------------------+----------------------------+
1 row in set (0.00 sec)

MariaDB [test]>
```

How it works...

Configuring the Audit Plugin is similar to configuring any other feature of MariaDB. Like many variables, the Audit Plugin variables can be set dynamically while the server is running. To make our settings permanent, we need to add them to the `[mysqld]` section of our `my.cnf` or `my.ini` file.

By default, the Audit Plugin will track all users. We can limit the plugin to just track certain users by using the `server_audit_incl_users` variable. Likewise, we can exclude specific users from being audited by using the `server_audit_excl_users` variable.

When we use these variables, the Audit Plugin tracks the users listed without regard to the user's hostname. This is because for auditing and regulatory purposes, where the user is connecting from is not as important as what they are doing while connected. The location of users is still tracked, but if we, for example, add the `untrusted_user` to the `server_audit_incl_users` variable, all the following users will be tracked:

- `untrusted_user@'localhost'`
- `untrusted_user@'192.168.1.%'`
- `untrusted_user@'%'`

There's more...

If a user appears in both the `server_audit_incl_users` and `server_audit_excl_users` variables, the user will be logged. This is because the include variable has priority over the exclude variable.

See also

- The full documentation of the Audit Plugin is available from SkySQL or in the MariaDB Knowledge Base at `https://mariadb.com/kb/en/mariadb-audit-plugin/`
- The previous *Installing the Audit Plugin* recipe covers downloading and installing the plugin

Using engine-independent table statistics

MariaDB includes a facility to gather statistics on all tables, no matter what storage engine those tables use. The MariaDB optimizer can use these statistics to better calculate the optimum query plans.

How to do it...

1. Connect to MariaDB using the `mysql` command-line client with a user that has the `SUPER` privilege.

2. Run the following command:

```
SET GLOBAL use_stat_tables=complementary;
```

3. Force an update of the table statistics for a table with the following command (change `table_name` to the name of an existing table):

```
ANALYZE TABLE table_name;
```

4. View the collected table, index, and column statistics with the following commands:

```
SELECT * FROM mysql.table_stats;
SELECT * FROM mysql.index_stats;
SELECT * FROM mysql.column_stats;
```

How it works...

How MariaDB uses the engine-independent table statistics is controlled by the `use_stat_tables` variable. There are three valid values: `never` means that MariaDB will not use the statistics, `complementary` means that MariaDB will use the statistics if similar statistics are not provided by the storage engine, and `preferably` means that MariaDB will always use the statistics and only fall back on the statistics provided by the storage engine if they don't exist elsewhere.

We can force an update of the table's statistics using the `ANALYZE TABLE` command. If the table's statistics are already up to date when we force an update, the output of the `ANALYZE TABLE` command will say so.

Full table and index scans are used when collecting statistics. Depending on the size of our table or index and how busy our server is, this could be an expensive operation. Often, the benefits outweigh the cost, but it is something to keep in mind.

In certain cases, it may be preferable to only collect statistics on certain columns or indexes. The `ANALYZE TABLE` command in MariaDB allows this. For example, to only gather statistics on certain columns and indexes of a table, the following syntax is used:

```
ANALYZE TABLE table_name PERSISTENT FOR
   COLUMNS (column_1,column_2,...)
   INDEXES (index_1,index_2,...);
```

There's more...

The `use_stat_tables` variable also controls the behavior of the `ANALYZE TABLE` command. When the variable is set to `never`, the command will only update the statistics provided by the storage engine, and engine-independent statistics will not be gathered. If the variable is set to either `complementary` or `preferably`, then both the engine-independent and storage-engine-provided statistics will be updated when the `ANALYZE TABLE` command is run.

See also

▸ The full documentation of engine-independent table statistics is available at `https://mariadb.com/kb/en/engine-independent-table-statistics/`

Using extended statistics

MariaDB includes a powerful feature for collecting extended user statistics. These statistics can be used to better understand how our server is behaving and to locate and identify the sources of our server's load.

How to do it...

1. Connect to MariaDB using the `mysql` command-line client with a user that has the `SUPER` privilege.

2. Enable statistics collection with the following command:

   ```
   SET GLOBAL userstat=1;
   ```

3. Run the following commands to show the statistics collected since collection was enabled:

   ```
   SHOW CLIENT_STATISTICS;
   SHOW INDEX_STATISTICS;
   SHOW TABLE_STATISTICS;
   SHOW USER_STATISTICS;
   ```

4. Run the following commands to flush the statistics by resetting the statistics counters to zero:

   ```
   FLUSH CLIENT_STATISTICS;
   FLUSH INDEX_STATISTICS;
   FLUSH TABLE_STATISTICS;
   FLUSH USER_STATISTICS;
   ```

How it works...

Extended statistics collection is off by default so that it does not cause unnecessary or unwanted load on the server. Enabling it is easy though and if desired, statistics gathering can be turned on and off at will. This can be very useful for gathering statistics on a busy server while minimizing the impact on that server.

There are four types of statistics that are collected: `CLIENT`, `INDEX`, `TABLE`, and `USER` statistics. The statistics are stored in the `information_schema` database in the `CLIENT_STATISTICS`, `INDEX_STATISTICS`, `TABLE_SATISTICS`, and `USER_STATISTICS` tables respectively. The `SHOW` command provides an easy way to view the collected statistics, but we can also directly query the tables in the `information_schema` database if we want a custom view of the data.

The type of data gathered includes features such as the total number of connections; the number of simultaneous (concurrent) connections; the number of bytes sent and received; the number of rows read, sent, or deleted; and so on.

There's more...

To turn on extended statistics so that it is always on, we need to add the following code to the `[mysqld]` section of our `my.cnf` or `my.ini` file:

```
userstat = 1
```

Keeping the extended statistics collection on all the time is OK if our database server is not very busy. However, if it is very busy and we need to gather statistics so that we know how the server is being used, we should only enable the statistics collection manually and then only for brief periods.

See also

 ▶ The full documentation of the user statistics feature is available at
    `https://mariadb.com/kb/en/user-statistics/`

Enabling the performance schema

The performance schema is a tool that we can use to monitor our server performance. It is disabled by default, but it can easily be enabled.

How to do it...

1. Open our `my.cnf` or `my.ini` file and add the following code to the `[mysqld]` section:

    `performance_schema`

2. Restart MariaDB.

3. Connect to MariaDB using the `mysql` command-line client.

4. Run the `SHOW ENGINES;` command and verify that `PERFORMANCE_SCHEMA` is listed. The performance schema entry will look similar to the following screenshot:

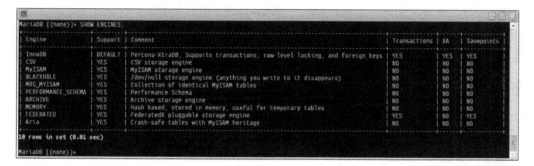

5. Switch to the `performance_schema` database using the following command:

    USE performance_schema;

6. Show the performance schema tables using the following command:

    SHOW TABLES;

How it works...

The performance schema is implemented as a storage engine. This is why it shows up alongside other storage engines when we use the `SHOW ENGINES;` command. However, it is not a storage engine for storing data. The purpose of the performance schema is to help us monitor server performance and when it is enabled, the performance schema creates a special `performance_schema` database that includes several tables that we can query to monitor our server performance.

There's more...

If we try to create a table with the performance schema as the engine, we will get the following error:

```
ERROR 1005 (HY000): Can't create table 'test'.'t1' (errno: 131
  "Command not supported by database")
```

See also

▶ The full documentation of the performance schema is available at
  `https://mariadb.com/kb/en/performance-schema/`

Using the performance schema

Using the performance schema is similar to querying a table or set of tables.

Getting ready

Enable the performance schema as described in the *Enabling the performance schema* recipe earlier in this chapter.

How to do it...

1. Connect to MariaDB using the `mysql` command-line client. List how many current connections the users have and how many connections they had in total (we might want to log in and out a few times with example users to populate this table):

   ```
   SELECT * FROM performance_schema.users;
   ```

   The preceding commands display an output similar to the following screenshot:

   ```
   daniel@pippin ~
   MariaDB [(none)]> SELECT * FROM performance_schema.users;
   +--------+---------------------+-------------------+
   | USER   | CURRENT_CONNECTIONS | TOTAL_CONNECTIONS |
   +--------+---------------------+-------------------+
   | other  |                   0 |                 2 |
   | daniel |                   0 |                 3 |
   | dbart  |                   1 |                 2 |
   | root   |                   1 |                 2 |
   | NULL   |                  19 |                22 |
   +--------+---------------------+-------------------+
   5 rows in set (0.00 sec)

   MariaDB [(none)]>
   ```

2. Look up for the detailed information on all of the currently running user connection threads:

```
SELECT * FROM performance_schema.threads
    WHERE type="foreground"\G
```

The preceding commands display an output similar to the following screenshot:

```
MariaDB [(none)]> SELECT * FROM performance_schema.threads
    -> WHERE type="foreground"\G
*************************** 1. row ***************************
          THREAD_ID: 22
               NAME: thread/sql/one_connection
               TYPE: FOREGROUND
     PROCESSLIST_ID: 2
   PROCESSLIST_USER: root
   PROCESSLIST_HOST: localhost
     PROCESSLIST_DB: NULL
PROCESSLIST_COMMAND: Query
   PROCESSLIST_TIME: 0
  PROCESSLIST_STATE: Sending data
   PROCESSLIST_INFO: SELECT * FROM performance_schema.threads
WHERE type="foreground"
   PARENT_THREAD_ID: 1
               ROLE: NULL
       INSTRUMENTED: YES
1 row in set (0.01 sec)

MariaDB [(none)]>
```

3. Add the following code to the `[mysqld]` section of our `my.cnf` or `my.ini` file and then restart MariaDB to disable the collection of user connection statistics:

```
performance_schema_users_size=0
```

4. Log in and out a few times with various users (real or example) and then rerun the command we ran in step 2 to look at the user connection statistics. Since we disabled the collection, the output of this information will look similar to the following screenshot:

```
MariaDB [(none)]> SELECT * FROM performance_schema.users;
Empty set (0.00 sec)

MariaDB [(none)]>
```

5. Remove the `performance_schema_users_size=0` line we added to our `my.cnf` or `my.ini` file in step 4 and then restart MariaDB.

6. Rerun the command from step 2 to verify that the user connection statistics are being collected again (there will be limited output because we just restarted MariaDB).

How it works...

Looking up the data in the performance schema is just like looking up the data in any other database table. We simply use the SELECT statements to query the performance schema for the information we are interested in.

Performance schema variables are not dynamic; this means that they can't be set while MariaDB is running. So, at any time, if we want to add or alter a performance schema variable, we need to add it to the [mysqld] section of our my.cnf or my.ini file and then restart MariaDB.

There's more...

Another way to set performance schema variables is to specify them on the command line when starting MariaDB. For example, to turn off the collection of user connection statistics on the command line, we will add the following line to our command to start the mysqld server:

```
--performance_schema_users_size=0
```

While this is a valid way to do it, it is easier and better to just add the variable we want to set to our configuration file.

See also

▶   The full documentation of the performance schema is available at
    https://mariadb.com/kb/en/performance-schema/

▶   A full list of all the performance schema tables and links to detailed information
    on each one is available at https://mariadb.com/kb/en/list-of-
    performance-schema-tables/

9

Searching Data Using Sphinx

In this chapter, we will cover the following recipes:

- ▶ Installing SphinxSE in MariaDB
- ▶ Installing the Sphinx daemon on Linux
- ▶ Installing the Sphinx daemon on Windows
- ▶ Configuring the Sphinx daemon
- ▶ Searching using the Sphinx daemon and SphinxSE

Introduction

With any growing or evolving database, there comes a time when the limitations of MariaDB's built in, full text-searching functionality becomes more of a hindrance than its convenience is worth. At that point, another method is needed to efficiently index and search through our textual data. This is where Sphinx comes in.

There are actually two parts to Sphinx: an external daemon called **Sphinx** that does the work of building and maintaining the search index using that we use to search our data, and a storage engine component called SphinxSE that is part of MariaDB, which the Sphinx daemon uses to talk to MariaDB. The recipes in this chapter will cover setting up and using both these.

Installing SphinxSE in MariaDB

Before we can start using Sphinx, we need to enable SphinxSE in MariaDB.

How to do it...

1. Open the `mysql` command-line client and connect to our database server with a user that has the `SUPER` privilege.

2. Run the following command to install `SphinxSE`:

    ```
    INSTALL SONAME 'ha_sphinx';
    ```

3. Run the following command, shown as follows, to check that the **Sphinx Storage Engine** (**SphinxSE**) is enabled (the `Support` column will say `YES`):

    ```
    SHOW storage engines;
    ```

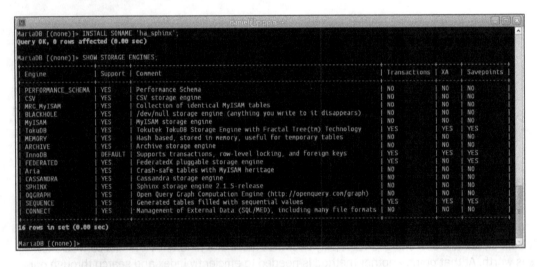

4. Run the following command to view the SphinxSE status variables (they will be empty):

```
SHOW STATUS LIKE 'sphinx_%';
```

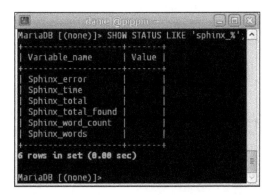

How it works...

SphinxSE is included in MariaDB, but it is disabled by default. To enable it, we run the `INSTALL SONAME` command with the name of the plugin (`ha_sphinx`). This is a one-time operation.

Once SphinxSE is enabled in this manner and if we have the external Sphinx daemon installed and running, we can start using Sphinx to search our data. This is the topic of the following two recipes.

There's more...

The following are a couple of minor things to keep in mind when working with SphinxSE.

SphinxSE versus Sphinx

Despite its name, SphinxSE does not actually store data. It's called a storage engine because it uses the storage engine API to communicate with the rest of MariaDB. In reality, SphinxSE is a client that talks to an externally running indexing and searching program (or daemon) called Sphinx. SphinxSE's purpose is to allow us to talk to the Sphinx daemon from within MariaDB.

Getting SphinxSE's status

Another way to get the status of SphinxSE is to use the following command:

```
SHOW ENGINE SPHINX STATUS;
```

For the SHOW STATUS command, if we haven't actually started using Sphinx, there won't be any status to display. The difference is that with SHOW ENGINE SPHINX STATUS; if there is nothing to display, then there will be no output. The output of the preceding statement is shown as follows:

So, with the SHOW STATUS command, all the status variables are shown even if they have no values to display, and with the **SHOW ENGINE SPHINX STATUS** command, only status variables that have something to tell us will be shown.

See also

▸ The full documentation of SphinxSE is available at:
  `https://mariadb.com/kb/en/sphinx-storage-engine/`

Installing the Sphinx daemon on Linux

In order to use SphinxSE and Sphinx, we must install the daemon on our server. This recipe covers the process for Linux servers running Ubuntu, Debian, Red Hat, Fedora, or CentOS.

How to do it...

1. On Red Hat, CentOS, Ubuntu, or Debian, go to the Sphinx download site at `http://sphinxsearch.com/downloads/release/` and download the latest Sphinx package for our Linux distribution.

2. On Debian or Ubuntu servers, run the following statement to install the Sphinx daemon:

   ```
   sudo apt-get install unixodbc libpq5 mariadb-client
   sudo dpkg -i sphinxsearch*.deb
   ```

3. On Red Hat and CentOS, run the following statement to install the Sphinx daemon:

   ```
   sudo yum install postgresql-libs unixODBC
   sudo rpm -Uhv sphinx*.rpm
   ```

4. On Fedora, run the following command to install Sphinx:

   ```
   sudo yum install sphinx
   ```

5. On all server types, configure the Sphinx daemon as described in the *Configuring the Sphinx daemon* recipe in this chapter.

6. On Ubuntu and Debian, edit the `/etc/default/sphinxsearch` file and set `START=yes`. Then run the following command to `start` the Sphinx daemon:

```
sudo service sphinxsearch start
```

7. On Fedora, CentOS, or Red Hat, run the following command to `start` the Sphinx daemon:

```
sudo service searchd start
```

8. To stop the Sphinx daemon, run the `service` command again, this time with `stop` instead of `start`.

How it works...

The Sphinx daemon is in the package repositories for CentOS, RedHat, Fedora, Ubuntu, and Debian. However, it is usually older than the version available directly from the official Sphinx website. The versions included in the package repositories also do not include the API files that let us easily integrate searching using Sphinx into our applications. These files are sometimes available as separate packages, but not always, so it's better to get Sphinx straight from the source so that we have everything we may need.

In Debian and Ubuntu, the Sphinx package and daemon are called `sphinxsearch`. In Red Hat, Fedora, and CentOS, the package is called `sphinx` and the daemon is called `searchd`.

See also

▸ The complete documentation of installing and using Sphinx is available on the Sphinx website: `http://sphinxsearch.com/docs/current.html`.

Installing the Sphinx daemon on Windows

In order to use Sphinx, we must install the daemon on our server. This recipe is all about installing the Windows version of the Sphinx daemon.

How to do it...

1. Go to `http://sphinxsearch.com/downloads/release/` and download the latest version of Sphinx for MySQL, either the 64-bit or 32-bit version depending on our version of Windows. For this recipe, we'll assume that we're running a 64-bit version of Windows.

2. Navigate to the `Downloads` folder and extract the ZIP file.

3. Extract the file to a location that is convenient. This recipe will assume that we extracted the files to `C:\Sphinx` (as the Sphinx docs recommend).

4. If the unzipping process creates a Sphinx subfolder (such as `sphinx-2.1.3-release-win64`) under `C:\Sphinx` move the contents of that subdirectory to the `C:\Sphinx` folder and then remove the empty directory using the following statements:

    ```
    cd C:\Sphinx
    mv .\sphinx-2.1.3-release-win64\* .\
    rmdir sphinx-2.1.3-release-win64
    ```

5. Configure Sphinx as described in the *Configuring the Sphinx daemon* recipe in this chapter

6. Complete the *Getting ready* portion of the *Searching with the Sphinx daemon* and *SphinxSE* recipe in this chapter and then run the following command:

    ```
    C:\Sphinx\bin\indexer --all
    ```

7. Open a PowerShell or terminal window and install the Sphinx `searchd` program as a Windows service with the following commands:

    ```
    cd C:\Sphinx
    C:\Sphinx\bin\searchd --install --config C:\Sphinx\sphinx.conf
    --servicename SphinxSearch
    ```

8. The output of the previous step will be similar to the following screenshot:

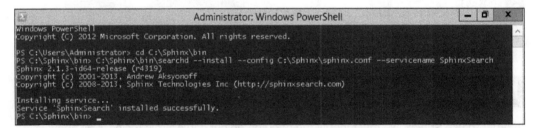

9. Open the Windows Management Console (also called **Computer Management** under the **Tools** menu of the Server Manager), click on the **Services and Applications** toggle, and then click on **Services**.

10. Locate **SphinxSearch** in the list of services. Right-click on it and choose **Start** as shown in the following screenshot:

How it works...

The Sphinx developers do not provide an MSI install package for Windows like the MariaDB developers do. Instead, they simply offer a ZIP file that we can download and use to install Sphinx manually.

There are several different versions of Sphinx that we can download. Any of the ones that mention MySQL is fine. We can download the ones that also include PostgreSQL and PgSQL support if we want, but they are only needed if we are using those databases in addition to MariaDB.

When we unzip the files, it helps if we put them in an easy-to-remember and easy-to-use location. So in this recipe we use C:\Sphinx\. In order to successfully start the Sphinx service, we need to bootstrap the search database by creating and populating our documents table and then use the indexer program to create our initial search index. After that is done we can run the command to install the SphinxSearch service and then start it.

There's more...

We can name the Windows service whatever we want. The Sphinx documentation recommends using the name SphinxSearch. Another popular choice is to name it searchd just like it is named in CentOS, Red Hat, and Fedora Linux.

See also

▶ The complete documentation of the various Sphinx configuration options is available on the Sphinx website at `http://sphinxsearch.com/docs/current.html`

Configuring the Sphinx daemon

In order to use Sphinx, we need to add a user to our MariaDB database and configure the Sphinx daemon so that it indexes the content we want it to.

Getting ready

Install the SphinxSE as described in the *Installing SphinxSE in MariaDB* recipe in this chapter. Install the Sphinx daemon as described in either the *Installing the Sphinx daemon on Linux* recipe or the *Installing the Sphinx daemon on Windows* recipe, both in this chapter, depending on which operating system we are using.

How to do it...

1. Open the `mysql` command-line client and create a user with `SELECT` rights for the tables in the databases we want the Sphinx daemon to index, using the following statements:

```
CREATE USER 'sphinx'@localhost
  IDENTIFIED BY 'sphinxsecretpassword';
GRANT SELECT on test.* to 'sphinx'@localhost;
```

2. Move the default `sphinx.conf` file out of the way; for example, the following will work on Linux:

```
sudo mv -vi sphinx.conf sphinx.conf.dist
```

3. Create a new `sphinx.conf` file in a text editor (such as vim, gedit, or pluma on Linux or Notepad on Windows) with the following statements:

```
#-----------------------------------------------------------------
# Example data source and index config
#-----------------------------------------------------------------
source docstbl {
  type = mysql
  sql_host = localhost
  sql_user = sphinx
```

```
    sql_pass = sphinxsecretpassword
    sql_db   = test
    sql_port = 3306
    sql_attr_timestamp = date_added
    sql_query = \
      SELECT id, UNIX_TIMESTAMP(date_added) AS date_added, \
      title, content FROM documents
    sql_query_info = SELECT * FROM documents WHERE id=$id
}

index docsidx {
  source = docstbl
  path = /tmp/docsidx
  dict = keywords
}

indexer {
  mem_limit = 32M
}

searchd {
  pid_file = /var/run/sphinxsearch/searchd.pid
}
```

4. On Windows, the `pid_file` and `path` lines will need to be changed to valid paths. They are as follows:

```
path = C:\Sphinx\docsidx
pid_file = C:\Sphinx\sphinx.pid
```

How it works...

The Sphinx daemon indexes our data using a database user that has the SELECT privilege on the tables we specify. We could use an existing user, but it's far better to create one specifically for the Sphinx daemon that only has the SELECT right on specific databases and tables we want it to have access to. For our recipe, we create a user named sphinx and grant it the SELECT right on all of the tables in the test database.

After creating the user, we need to inform the Sphinx daemon of the name and password of the user, the database to connect to, and the query to use when building our index, among other things. The Sphinx daemon's configuration file is named sphinx.conf, and it will be in one of the few different locations depending on our operating system. The actual configuration files are very similar; the main differences are the paths to various locations, which are different depending on where those locations are on our operating system.

On Windows, the `sphinx.conf` file is located wherever we unzipped the files. A common location is `C:\Sphinx\sphinx.conf`. On Red Hat, Fedora, or CentOS, the `sphinx.conf` file is located in `/etc/sphinx/sphinx.conf`. On Ubuntu and Debian, the `sphinx.conf` file is located in `/etc/sphinxsearch/sphinx.conf`.

The default configuration file contains examples of every possible option with short descriptions for each of them. Most are commented out in the file as they aren't needed.

The actual variables we need to set are quite minimal. To make it easy, the book's website has a file, `43990S_09_sphinx.conf`, with the configuration from the recipe. We can simply add the contents of this file to our local `sphinx.conf` file instead of manually typing it in.

One important note is that in the example, the path to the index is set to `/tmp/docsidx`. In reality, we would likely never want to store our index in the `/tmp/` directory. This location is fine for our test index though. A better place on Linux would be under `/var/lib/`. For example, the default location for our index file on Ubuntu and Debian would be `/var/lib/sphinxsearch/data/docsidx`

The descriptions in the example configuration file are often enough to understand what the variable in question does, so there is no need to go through all of them here. The main purpose of the configuration file is to define our data sources in the `source{}` sections, define indexes attached or based on those data sources in the `index{}` sections, and set options for Sphinx's `indexer` and `searchd`, the two main parts of the Sphinx daemon, which do the work of indexing and searching through our data, respectively.

There's more...

There are a few things to keep in mind when configuring Sphinx. They are discussed in the following sections.

The Sphinx daemon and MariaDB on different hosts

First, the Sphinx daemon doesn't have to run on the server running MariaDB. It can talk to our database over a network connection just like any other MariaDB client. In that case, we just set the `sql_host` option to the hostname or IP address of our MariaDB server and configure everything else in the same manner as if we were running both on the same server. We just need to remember that the user we create must be able to login from the server on which Sphinx is running.

Sphinx queries

Another thing to study when looking at the example configuration file is that when we set up our data sources, one of the things we do is to define a query with the `sql_query` variable. This query could be something simple like the following code:

```
SELECT id, data FROM documents
```

Or it could be something more complex like what we used in the recipe:

```
sql_query = \

  SELECT id, group_id, \
  UNIX_TIMESTAMP(date_added) AS date_added, \
  title, content \

FROM documents
```

In either case, the very first column must be an integer. This first column is the document ID in Sphinx and it is mandatory. The second thing is that any data we want to be searchable must be returned by this query (or in the query part of another data source section). If it isn't, Sphinx won't know about it, so it won't be able to help us search for it.

This goes both ways as there may be cases where we don't want some data to be searchable. In this case, just don't include it in the `sql_query` and Sphinx will not even see it.

Now that we have the Sphinx daemon configured, we can test it by searching for our data. That is the topic of the following recipe.

See also

> ▸ The complete, detailed documentation for configuring Sphinx is available on the Sphinx website at `http://sphinxsearch.com/docs/current.html`

Searching with the Sphinx daemon and SphinxSE

After completing the other recipes in this chapter, this is the recipe where we actually get to see Sphinx doing something.

Getting ready

This recipe requires that we install and configure SphinxSE and the Sphinx daemon. See the previous recipes in this chapter for instructions.

In the previous recipe, we configured the Sphinx daemon to index and search a table called `documents` in the `test` database. For the purposes of this recipe and to match the previous recipe, we need to create this table with the following `CREATE TABLE` command:

```
CREATE TABLE documents (
    id SERIAL PRIMARY KEY,
    date_added TIMESTAMP,
    title VARCHAR(256),
    content TEXT
);
```

We also need to add some example data to the table. The `43990S_09_documents.sql` file, available from this book's website, will create the table and populate it with some example data. We can load the file using the following statement:

```
mysql -u user -p test < 43990S_09_documents.sql
```

We'll need to change the `user` to a valid username and provide a valid password when prompted.

How to do it...

1. In a terminal window, stop the Sphinx daemon if it is running and then start it again.

2. Run the following `indexer` command:

   ```
   indexer --rotate -all
   ```

   ```
   daniel@pippin:~$ sudo service sphinxsearch stop
   sphinxsearch stop/waiting
   daniel@pippin:~$ sudo service sphinxsearch start
   sphinxsearch start/running, process 22304
   daniel@pippin:~$ sudo indexer --rotate --all
   Sphinx 2.1.3-id64-dev (r4319)
   Copyright (c) 2001-2013, Andrew Aksyonoff
   Copyright (c) 2008-2013, Sphinx Technologies Inc (http://sphinxsearch.com)

   using config file '/etc/sphinxsearch/sphinx.conf'...
   indexing index 'docsidx'...
   collected 13 docs, 0.0 MB
   sorted 0.0 Mhits, 100.0% done
   total 13 docs, 9257 bytes
   total 0.003 sec, 2398807 bytes/sec, 3368.74 docs/sec
   total 4 reads, 0.000 sec, 3.7 kb/call avg, 0.0 msec/call avg
   total 11 writes, 0.000 sec, 2.3 kb/call avg, 0.0 msec/call avg
   rotating indices: successfully sent SIGHUP to searchd (pid=22304).
   daniel@pippin:~$
   ```

3. Run the following `search` command:

   ```
   search -q nosql
   ```

4. Open the `mysql` command-line client, connect to the `test` database, and create a SphinxSE table connected to our local Sphinx daemon:

```
CREATE TABLE documents_search (
    id BIGINT UNSIGNED NOT NULL,
    weight INT NOT NULL,
    query VARCHAR(3072) NOT NULL,
    INDEX(query)
) ENGINE=SPHINX;
```

5. Test your `documents_search` table by running some queries, such as the following:

```
SELECT * FROM documents_search WHERE query='nosql';
SELECT * FROM documents_search WHERE query='sphinx';
```

6. Exit the `mysql` command-line client, stop MariaDB, relaunch the `mysql` command-line client by connecting directly to the Sphinx daemon, and run the following queries:

```
mysql -u root -h 0 -P 9306
```

```
SELECT * FROM docsidx WHERE MATCH('syntax diagrams');
```

```
SELECT * FROM docsidx WHERE MATCH('diving');
```

```
SELECT * FROM docsidx WHERE MATCH('tokudb|cassandra');
```

```
daniel@pippin:~$ sudo service mysql stop
 * Stopping MariaDB database server mysqld                              [ OK ]
daniel@pippin:~$ mysql -u root -h 0 -P 9306
Welcome to the MariaDB monitor.  Commands end with ; or \g.
Your MySQL connection id is 1
Server version: 2.1.3-id64-dev (r4319)

Copyright (c) 2000, 2013, Oracle, Monty Program Ab and others.

Type 'help;' or '\h' for help. Type '\c' to clear the current input statement.

MySQL [(none)]> SELECT * FROM docsidx WHERE MATCH('syntax diagrams');
+------+------------+
| id   | date_added |
+------+------------+
|   10 | 1234567980 |
|   11 | 1234567990 |
+------+------------+
2 rows in set (0.01 sec)

MySQL [(none)]> SELECT * FROM docsidx WHERE MATCH('diving');
+------+------------+
| id   | date_added |
+------+------------+
|    2 | 1234567900 |
+------+------------+
1 row in set (0.00 sec)

MySQL [(none)]> SELECT * FROM docsidx WHERE MATCH('tokudb|cassandra');
+------+------------+
| id   | date added |
+------+------------+
|   12 | 1234568000 |
|    4 | 1234567920 |
+------+------------+
2 rows in set (0.01 sec)

MySQL [(none)]>
```

How it works...

There are several ways to search through our data using SphinxSE and the Sphinx daemon. However, before doing that, we need to index our data using the `indexer` command; so, that's what we do first.

The Sphinx daemon ships with a command-line utility called `search`, which we can use to search through our indexes directly. This is useful for testing to make sure our data has been indexed correctly and in shell scripts.

The second way of searching our data is with SphinxSE. As a storage engine, to use SphinxSE, we need to create a table. This table looks like a regular table for the most part, but when creating it, what we are really doing is defining our connection to the Sphinx daemon. The table has three columns and an index. We can name them what we want, but their datatypes need to match what SphinxSE and the Sphinx daemon expect. The first column is for the `id` of our documents; it must be defined as `BIGINT` and its natural name is `id`. The second column is the `weight`. This column will show us an integer. The higher the number, the better the document matches our query. The third column is for our queries. In our recipe, we name this column `query`, but another common name is `q`.

The last part of the SphinxSE table definition is to set the `ENGINE` for the table to `SPHINX`. We could also set a `CONNECTION` parameter, which has the following form:

```
CONNECTION="sphinx://HOST:PORT/INDEXNAME"
```

By leaving this parameter off in our table definition, SphinxSE goes with the default values, which are as follows:

```
CONNECTION="sphinx://localhost:9312/*"
```

After setting up our special SphinxSE table, we can search for data using a simple `SELECT` statement with our query in the `WHERE` clause. SphinxSE will reply with the ID of the documents that match along with three columns of information. The first will be an `id` column containing the IDs of the matching documents. The second column, named `weight` contains an integer. The higher this number, the better it matches our query. The third column contains our actual query.

Finally, in our recipe, we have some fun and connect directly to the Sphinx daemon. We can do this because it speaks the MariaDB binary network protocol. We're not actually connecting to MariaDB; we turned it off after all. Here, we use the `mysql` command-line client but we could use any MariaDB-compatible client.

The SQL we use in queries using this special mode is actually a Sphinx-specific variant called SphinxQL. It is a subset of the regular SQL and is used specifically for Sphinx queries from the command-line (or another) client.

There's more...

To get the most out of SphinxSE and the Sphinx daemon, we probably want to make use of the Sphinx API.

There isn't time here to go into how to use the Sphinx APIs for the various programming languages that Sphinx supports. Thankfully, there are example test programs included with the Sphinx daemon for all of them.

On Windows, they can be found under the `C:\Sphinx\api` folder (if we unzipped Sphinx to `C:\Sphinx`). On Linux, the examples are generally found under `/usr/share/sphinxsearch/api/` or `/usr/share/sphinx/api/` depending on whether we're using `.deb` or `.rpm` packages, respectively.

See also

- The full documentation of SphinxQL can be found at
  `http://sphinxsearch.com/docs/current.html#sphinxql-reference`

- The full documentation of *rt* indexes can be found
  at `http://sphinxsearch.com/docs/current.html#rt-indexes`

- Some examples showing the differences between using SphinxQL and the API can
  be found at `http://sphinxsearch.com/blog/2013/07/23/from-api-to-sphinxql-and-back-again/`

10
Exploring Dynamic and Virtual Columns in MariaDB

In this chapter, we will cover the following recipes:

- ▶ Creating tables with dynamic columns
- ▶ Inserting, updating, and deleting dynamic column data
- ▶ Reading data from a dynamic column
- ▶ Using virtual columns

Introduction

One recent trend in the database world has been the development and use of **NoSQL databases**. This trend arose from a realization that relational database servers that use SQL, such as MariaDB, are not always the right tool for the job. Sometimes nonrelational, specialized, scalable, and clustered key-value databases work better for specific tasks.

Another trend is the addition of virtual columns to databases. These columns don't change how the data is accessed as dynamic columns do. What they do is change how the data in them is stored. In short, the data is derived from the values of other columns in the row, similar to a spreadsheet.

The MariaDB developers see the value in such nontraditional database features, and have implemented these and others in MariaDB to make it as flexible and as capable a database server as possible.

Both the chapters following this one delve into a couple of additional NoSQL features of MariaDB, HandlerSocket and the Cassandra storage engine, respectively.

 This chapter includes several syntax diagrams and data type definitions. The parts of these diagrams and definitions in square brackets [] are optional. Also, a series of three dots . . . (also called an ellipsis) means that the previous part in the bracket can be repeated.

Creating tables with dynamic columns

Tables with dynamic columns are similar to regular tables, but not quite the same. Similar to standard tables, they have columns and rows. The difference is that each row can have a different number of columns holding the data and the data types that are appropriate for that row.

How to do it...

1. Launch the mysql command-line client and connect to our MariaDB server.

2. Create a test database and use it with the following command:

   ```
   CREATE DATABASE IF NOT EXISTS test;

   USE test;
   ```

3. Create a table with a standard PRIMARY KEY column and a BLOB column using the following commands:

   ```
   CREATE TABLE dyn_example (

       id SERIAL PRIMARY KEY,

       dyn_cols BLOB

   );
   ```

How it works...

The dynamic columns feature in MariaDB is a set of special functions that allow us to define and redefine the number of columns and their data types as needed on a row-by-row basis without altering our table configuration. These special columns exist and are defined as a standard BLOB column in our CREATE TABLE command. But unlike a regular BLOB column, we will only interact with this column using several special dynamic columns helper functions. We will cover these helper functions in the *Inserting, updating, and deleting dynamic column data* and *Reading data from a dynamic column* recipes in this chapter.

The two things that a table with dynamic columns needs are an `id` column (or something similar) for `PRIMARY KEY` and a column with the type `BLOB`. Other columns can also be a part of the definition, but these are the ones that need to be there.

There's more...

When using dynamic columns, there are a couple of limitations to know about. The first is that the maximum number of dynamic columns we can define inside a single dynamic column `BLOB` is `65,535`. Next, the total length of a packed dynamic `BLOB` column is whatever the `max_allowed_packet` size variable is set to, up to one gigabyte.

Normally, the server handles all the interactions with dynamic columns and the client only calls the various dynamic columns functions. It is possible, however, for clients to directly manipulate and interact with dynamic columns using an API. The API is part of the `libmysql` client library.

See also

- The full documentation of dynamic columns can be found at `https://mariadb.com/kb/en/dynamic-columns/` and `https://mariadb.com/kb/en/dynamic-columns-in-mariadb-10/`
- The documentation of the dynamic columns API is available at `https://mariadb.com/kb/en/dynamic-columns-api/`
- Refer to the *Inserting, updating, and deleting dynamic column data* and *Reading data from a dynamic column* recipes in this chapter

Inserting, updating, and deleting dynamic column data

Inserting new data and updating existing data in a dynamic column is not the same as with traditional columns. Without some help from a set of special dynamic columns functions, the standard MariaDB `INSERT`, `UPDATE`, and `DELETE` statements do not understand how to work with a dynamic column or the data stored in it. They will only see it as a `BLOB` column. This recipe introduces and demonstrates the basic functions used when interacting with a dynamic column.

Getting ready

First, you need to complete the *Creating tables with dynamic columns* recipe.

How to do it...

1. Launch the `mysql` command-line client and connect to the `test` database in our MariaDB server.

2. Insert some values into the `dyn_example` table we created earlier:

```
INSERT INTO dyn_example (dyn_cols) VALUES
    (COLUMN_CREATE('name','t-shirt', 'color','blue'
        AS CHAR, 'size','XL' AS CHAR)),
    (COLUMN_CREATE('name','t-shirt', 'color','blue'
        AS CHAR, 'size','L' AS CHAR)),
    (COLUMN_CREATE('name','t-shirt', 'color','black'
        AS CHAR, 'size','M' AS CHAR)),
    (COLUMN_CREATE('name','flashlight', 'color','black'
        AS CHAR, 'size','AAA' AS CHAR, 'num', 2 AS INT)),
    (COLUMN_CREATE('name','shovel', 'length','5'));
```

3. Update a dynamic column in a single row using the following command:

```
UPDATE dyn_example SET
    dyn_cols=COLUMN_ADD(dyn_cols, 'name', 'torch')
WHERE COLUMN_GET(dyn_cols, 'name' AS CHAR) = 'flashlight';
```

4. Add a dynamic column to a single row using the following command:

```
UPDATE dyn_example SET
    dyn_cols=COLUMN_ADD(dyn_cols,'length', 6)
WHERE COLUMN_GET(dyn_cols, 'name' AS CHAR) = 'torch';
```

5. Delete a column from a single row using the following command:

```
UPDATE dyn_example SET
    dyn_cols=COLUMN_DELETE(dyn_cols,'length')
WHERE COLUMN_GET(dyn_cols, 'name' AS CHAR) = 'shovel';
```

How it works...

The standard SQL `INSERT`, `UPDATE`, and `DELETE` statements do not work as expected on a dynamic column. These statements see the dynamic column as a regular `BLOB` column, and if we try to insert or update it directly, we will likely end up corrupting the row. To properly interact with this column, we need to use special dynamic columns functions. The functions for inserting, updating, and deleting data are `COLUMN_CREATE`, `COLUMN_ADD`, and `COLUMN_DELETE`.

Each dynamic column in a row can have a different number of columns, and each of these dynamically defined columns can have the following different data types:

Type	Description
BINARY [(N)]	A variable-length binary string
CHAR [(N)]	A variable-length string
DATE	A 3-byte date
DATETIME [(D)]	A 9-byte date and time. Microseconds are supported
DECIMAL [(M[,D])]	A variable-length binary decimal
INTEGER	A variable-length signed integer, up to 64 bits in length
SIGNED [INTEGER]	A variable-length signed integer, up to 64 bits in length
TIME [(D)]	A 6-byte time. Microseconds are supported and it may be negative
UNSIGNED [INTEGER]	A variable-length unsigned integer, up to 64 bits in length

Defining the data type is optional when creating a new dynamic column or updating an existing dynamic column, but it is mandatory to specify a data type when reading data from a dynamic column.

The COLUMN_CREATE function is used as part of an INSERT statement to both add a new row and to define the dynamic columns in that row. Unlike the COLUMN_ADD and COLUMN_DELETE functions, where we specify the dynamic columns BLOB column name inside the function, in the COLUMN_CREATE function, this is taken care of by the INSERT statement this function is a part of. The syntax of this function is as follows:

```
COLUMN_CREATE(column_name, value [AS type] [, column_name, value
    [AS type]]...);
```

The COLUMN_ADD function is used as part of an UPDATE statement to either update an existing dynamic column in one or more existing rows or to add a new column to one or more existing rows. The syntax of this function is as follows:

```
COLUMN_ADD(dyncol_blob_name, column_name, value [AS type] [,
    column_name, value [AS type]]...);
```

The COLUMN_DELETE function is used as part of an UPDATE statement to delete the specified dynamic column or columns. The syntax of this function is as follows:

```
COLUMN_DELETE(dyncol_blob_name, column_name[, column_name]...);
```

There's more...

The first version of the dynamic columns feature, introduced in MariaDB 5.3, only allowed for numbered columns. MariaDB 10.0 was the first version of MariaDB to support named dynamic columns. So, in MariaDB 5.3 and MariaDB 5.5, in the place where we now specify the column name, we will put a number instead. If we are working with the code that was developed originally for this first version of dynamic columns, we will see numbers instead of column names.

MariaDB 10.0 and later supports the old style of dynamic columns only so long as our code consistently refers to the columns by number. Once we start using names, our dynamic columns will be automatically upgraded to the new format for dynamic columns and we will be unable to continue using numbers to refer to our dynamic columns.

Nesting dynamic columns

Dynamic columns can be nested if we put one dynamic column function inside another. For example, we can perform the following query:

```
INSERT INTO dyn_example (dyn_cols) VALUES
  (COLUMN_CREATE('type','parent', 'name', 'Mary',
    'child1', COLUMN_CREATE('name', 'Sue', 'eyes','brown'),
    'child2', COLUMN_CREATE('name', 'Bob',
      'grandchild', COLUMN_CREATE('name', 'baby'))
  ));
```

This `INSERT` statement creates a dynamic column with two nested dynamic columns inside it, one of which has its own nested dynamic column. The names of each column in a dynamic column have to be unique, but we can duplicate names as long as they are in their own uniquely-named nested dynamic column.

The *Reading nested dynamic columns* section of the *Reading data from a dynamic column* recipe in this chapter has instructions on how to query and read nested dynamic column's data.

See also

▶ The full documentation of dynamic columns can be found at https://mariadb. com/kb/en/dynamic-columns/ and https://mariadb.com/kb/en/ dynamic-columns-in-mariadb-10/

▶ Refer to the *Creating tables with dynamic columns* and *Reading data from a dynamic column* recipes in this chapter

Reading data from a dynamic column

Reading data from a dynamic column is not the same as with traditional columns. Without some help from a set of special dynamic columns functions, the standard MariaDB SELECT statements will not understand how to properly read the data stored in a dynamic columns BLOB. They will see it as a BLOB column and treat it like any other BLOB. This recipe introduces and demonstrates the basic functions used when reading a dynamic column.

Getting ready

Complete the *Creating tables with dynamic columns* recipe and the *Inserting, updating, and deleting dynamic column data* recipe in this chapter.

How to do it...

1. Launch the mysql command-line client. Connect to our MariaDB server and the test database.

2. Discover the columns in our data:

   ```
   SELECT id, COLUMN_LIST(dyn_cols) FROM dyn_example;
   ```

   The following screenshot displays the columns in our data:

3. Read data from our table using the following commands:

```
SELECT id,
    COLUMN_GET(dyn_cols, 'name' AS CHAR) AS 'name',
    COLUMN_GET(dyn_cols, 'color' AS CHAR) AS 'color',
    COLUMN_GET(dyn_cols, 'size' AS CHAR) AS 'size',
    COLUMN_GET(dyn_cols, 'num' AS INT) AS 'num'
FROM dyn_example;
```

The following screenshot displays data selected using the preceding command:

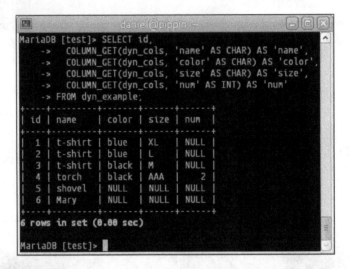

4. Select everything from our table and output each dynamic columns BLOB as a JSON object using the following command:

```
SELECT id, COLUMN_JSON(dyn_cols) FROM dyn_example;
```

The preceding command displays the following screenshot:

```
MariaDB [test]> SELECT id, COLUMN_JSON(dyn_cols) FROM dyn_example;
+----+-----------------------------------------------------------------------------------------------------------------------------+
| id | COLUMN_JSON(dyn_cols)                                                                                                       |
+----+-----------------------------------------------------------------------------------------------------------------------------+
|  1 | {"name":"t-shirt","size":"XL","color":"blue"}                                                                               |
|  2 | {"name":"t-shirt","size":"L","color":"blue"}                                                                                |
|  3 | {"name":"t-shirt","size":"M","color":"black"}                                                                               |
|  4 | {"num":2,"name":"torch","size":"AAA","color":"black","length":6}                                                            |
|  5 | {"name":"shovel"}                                                                                                           |
|  6 | {"name":"Mary","type":"parent","child1":{"eyes":"brown","name":"Sue"},"child2":{"name":"Bob","grandchild":{"name":"baby"}}} |
+----+-----------------------------------------------------------------------------------------------------------------------------+
6 rows in set (0.00 sec)

MariaDB [test]>
```

5. Check each dynamic columns `BLOB` to see if the `num` column exists in it:

```
SELECT id, COLUMN_EXISTS(dyn_cols, 'num')
    FROM dyn_example;
```

The preceding command displays the following screenshot:

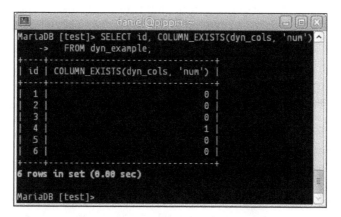

6. Check that each dynamic columns `BLOB` columns in each row is valid using the following command:

```
SELECT id, COLUMN_CHECK(dyn_cols)
    FROM dyn_example;
```

The preceding command displays the following screenshot:

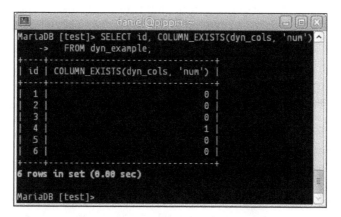

How it works...

To read dynamic columns, we must use either the COLUMN_GET or COLUMN_JSON helper functions. If we try to use a standard SELECT statement without using these functions, we will get data that appears to be garbled. In fact, it is a binary representation of our data that the dynamic column's API understands and can read but that SELECT, by itself, cannot. This is similar to how a music program understands how to read a binary MP3 file, but not a file containing a 3D model of an airplane.

The COLUMN_GET function requires us to specify the name of our dynamic columns BLOB column along with the name of the dynamic column inside the blob we want to read and the data type of that dynamic column. This is in contrast to the COLUMN_ADD and COLUMN_CREATE functions, where defining the data type is optional. Also, we must call this function for each individual column we want to retrieve, as it does not allow us to specify multiple columns at once. The syntax of the COLUMN_GET function is as follows:

```
COLUMN_GET(dyncol_blob_name, column_name AS type);
```

To discover what columns exist in a given dynamic columns BLOB of a row or of several rows, we use the COLUMN_LIST function. If we omit the WHERE clause, we will get a list of the columns in every dynamic columns BLOB for every row in our table. The syntax of this function is as follows:

```
COLUMN_LIST(dyncol_blob_name);
```

The COLUMN_EXISTS function allows us to check if a given column exists in a given dynamic columns BLOB of a given row or rows (or all rows if we omit a WHERE clause). The function returns 1 if the column exists, and 0 if it doesn't. The syntax of this function is as follows:

```
COLUMN_EXISTS(dyncol_blob_name, column_name);
```

The COLUMN_JSON function allows us to easily grab all of the columns in a dynamic columns BLOB and output it as a standard JSON object sentence. Because this function outputs all of the dynamic columns, we do not need to specify or know what columns are in the row or rows we are selecting. The syntax of this function is as follows:

```
COLUMN_JSON(dyncol_blob_name);
```

The COLUMN_CHECK function allows us to verify that a given dynamic columns BLOB is valid and not corrupted. The syntax of this function is as follows:

```
COLUMN_CHECK(dyncol_blob_name);
```

There's more...

The first version of dynamic columns included in MariaDB 5.3 and MariaDB 5.5 did not allow for column names. Instead, columns were referred to with numbers. These old-style dynamic columns are still supported in MariaDB 10.0 and above, but the output is slightly different. For example, the COLUMN_LIST function, if it is used to query one of these old-style dynamic column's blobs, will return a comma-separated list of column numbers instead of a comma-separated list of column names.

Reading nested dynamic columns

Nested dynamic columns represent a particular challenge when we want to read the data. For example, if we input the example nested dynamic columns as demonstrated in the *Nesting dynamic columns* section of the *Inserting, updating, and deleting dynamic column data* recipe, and if we try to get the data using the COLUMN_GET function as follows, our output result will appear garbled:

```
SELECT
  COLUMN_GET(dyn_cols, 'child1' AS CHAR) as 'child1',
  COLUMN_GET(dyn_cols, 'child2' AS CHAR) as 'child2'
FROM dyn_example WHERE
  COLUMN_GET(dyn_cols, 'type' AS CHAR) = 'parent';
```

The output result will appear as shown in the following screenshot:

Instead, we must use the COLUMN_JSON function to properly select the nested dynamic columns data, using the following command:

```
SELECT COLUMN_JSON(dyn_cols)
FROM dyn_example WHERE
  COLUMN_GET(dyn_cols, 'type' AS CHAR) = 'parent';
```

The preceding command displays the output shown in the following screenshot:

```
MariaDB [test]> SELECT COLUMN_JSON(dyn_cols)
    -> FROM dyn_example WHERE
    ->   COLUMN_GET(dyn_cols, 'type' AS CHAR) = 'parent';
+-----------------------------------------------------------------------------------------------------+
| COLUMN_JSON(dyn_cols)                                                                               |
+-----------------------------------------------------------------------------------------------------+
| {"name":"Mary","type":"parent","child1":{"eyes":"brown","name":"Sue"},"child2":{"name":"Bob","grandchild":{"name":"baby"}}} |
+-----------------------------------------------------------------------------------------------------+
1 row in set (0.00 sec)

MariaDB [test]>
```

See also

▶ The full documentation of dynamic columns can be found at https://mariadb.com/kb/en/dynamic-columns/ and https://mariadb.com/kb/en/dynamic-columns-in-mariadb-10/

▶ Refer to the *Creating tables with dynamic columns* and *Inserting, updating, and deleting dynamic column data* recipes in this chapter

Using virtual columns

The virtual columns feature of MariaDB allows us to create columns which contain precalculated or calculated on-the-fly values.

How to do it...

1. Launch the `mysql` command-line client and connect to our MariaDB database.

2. Create a `test` database and switch to that database using the following command:

   ```
   CREATE DATABASE IF NOT EXISTS test;
   USE test;
   ```

3. Create a table with virtual columns using the following command:

   ```
   CREATE TABLE virt_cols (
     id SERIAL PRIMARY KEY,
     surname VARCHAR(64),
     givenname VARCHAR(64),
     uid INT AS (id + 1000) VIRTUAL,
     username VARCHAR(6) AS
       (LOWER(CONCAT(LEFT(givenname,1),(LEFT(surname,5)))))
         PERSISTENT);
   ```

4. Examine the structure of the table using the following command:

   DESCRIBE virt_cols;

   The DESCRIBE command displays the structure of the table as shown in the following screenshot:

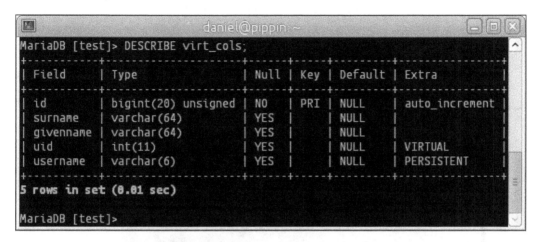

5. Show a CREATE TABLE command that will recreate the exact table (including the virtual columns):

   SHOW CREATE TABLE virt_cols\G

   The preceding command displays the following output:

```
MariaDB [test]> SHOW CREATE TABLE virt_cols\G
*************************** 1. row ***************************
       Table: virt_cols
Create Table: CREATE TABLE `virt_cols` (
  `id` bigint(20) unsigned NOT NULL AUTO_INCREMENT,
  `surname` varchar(64) DEFAULT NULL,
  `givenname` varchar(64) DEFAULT NULL,
  `uid` int(11) AS (id + 1000) VIRTUAL,
  `username` varchar(6) AS (LOWER(CONCAT(LEFT(givenname,1),(LEFT(surname,5))))) PERSISTENT,
  PRIMARY KEY (`id`),
  UNIQUE KEY `id` (`id`)
) ENGINE=InnoDB DEFAULT CHARSET=latin1
1 row in set (0.00 sec)

MariaDB [test]>
```

6. Insert some data as follows:

```
INSERT INTO virt_cols (surname,givenname) VALUES
    ('Packer','Boyd'),('Uchtdorf','Dieter'),
    ('Ballard','Russell'),('Holland','Jeffrey'),
    ('Cook','Quentin'),('Bednar','David');
INSERT INTO virt_cols (surname,givenname,uid,username) VALUES
    ('Christofferson','Todd', DEFAULT, DEFAULT),
    ('Andersen','Neil', DEFAULT, DEFAULT);
```

7. Select the data from our `virt_cols` table using the following command:

```
SELECT * FROM virt_cols;
```

The preceding command displays the following output:

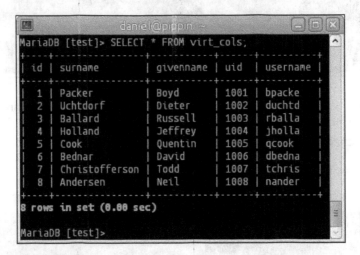

How it works...

The virtual columns feature of MariaDB allows us to create special columns in our table that have calculated values based on the output of a function (or a combination of functions). These values can be either `PERSISTENT`, meaning the value is stored in the database and only updated when the row is updated, or `VIRTUAL`, meaning the value is calculated each time the row is read.

When using a standard DESCRIBE statement to examine the structure of a table with virtual columns, the EXTRA column in the output will tell us whether a column is virtual or not with the presence of the text VIRTUAL or PERSISTENT to identify each type of virtual column. What the DESCRIBE statement will not do is show us the function or combination of functions and operators which determine the value of the virtual column. For that, we need to use the SHOW CREATE TABLE command.

When inserting or updating data in a table with virtual columns, we can either choose to not specify the columns in our SQL statement or to go ahead and specify them but use the DEFAULT key word instead of providing a value. In our recipe, we perform both actions.

Selecting data from a table with virtual columns is just like selecting from a table without virtual columns. The only difference will be if the function calculating the value of a VIRTUAL column takes a noticeable amount of time to run. A PERSISTENT virtual column, because its calculated value is stored in the database, will return results as fast as regular columns in the table, but a VIRTUAL column's value is calculated every time the table is queried.

There's more...

Virtual columns have some limitations. For starters, they can only be used with InnoDB, XtraDB, Aria, and MyISAM tables.

Also, indexes are only partially supported for virtual columns. This is because virtual columns do not support primary keys. It is possible to have an index on a PERSISTENT virtual column, but even then statements such as UPDATE CASCADE, ON UPDATE SET NULL, and ON DELETE SET NULL are not allowed.

That said, things such as triggers and stored procedures are fully supported by virtual columns.

See also

- ▸ The full documentation of virtual columns in MariaDB is available at https://mariadb.com/kb/en/virtual-columns/

11
NoSQL with HandlerSocket

In this chapter, we will cover the following recipes:

- Installing and configuring HandlerSocket
- Installing the libhsclient library
- Installing the HandlerSocket PERL client libraries
- Reading data using HandlerSocket and PERL
- Inserting data using HandlerSocket and PERL
- Updating and deleting data using HandlerSocket and PERL
- Installing the HandlerSocket Python client libraries
- Reading data using HandlerSocket and Python
- Inserting data using HandlerSocket and Python
- Updating and deleting data using HandlerSocket and Python
- Installing the HandlerSocket Ruby client libraries
- Reading data using HandlerSocket and Ruby
- Inserting data using HandlerSocket and Ruby
- Updating and deleting data using HandlerSocket and Ruby
- Using HandlerSocket directly with Telnet

Introduction

This chapter is all about installing, configuring, and most importantly, using HandlerSocket, a NoSQL interface for MariaDB. We'll start with installing and configuring the HandlerSocket plugin for MariaDB and compiling and installing the `libhsclient` library that other languages use to talk directly to our MariaDB databases through HandlerSocket.

We then go through the same basic recipes for three popular scripting languages: PERL, Python, and Ruby. For each of these three languages, we first install the client library, and then go through reading, inserting, updating, and deleting data. After installing the HandlerSocket plugin, feel free to jump directly to a preferred language. To finish off the chapter, we have a recipe on interacting with HandlerSocket directly using `telnet`.

Installing and configuring HandlerSocket

The HandlerSocket plugin is included with MariaDB, but like other optional plugins, it is not enabled or configured by default.

How to do it...

1. Launch the `mysql` command-line client and connect to our MariaDB database.

2. Install the HandlerSocket plugin using the following command:

   ```
   INSTALL SONAME 'handlersocket';
   ```

3. Open our `my.cnf` or `my.ini` file and add the following command to the `[mysqld]` section:

   ```
   #
   # * HandlerSocket
   #
   handlersocket_address="127.0.0.1"
   handlersocket_port="9998"
   handlersocket_port_wr="9999"
   ```

4. Stop and restart MariaDB.

5. Reconnect to MariaDB using the `mysql` command-line client and see the HandlerSocket worker threads using the following statement:

```
SHOW PROCESSLIST;
```

How it works...

The HandlerSocket plugin allows us to completely bypass the SQL layer of MariaDB. This offers an incredible speed for simple operations. The downside is that HandlerSocket only handles simple operations. It cannot handle anything beyond the basic `SELECT`, `INSERT`, `UPDATE`, and `DELETE` statements, and it can only search on a primary or other indexed key.

The HandlerSocket plugin is included with MariaDB, but like other optional plugins, it is not activated by default. To activate it, we use the `INSTALL SONAME` command. This is a one-time operation.

After running the `INSTALL` command, there are a few settings we need to add to our local `my.cnf` file in order for HandlerSocket to work properly. So, after installing the plugin, we edit our main configuration file and add it.

The `handlersocket_address` setting is the IP address that the plugin will listen on for requests. The `handlersocket_port` variable sets the port number we connect to for read-only requests. The `handlersocket_port_wr` variable defines the port number we connect to for inserts, updates, and other operations that require write access.

When installing and configuring HandlerSocket, we need to make sure that we run the `INSTALL SONAME` command before adding the settings to our `my.cnf` file. The HandlerSocket configuration options are only valid if the plugin is installed. They will cause an error and prevent MariaDB from starting if they are present in our configuration file when the HandlerSocket plugin is not installed.

When HandlerSocket is configured and running, it will spawn several worker threads. These threads handle requests from our applications. While HandlerSocket is running, looking for the worker threads is a good way to verify that we have installed and configured HandlerSocket correctly. When HandlerSocket is running, the output of the SHOW PROCESSLIST; command will look similar to the following screenshot:

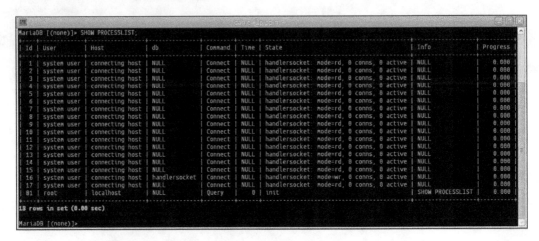

To remove the HandlerSocket plugin, we use the UNINSTALL SONAME command. If we choose to UNINSTALL the plugin, we must also remove the configuration settings we added after installing the plugin.

There's more...

By default, the HandlerSocket plugin will launch 16 read threads and 1 write thread. Both of them can be controlled by adding the following variables to the [mysqld] section of our main my.cnf file:

```
# HandlerSocket Read Threads:
handlersocket_threads     = 16


# HandlerSocket Write Threads:
handlersocket_threads_wr = 1
```

The maximum permissible value for each of them is 3000, but it's not recommended to ever set them that high. In fact, the developers recommend leaving the number of write threads set to 1. For the read threads, they recommend setting it to double the number of CPU cores on the server.

We can also set plain text passwords for clients to use when connecting with HandlerSocket. Along with completely bypassing the SQL layer of MariaDB, HandlerSocket also bypasses MariaDB's security layer. This adds back a measure of security that is otherwise missing when using this plugin. We can set separate passwords for both the read-only and write ports. The two variables are as follows:

```
handlersocket_plain_secret = 'readSocketPassword'

handlersocket_plain_secret_wr = 'writeSocketPassword'
```

See also

▸ The full documentation of the HandlerSocket plugin can be found at `https://mariadb.com/kb/en/handlersocket/`

▸ The various HandlerSocket configuration options are documented at `https://mariadb.com/kb/en/handlersocket-configuration-options/`

▸ The HandlerSocket protocol is documented at `https://github.com/DeNA/HandlerSocket-Plugin-for-MySQL/blob/master/docs-en/protocol.en.txt`

Installing the libhsclient library

The `libhsclient` library is what client libraries use to talk to HandlerSocket. This library is not included with MariaDB; so, we need to either install it from our Linux distribution's package repositories or build and install it ourselves.

Getting ready

Install and configure the HandlerSocket plugin as described in the *Installing and configuring HandlerSocket* recipe earlier in this chapter. In order to build the `libhsclient` library, we need to have some development tools and packages installed.

On Red Hat, Fedora, or CentOS, run the following command to install the necessary tools:

```
sudo yum install make gcc-c++
```

On Debian or Ubuntu, run the following command to install the necessary tools:

```
sudo apt-get install make g++
```

We are now ready to build and install the `libhsclient` libraries.

How to do it...

1. Download the latest HandlerSocket source file as follows:

```
wget \
https://github.com/DeNA/HandlerSocket-Plugin-for-MySQL/archive/
master.tar.gz
```

2. Change to the `/usr/local/src` directory and untar the file we just downloaded as follows:

```
cd /usr/local/src/

sudo tar -zxvf /path/to/master*
```

3. Change to the `libhsclient/` directory and rename `Makefile.plain` to `Makefile` as follows:

```
cd HandlerSocket-Plugin-for-MySQL-master/libhsclient

sudo mv -vi Makefile.plain Makefile
```

4. Compile `libhsclient` and install it as follows:

```
sudo make

sudo mkdir -vp /usr/local/include/handlersocket

sudo install -vm 644 *.hpp /usr/local/include/handlersocket


sudo install -vm 644 libhsclient.a /usr/local/lib


cd /usr/local/include/

sudo ln -vs handlersocket/*.hpp ./
```

How it works...

Compiling and installing the `libhsclient` library is much like compiling and installing other software from a source on Linux. The main difference is that because it is part of the larger HandlerSocket plugin source package and because we don't need the MariaDB plugin parts (they are already in MariaDB), we don't use the usual `./configure && make && sudo make install` three-step dance that is so common with the other source code. Instead, we navigate directly to the `libhsclient/` subdirectory, put the default `Makefile` in place, and use the `make` process.

The library is not very large, so the `make` process does not take long. When the process is completed, we will have several files that end in `.hpp` in the `libhsclient/` directory. These files need to be moved to a location from where our client libraries can see them, so that's what we do in the last few commands we run in step 4.

Installing the HandlerSocket PERL client libraries

The HandlerSocket client libraries for PERL are included with the HandlerSocket source code. In this recipe, we'll compile and install them.

Getting ready

In order to build the HandlerSocket PERL client library, we need to install some development tools and packages. First, we need to install the `libhsclient` library as described in the *Installing the libhsclient library* recipe earlier in this chapter. Then, we need to install some PERL development tools.

On Red Hat, Fedora, or CentOS, run the following command:

```
sudo yum install perl-devel perl-Test-Simple
```

On Debian or Ubuntu, run the following command to install the necessary packages:

```
sudo apt-get install libperl-dev
```

We are now ready to install the HandlerSocket PERL client library.

How to do it...

1. Open a command-line window.

2. Change to the `perl-Net-HandlerSocket` directory in the `HandlerSocket` source directory as follows:

   ```
   cd /usr/local/src/HandlerSocket-Plugin-for-MySQL-master/
   cd perl-Net-HandlerSocket/
   ```

3. Run the following commands to install the PERL HandlerSocket client libraries:

   ```
   sudo perl Makefile.PL
   sudo make
   sudo make test
   sudo make install
   ```

How it works...

The HandlerSocket plugin source code includes a PERL client library, but this library is not included with MariaDB binaries, so we have to install it manually. We already had the HandlerSocket source code from the recipe we followed to install the `libhsclient` library, so we don't have to download it again.

Actually, compiling and installing the library is extremely easy. When the `make test` portion is run, the following text should be the last line of the output:

```
Result: PASS
```

Reading data using HandlerSocket and PERL

In this recipe, we will create a simple PERL script that reads data using HandlerSocket.

Getting ready

Install the HandlerSocket PERL client libraries as described in the *Installing the HandlerSocket PERL client libraries* recipe earlier in this chapter.

Launch the `mysql` command-line client and run the following commands to create a test table with some data:

```
CREATE DATABASE IF NOT EXISTS test;
USE test;
DROP TABLE IF EXISTS hs_test;
CREATE TABLE hs_test (
  id SERIAL PRIMARY KEY,
  givenname varchar(64),
  surname varchar(64)
);
INSERT INTO hs_test VALUES
  (1,"William","Hartnell"), (2,"Patrick","Troughton"),
  (3,"John","Pertwee"), (4,"Tom","Baker"),
  (5,"Peter","Davison"), (6,"Colin","Baker");
```

This sample data is also in the `hs_sample_data.sql` file available on the book's website.

How to do it...

1. Create a file named `hs_read_test.pl` with the following content:

```perl
#!/usr/bin/perl
use strict;
use warnings;

use Net::HandlerSocket;
my $read_args = { host => 'localhost', port => 9998 };
my $hs = new Net::HandlerSocket($read_args);

my $res = $hs->open_index(0, 'test', 'hs_test', 'PRIMARY',
'id,givenname,surname');
  die $hs->get_error() if $res != 0;

my $pk = 1;

$res = $hs->execute_single(0, '=', [ "$pk" ], 10, 0);
  die $hs->get_error() if $res->[0] != 0;
shift(@$res);

while ( $res->[0] ) {
  printf("%s\t%s\t%s\n",$res->[0],$res->[1],$res->[2]);
  $pk++;
  $res = $hs->execute_single(0, '=', [ "$pk" ], 20, 0);
    die $hs->get_error() if $res->[0] != 0;
  shift(@$res);
}

$hs->close();
```

2. Run the file with the following command:

```
perl hs_read_test.pl
```

 This file is also available on the book's website.

How it works...

To read data using the HandlerSocket PERL library, we first need to create a `Net::HandlerSocket` object. This is done in our recipe with the `use Net::HandlerSocket` line and the two lines following it, where we supply the host and port information.

With the object now created, we can open a connection to a specific table using the `open_index` method. When doing so, we give our connection a number (0 in our recipe) and then specify the database we want to access (`test`), the table (`hs_test`), the index we want to open (we use `PRIMARY` in our recipe, which is a key word that means the `primary key`), and finally, a comma-separated list of the columns we want to read (`id,givenname,surname`).

To execute a single read, we use the `execute_single` method. This method takes five arguments. The first is the connection number (0) we set when calling the `open_index` method. The second is the search operator (= in our recipe). Supported operators include =, >=, <=, >, and <. The third argument is an array of the key we want to find. The array must have the same number of elements as the number of columns the key we are searching has. As we are searching the primary key in our recipe and it only has a single column, our array only has one element. The fourth and fifth arguments are the maximum number of records to retrieve and the number of columns to skip before retrieving anything, respectively (10 and 0 in our recipe).

The result we get back is an array with elements corresponding to the columns we defined with our `open_index` call. In our recipe, we use `printf` to print them to our terminal.

To cycle through all of the records in our test database, we use a `while` loop to increment our $pk variable until it doesn't find a record.

Lastly, we call the `close` method to close our connection. The output of this script will look like the following screenshot:

```
daniel@pippin: ~
daniel@pippin:~$ perl hs_read_test.pl
1        William Hartnell
2        Patrick Troughton
3        John    Pertwee
4        Tom     Baker
5        Peter   Davison
6        Colin   Baker
daniel@pippin:~$
```

There's more...

We can execute multiple queries in a single operation using the `execute_multi` method.
Instead of a single set of arguments, this method accepts an array of arguments. Each entry
in the array contains the same five arguments used in the `execute_single` method. For
example, consider the following statements:

```
my $mres = $hs->execute_multi([
  [0, '=', [ "1" ], 1, 0],
  [0, '>', [ "3" ], 5, 0],
  [0, '>=', [ "5" ], 2, 0],
  [0, '<', [ "6" ], 4, 3]
]);
```

As we are dealing with multiple requests, error handling goes in a `for` loop as follows:

```
for my $res (@$mres) {
  die $hs->get_error() if $res->[0] != 0;
  shift(@$res);
  # and etc...
}
```

See also

▸ The documentation for the PERL client library is available at `https://github.com/DeNA/HandlerSocket-Plugin-for-MySQL/blob/master/docs-en/perl-client.en.txt`

Inserting data using HandlerSocket and PERL

To insert data with HandlerSocket, we need to use a different port, but we still use the
`execute_single` command with extra options.

Getting ready

Complete the *Reading data using HandlerSocket and PERL* recipe before starting
this recipe.

How to do it...

1. Create a file named `hs_insert_test.pl` with the following content (this script is also available on the book's website):

```perl
#!/usr/bin/perl
use strict;
use warnings;


use Net::HandlerSocket;
my $write_args = { host => 'localhost', port => 9999 };
my $hsw = new Net::HandlerSocket($write_args);


my $resw = $hsw->open_index(1, 'test', 'hs_test', 'PRIMARY',
'id,givenname,surname');
  die $hsw->get_error() if $resw != 0;


$resw = $hsw->execute_single(1, '+', [ '7', 'Sylvester', 'McCoy'
],0,0);
  die $hsw->get_error() if $resw->[0] != 0;


$resw = $hsw->execute_single(1, '+', [ '8', 'Paul', 'McGann'
],0,0);
  die $hsw->get_error() if $resw->[0] != 0;


$hsw->close();
```

2. Run the file using the following command:

```
perl hs_insert_test.pl
```

3. Run the `hs_read_test.pl` script to verify that our inserts worked:

```
perl hs_read_test.pl
```

How it works...

Creating the `Net::HandlerSocket` object and opening a connection are very similar to how we open a read-only connection. The main difference is that we specify the write port (9999) instead of the read-only port (9998). Opening an index is also the same as what we do for a read-only connection.

Performing an insert is different. We do use the same `execute_single` method, but instead of using a comparison operator, like we would for reading data, we use a + operator to indicate that we are adding a new row.

The third argument of the `execute_single` method is also different. Instead of specifying what we are searching for, we put in the data we are inserting. These values correspond to the columns we specified in the `open_index` call. The fourth and fifth arguments of the `execute_single` method are not used when inserting and so, both can be set to `0`.

The `hs_insert_test.pl` script will not produce any output, so after running it, we can rerun the `hs_read_test.pl` script we created in the *Reading data using HandlerSocket and PERL* recipe. Thus, we can confirm the data was entered. The output will look like the following screenshot:

```
daniel@pippin: ~$ perl hs_insert_test.pl
daniel@pippin: ~$ perl hs_read_test.pl
1        William Hartnell
2        Patrick Troughton
3        John    Pertwee
4        Tom     Baker
5        Peter   Davison
6        Colin   Baker
7        Sylvester       McCoy
8        Paul    McGann
daniel@pippin: ~$
```

See also

The documentation for the PERL client library is available at `https://github.com/DeNA/HandlerSocket-Plugin-for-MySQL/blob/master/docs-en/perl-client.en.txt`

Updating and deleting data using HandlerSocket and PERL

In addition to reading and inserting data, updating and deleting data round out the abilities of HandlerSocket.

Getting ready

Complete the *Inserting data using HandlerSocket and PERL* recipe before starting this recipe.

1. Create a file named hs_update_test.pl with the following content (this script is also available on the book's website):

```perl
#!/usr/bin/perl
use strict;
use warnings;


use Net::HandlerSocket;
my $update_args = { host => 'localhost', port => 9999 };
my $hsu = new Net::HandlerSocket($update_args);


my $resu = $hsu->open_index(2, 'test', 'hs_test', 'PRIMARY',
'givenname');
    die $hsu->get_error() if $resu != 0;


$resu = $hsu->execute_single(2, '=', [ '3' ],1,0, 'U', [ 'Jon' ]);
    die $hsu->get_error() if $resu->[0] != 0;
printf("Number of Updated Rows:\t%s\n",$resu->[1]);


$hsu->close();
```

2. Create a file called hs_delete_test.pl with the following contents (this script is also available on the book's website):

```perl
#!/usr/bin/perl
use strict;
use warnings;


use Net::HandlerSocket;
my $delete_args = { host => 'localhost', port => 9999 };
my $hsd = new Net::HandlerSocket($delete_args);


my $resd = $hsd->open_index(3, 'test', 'hs_test', 'PRIMARY',
'id,givenname,surname');
    die $hsd->get_error() if $resd != 0;


$resd = $hsd->execute_single(3, '+', [ '101', 'Junk', 'Entry'
],1,0);
```

```
    die $hsd->get_error() if $resd->[0] != 0;


$resd = $hsd->execute_single(3, '+', [ '102', 'Junk', 'Entry'
],1,0);
    die $hsd->get_error() if $resd->[0] != 0;


$resd = $hsd->execute_single(3, '+', [ '103', 'Junk', 'Entry'
],1,0);
    die $hsd->get_error() if $resd->[0] != 0;


$resd = $hsd->execute_single(3, '>', [ '100' ],10,0, 'D');
    die $hsd->get_error() if $resd->[0] != 0;


printf("Number of Deleted Rows:\t%s\n",$resd->[1]);


$hsd->close();
```

3. Run the files with the following commands:

    ```
    perl hs_update_test.pl
    perl hs_delete_test.pl
    ```

4. Run the `hs_read_test.pl` script to verify that our `update` and `delete` commands have worked:

    ```
    perl hs_read_test.pl
    ```

How it works...

To update and delete data, we use the `execute_single` method but with extra arguments. To update data, there are two extra arguments. The first five are just like the ones used for reading a row. The sixth argument is the letter `U` that stands for update. The seventh argument contains the values we want to update. These must correspond to the columns we specify in the `open_index` call.

In our recipe, we specified just the `givenname` column, so that's the only value we need to provide. Our recipe searches for the primary key 3 and then updates the `givenname` column of the row with that key to `Jon`, which is how his given name is actually spelled.

Lastly, in our update script, the result we get back from the `execute_single` method is the number of rows updated. So, to make things more user friendly, we print the value out. The output should be as follows:

```
Number of Updated Rows:  1
```

In our delete script, the calls are simpler than what we used to update data, but we first insert some data to give us something to delete (this lets us run the script multiple times, and it will always have those three rows to delete).

After inserting the three junk rows, we call `execute_single` with D (for delete) and with a comparison operator (>) and a record limit of `10` that lets us delete the records we just added. When we run the statement, the output will be as follows:

Number of Deleted Rows: 3

Finally, we run the `hs_read_test.pl` script we created in the *Reading data using HandlerSocket and PERL* recipe, so we can confirm that the given name was correctly updated (the deleted rows, obviously, will not appear in the output unless something went wrong).

The output will look like the following screenshot:

```
daniel@pippin: ~
daniel@pippin: ~$ perl hs_update_test.pl
Number of Updated Rows: 1
daniel@pippin: ~$ perl hs_delete_test.pl
Number of Deleted Rows: 3
daniel@pippin: ~$ perl hs_read_test.pl
1        William Hartnell
2        Patrick Troughton
3        Jon     Pertwee
4        Tom     Baker
5        Peter   Davison
6        Colin   Baker
7        Sylvester         McCoy
8        Paul    McGann
daniel@pippin: ~$
```

See also

▶ The documentation for the PERL client library is available at `https://github.com/DeNA/HandlerSocket-Plugin-for-MySQL/blob/master/docs-en/perl-client.en.txt`

Installing the HandlerSocket Python client libraries

Python is another popular scripting language. This recipe is about installing the Python `pyhs` client library for HandlerSocket so that we can use it in our scripts.

Getting ready

Install the `libhsclient` library as described in the *Installing the libhsclient library* recipe earlier in this chapter.

We need to also install the `mercurial` and `python-setuptools` packages so that we can get the latest copy of the `pyhs` source code and install it.

On Red Hat, Fedora, or CentOS, run the following command:

```
sudo yum install mercurial python-setuptools
```

On Debian or Ubuntu, run the following command:

```
sudo apt-get install mercurial python-setuptools
```

We are now ready to install the HandlerSocket client libraries for Python.

How to do it...

1. Clone a copy of the `pyhs` source code as follows:

    ```
    cd /usr/local/src/
    sudo hg clone http://bitbucket.org/excieve/pyhs
    ```

2. Change to the `pyhs` directory and edit the `setup.py` file by adding the following line after the four `from...` and `DistutilsPlatformError` lines at the top of the file:

    ```
    ext_errors = (CCompilerError, DistutilsExecError,
    DistutilsPlatformError)
    ```

3. Run the `setup.py` script to install `pyhs` as follows:

    ```
    sudo python setup.py install
    ```

How it works...

There are a couple of different HandlerSocket libraries for the Python language. The one we're installing is called `pyhs`. Its source code is hosted on `bitbucket.org` and uses `mercurial` for version control. The actual process of checking out and installing the library is quite simple. However, there's a bug in the file that requires a quick fix before we can actually complete the install. The bug is described at `https://bitbucket.org/excieve/pyhs/issue/11/setuppy-error-ext_errors-not-defined` and may actually be fixed in the current version of `pyhs`, so we should check before applying the fix described here.

If everything goes well, the last line of the output of the `install` step will be as follows:

```
Success
```

▶ The documentation of the `pyhs` library is available at
`http://python-handler-socket.readthedocs.org/en/latest/`

Reading data using HandlerSocket and Python

Now that we have installed `pyhs`, we can start using it to read data from our database.

Getting ready

Install the HandlerSocket PERL client libraries as described in the *Installing the HandlerSocket PERL client libraries* recipe earlier in this chapter. Launch the `mysql` command-line client and run the SQL commands from the *Getting ready* section of the *Reading data using HandlerSocket and PERL* recipe, described earlier in this chapter, to give us some sample data to read (and if we've already gone through the PERL or Ruby recipes, running the SQL commands again will reset the sample data to its default state).

How to do it...

1. Launch the interactive Python interpreter in a terminal window as follows:

   ```
   python
   ```

2. Run the following commands in the interpreter:

   ```
   from pyhs import Manager
   hs = Manager()
   data = hs.get('test', 'hs_test', ['id', 'givenname', 'surname'],
   '5')
   print dict(data)
   ```

3. Then, run the following commands in the interpreter:

   ```
   from pyhs.sockets import ReadSocket
   hsr = ReadSocket([('inet', '127.0.0.1', 9998)])

   r_id = hsr.get_index_id('test', 'hs_test', ['id', 'givenname',
   'surname'])

   hsr.find(r_id, '=', ['5'])
   hsr.find(r_id, '=', ['6'])
   hsr.find(r_id, '>=', ['1'],20)
   ```

4. Press *Ctrl + D* to exit the interactive Python interpreter.

How it works...

The `pyhs` libraries provide us with both high- and low-level methods of getting data. In our recipe, we used the high-level method first.

We start by importing the high-level `Manager` object. We then assign it to a variable and use the `get` method to search for a row in our database. This method takes four arguments. First, the name of the database, then the table name, an array of the columns we want to get, and lastly, the primary key value we want to search for (5 in our recipe). We assign the result to a variable and then print it out to our screen with `print dict()`. The output of the `print dict(data)` line will look like the following command:

```
{'givenname': 'Peter', 'surname': 'Davison', 'id': '5'}
```

Next, we import the lower level `ReadSocket` object. With the `Manager` object we can simply request what we want and get it all in one step, but we can't do that with `ReadSocket`. Instead, with `ReadSocket`, we first open a connection to the HandlerSocket read-only port, then we call the `get_index_id` method to define the database, table, and columns we are interested in. This method takes three arguments: the database name, the table name, and an array of the columns we are interested in.

We are then able to read data using the `find` method. This method takes three arguments. First is the variable we used when calling `get_index_id`. Second is the comparison operator we want to use; the supported operators are =, >, <, >=, and <=. The third argument is the key value we want to search for. There are fourth and fifth arguments that are optional. They set the maximum number of rows to return and the number of records to skip before retrieving records. If these arguments are not specified, the `find` method will set them both to 0.

The results of the `find` method are returned as an array. Of the three calls to this method in our recipe, the first two return single rows and the last returns all of the records in our example table. The returned values in the Python interpreter will look like the following command:

```
[('5', 'Peter', 'Davison')]
```

```
[('6', 'Colin', 'Baker')]
```

```
[('1', 'William', 'Hartnell'), ('2', 'Patrick', 'Troughton'), ('3',
'John', 'Pertwee'), ('4', 'Tom', 'Baker'), ('5', 'Peter', 'Davison'),
('6', 'Colin', 'Baker')]
```

The complete output of the recipe will look like the following screenshot:

```
daniel@pippin: ~$ python
Python 2.7.5+ (default, Sep 19 2013, 13:48:49)
[GCC 4.8.1] on linux2
Type "help", "copyright", "credits" or "license" for more information.
>>> from pyhs import Manager
>>> hs = Manager()
>>> data = hs.get('test', 'hs_test', ['id', 'givenname', 'surname'], '5')
>>> print dict(data)
{'givenname': 'Peter', 'surname': 'Davison', 'id': '5'}
>>> from pyhs.sockets import ReadSocket
>>> hsr = ReadSocket([('inet', '127.0.0.1', 9998)])
>>> r_id = hsr.get_index_id('test', 'hs_test', ['id', 'givenname', 'surname'])
>>> hsr.find(r_id, '=', ['5'])
[('5', 'Peter', 'Davison')]
>>> hsr.find(r_id, '=', ['6'])
[('6', 'Colin', 'Baker')]
>>> hsr.find(r_id, '>=', ['1'],20)
[('1', 'William', 'Hartnell'), ('2', 'Patrick', 'Troughton'), ('3', 'John', 'P
ertwee'), ('4', 'Tom', 'Baker'), ('5', 'Peter', 'Davison'), ('6', 'Colin', 'Ba
ker')]
>>>
daniel@pippin: ~$
```

See also

▶   The documentation of the `pyhs` library is available at
    `http://python-handler-socket.readthedocs.org/en/latest/`

Inserting data using HandlerSocket and Python

Inserting data using Python is similar to how it is done in other languages, but with a bit of Python flair.

Getting ready

Complete the *Reading data using HandlerSocket and Python* recipe, described earlier in this chapter, prior to starting this recipe.

How to do it...

1. Launch the interactive Python interpreter in a terminal window as follows:

    ```
    python
    ```

2. Then, run the following commands in the Python interpreter:

    ```
    from pyhs import Manager
    hs = Manager()
    hs.insert('test', 'hs_test', [('id', '7'), ('givenname',
    'Sylvester'), ('surname', 'McCoy')])
    ```

3. Finally, run the following commands in the interpreter:

    ```
    from pyhs.sockets import WriteSocket
    hsw = WriteSocket([('inet', '127.0.0.1', 9999)])
    w_id = hsw.get_index_id('test', 'hs_test', ['id', 'givenname',
    'surname'])

    hsw.insert(w_id, ['8','Paul','McGann'])
    ```

How it works...

Similar to how data was read, when inserting data with `pyhs` there are two ways to do it. First is at a high level using the `Manager` object, and the second is at a low-level using the `WriteSocket` object.

The `Manager` object's `insert` method takes three arguments. First, we set the database name and then the table name. Finally, we provide an array that contains the column names and the values we want to insert.

For the `WriteSocket` object, we first open a connection to the `HandlerSocket` write port and then call the `get_index_id` method to define the database, table, and columns we want to insert.

We are then able to insert data using the `insert` method. This method takes two arguments. First is the variable we used when calling `get_index_id` (we used `w_id` in our recipe), and the second is an array of the values we want to insert. After successful insertion, the `insert` method will return `True`.

The `WriteSocket` object doesn't have a `find` method, so if we want to read back the data we just entered, we need to use the `ReadSocket` object as described in the *Reading data using HandlerSocket and Python* recipe earlier in this chapter.

The output of the commands run in this recipe will look like the following screenshot:

```
daniel@pippin: ~$ python
Python 2.7.5+ (default, Sep 19 2013, 13:48:49)
[GCC 4.8.1] on linux2
>>> hs.insert('test', 'hs_test', [('id', '7'), ('givenname', 'Sylvester'), ('surname', 'McCoy')])
True
>>> from pyhs.sockets import WriteSocket
>>> hsw = WriteSocket([('inet', '127.0.0.1', 9999)])
>>> w_id = hsw.get_index_id('test', 'hs_test', ['id', 'givenname', 'surname'])
>>> hsw.insert(w_id, ['8','Paul','McGann'])
True
>>>
daniel@pippin: ~$ 
```

See also

▶ The documentation of the pyhs library is available at
   http://python-handler-socket.readthedocs.org/en/latest/

Updating and deleting data using HandlerSocket and Python

Updating and deleting data is similar to but not quite the same as inserting data.

Getting ready

Complete the *Inserting data using HandlerSocket and Python* recipe prior to starting this recipe.

How to do it...

1. Launch the interactive Python interpreter in a terminal window as follows:

   ```
   python
   ```

2. Run the following commands in the Python interpreter:

   ```
   from pyhs.sockets import WriteSocket
   hsu = WriteSocket([('inet', '127.0.0.1', 9999)])
   u_id = hsu.get_index_id('test', 'hs_test', ['givenname'])
   hsu.find_modify(u_id, '=', ['3'],'U',['Jon'],10,0)
   ```

3. Then, run the following commands in the Python interpreter to open new read and write connections to our test table:

```
from pyhs.sockets import ReadSocket
hsr = ReadSocket([('inet', '127.0.0.1', 9998)])
r_id = hsr.get_index_id('test', 'hs_test', ['id', 'givenname',
'surname'])


from pyhs.sockets import WriteSocket
hsd = WriteSocket([('inet', '127.0.0.1', 9999)])
d_id = hsd.get_index_id('test', 'hs_test', ['id', 'givenname',
'surname'])
```

4. Run the following commands to test the process of deleting data:

```
hsr.find(r_id, '>=', ['1'],20)
hsd.insert(d_id, ['101','Junk','Entry'])
hsd.insert(d_id, ['102','Junk','Entry'])
hsd.insert(d_id, ['103','Junk','Entry'])
hsr.find(r_id, '>=', ['1'],20)
hsd.find_modify(d_id, '>', ['100'],'D','',10)
hsr.find(r_id, '>=', ['1'],20)
```

How it works...

To update data, we use the `WriteSocket` object of the `pyhs` library. First, we open a connection to the HandlerSocket write port, and then we call the `get_index_id` method to define the database, table, and columns we want to update. In step 2 of our recipe, we're only updating the `givenname` column, so that's all we define.

We update data using the `find_modify` method. This method takes seven arguments. First is the variable we used when calling `get_index_id` (we used `u_id` in our recipe), and the second is the comparison operator we want to use for finding the values to update; the supported operators are =, >, <, >=, and <=. The third argument is the key value we want to search for (3 in our recipe). The fourth argument is the character U that tells the method that we are performing an update. Fifth, is an array of the values we want to update. This array corresponds to the columns we specified when we called the `get_index_id` method; just fill the `givenname` column in our recipe. The sixth and seventh arguments set the maximum number of rows to update and the number of records to skip before searching records, respectively. We set these to 10 and 0 in our recipe, respectively.

On a successful update, the `find_modify` method will return the number of rows updated as an array. The returned value in the Python interpreter will look like the following command:

```
[('1',)]
```

The complete output of the recipe will look like the following screenshot:

```
daniel@pippin: ~$ python
Python 2.7.5+ (default, Sep 19 2013, 13:48:49)
[GCC 4.8.1] on linux2
Type "help", "copyright", "credits" or "license" for more information.
>>> from pyhs.sockets import WriteSocket
>>> hsu = WriteSocket([('inet', '127.0.0.1', 9999)])
>>> u_id = hsu.get_index_id('test', 'hs_test', ['givenname'])
>>> hsu.find_modify(u_id, '=', ['3'],'U',['Jon'],10,0)
[('1',)]
>>>
daniel@pippin: ~$
```

The `WriteSocket` object doesn't have a `find` method, so if we want to read back the row we just updated, we need to use the `ReadSocket` object as described in the *Reading data using HandlerSocket and Python* recipe earlier in this chapter.

To test the process of deleting data in steps 3 and 4 of our recipe, we first import the `ReadSocket` object in step 3 like we did in the *Reading data using HandlerSocket and Python* recipe earlier in this chapter, so we can easily read the data to show the before and after states of our table. We then open a new `WriteSocket` object, this time defining all of the columns in our table instead of just the `givenname` column.

Then, in step 4 of our recipe, we actually test the code by inserting some data, deleting it, and reading the data in our table before and after each step. When deleting rows in our recipe, we supply the `find_modify` method with six arguments. First is the variable we used when calling `get_index_id` (we used `d_id` in our recipe), and the second is the comparison operator we want to use for finding the rows to delete (> in our recipe). The third argument is the key value we want to search for (100 in our recipe). The fourth argument is the character D, which tells the method that we are performing a delete operation. The fifth argument of the `find_modify` method is an array of the values we want to update; this is only used when updating a row, which we aren't doing here, so we supply an empty value. We do this so that we can specify the sixth argument, which is the limit of the number of rows we want to modify. We do this because if this value is not specified, the method will default to only deleting a single row. In our recipe, we want to delete all rows with id greater than 100, so we set this to 10 (we could set it to 3 since there are only three that match, but in cases where we don't know the exact number of rows we are deleting and we want to make sure we delete them all, it's better to set this value to a larger value than we need to). The result we get back will be an array containing a single value equal to the number of rows deleted.

In our recipe, we print out our data in our example table twice; once before the deletion and then again after it. The key output is in between when the find_modify method returns the number of rows deleted. In our recipe, the output will be the following command:

```
[('3',)]
```

The complete output of steps 3 and 4 will look like the following screenshot:

```
daniel@pippin:~$ python
Python 2.7.5+ (default, Sep 19 2013, 13:48:49)
[GCC 4.8.1] on linux2
Type "help", "copyright", "credits" or "license" for more information.
>>> from pyhs.sockets import ReadSocket
>>> hsr = ReadSocket([('inet', '127.0.0.1', 9998)])
>>> r_id = hsr.get_index_id('test', 'hs_test', ['id', 'givenname', 'surname'])
>>> from pyhs.sockets import WriteSocket
>>> hsd = WriteSocket([('inet', '127.0.0.1', 9999)])
>>> d_id = hsd.get_index_id('test', 'hs_test', ['id', 'givenname', 'surname'])
>>> hsr.find(r_id, '>=', ['1'],20)
[('1', 'William', 'Hartnell'), ('2', 'Patrick', 'Troughton'), ('3', 'Jon', 'Pertw
ee'), ('4', 'Tom', 'Baker'), ('5', 'Peter', 'Davison'), ('6', 'Colin', 'Baker'),
('7', 'Sylvester', 'McCoy'), ('8', 'Paul', 'McGann')]
>>> hsd.insert(d_id, ['101','Junk','Entry'])
True
>>> hsd.insert(d_id, ['102','Junk','Entry'])
True
>>> hsd.insert(d_id, ['103','Junk','Entry'])
True
>>> hsr.find(r_id, '>=', ['1'],20)
[('1', 'William', 'Hartnell'), ('2', 'Patrick', 'Troughton'), ('3', 'Jon', 'Pertw
ee'), ('4', 'Tom', 'Baker'), ('5', 'Peter', 'Davison'), ('6', 'Colin', 'Baker'),
('7', 'Sylvester', 'McCoy'), ('8', 'Paul', 'McGann'), ('101', 'Junk', 'Entry'), (
'102', 'Junk', 'Entry'), ('103', 'Junk', 'Entry')]
>>> hsd.find_modify(d_id, '>', ['100'],'D','',10)
[('3',)]
>>> hsr.find(r_id, '>=', ['1'],20)
[('1', 'William', 'Hartnell'), ('2', 'Patrick', 'Troughton'), ('3', 'Jon', 'Pertw
ee'), ('4', 'Tom', 'Baker'), ('5', 'Peter', 'Davison'), ('6', 'Colin', 'Baker'),
('7', 'Sylvester', 'McCoy'), ('8', 'Paul', 'McGann')]
>>>
```

See also

▶ The documentation of the pyhs library is available at
   http://python-handler-socket.readthedocs.org/en/latest/

Installing the HandlerSocket Ruby client libraries

Ruby is the last language in our trio of scripting languages compatible with HandlerSocket in this chapter. Installing and using this library is easy.

Getting ready

Install the `libhsclient` library as described in the *Installing the libhsclient library* recipe earlier in this chapter. In order to build the HandlerSocket Ruby client libraries, we need to install some development tools and packages.

On Red Hat, Fedora, or CentOS, run the following command:

```
sudo yum install ruby-irb rubygems ruby-rdoc ruby-devel
```

On Debian or Ubuntu, run the following command:

```
sudo apt-get install irb rubygems rdoc ruby-dev
```

We are now ready to install the HandlerSocket Ruby client libraries.

How to do it...

1. Use `rubygems` to install the `handlersocket` gem in a terminal window, as follows:

   ```
   sudo gem install 'handlersocket'
   ```

2. Launch the `irb` interactive Ruby interpreter and check that the `handlersocket` library loads as follows:

   ```
   irb
   require 'rubygems'
   require 'handlersocket'
   ```

How it works...

The RubyGems package manager makes installing the HandlerSocket Ruby library easy. To test that the library is correctly installed, we just need to launch the `irb` interactive Ruby interpreter and try to run the `require handlersocket` command. If the library loads correctly, the interpreter will return the following output:

```
=> true
```

There's more...

On some systems, the `require 'rubygems'` line is not needed. If it is not required, the command will return `false` and the `require 'handlersocket'` line will still return `true`. So, if we want, we can just ignore the harmless `false` report or omit the `require 'rubygems'` line altogether. When the `require 'rubygems'` line is required, `irb` will complain that it cannot find the `handlersocket` library. Once we run the `require` command on the `rubygems` library, the `handlersocket` library can be found. The output of this recipe on Ubuntu and Debian will look like the following screenshot:

```
daniel@pippin: ~
daniel@pippin:~$ sudo gem install 'handlersocket'
Building native extensions.  This could take a while...
Successfully installed handlersocket-0.0.2
1 gem installed
Installing ri documentation for handlersocket-0.0.2...
Installing RDoc documentation for handlersocket-0.0.2...
daniel@pippin:~$ irb
irb(main):001:0> require 'rubygems'
=> false
irb(main):002:0> require 'handlersocket'
=> true
irb(main):003:0>
daniel@pippin:~$
```

See also

- The source code of the Ruby `handlersocket` library, along with examples, can be found at `https://github.com/miyucy/handlersocket`

Reading data using HandlerSocket and Ruby

In some ways, using the Ruby HandlerSocket client library is very similar to using the Python HandlerSocket client library described earlier in this chapter. This is mainly true in the commands we send to HandlerSocket, but there are differences that can trip us up if we're not careful.

Getting ready

Install the HandlerSocket Ruby client libraries as described in the *Installing the HandlerSocket Ruby client libraries* recipe earlier in this chapter. Launch the `mysql` command-line client and run the SQL commands from the *Getting ready* section of the *Reading data using HandlerSocket and PERL* recipe earlier in this chapter to give us some sample data to read (and if we've already gone through the PERL or Python recipes, running the SQL commands again will reset the sample data to its default state).

How to do it...

1. Launch the interactive Ruby interpreter in a terminal window as follows:

   ```
   irb
   ```

2. Open a connection to our database in the `irb` interpreter as follows:

   ```
   require 'rubygems'
   require 'handlersocket'
   hs = HandlerSocket.new(:host => '127.0.0.1',:port => '9998')
   hs.open_index(0,'test','hs_test','PRIMARY','id,givenname,surname')
   ```

3. Then, read some data in the `irb` interpreter as follows:

   ```
   p hs.execute_single(0,'=',[1])
   p hs.execute_single(0,'>',[1],2,2)
   p hs.execute_single(0,'>=',[1],20)
   ```

How it works...

To read data, we first create a connection to the HandlerSocket read-only port using the `HandlerSocket.new` method. This method takes two arguments: the host, which is the IP address or domain name of the host we are connecting to, and the port. We are connecting to the local host and the read-only port, so we put in `127.0.0.1` and `9998`, respectively. Then, we call the `.open_index` method to define the database, table, and columns we are interested in. This method takes five arguments. First is an identification number, which can be any integer we want; in our recipe we use `0`. The second and third arguments are the database name and table name we want to read, respectively. The fourth argument is the name of the key we want to search on. In our example table, the only key is the primary key, so we use the key word `PRIMARY`. The fifth argument is a comma-separated list of the columns we want to read. In our recipe, we name all of the columns in our example table (`id`, `givenname`, and `surname`).

We are then able to read data using the `execute_single` method. This method takes three arguments with the optional fourth and fifth arguments. First is the variable we used when calling `open_index` (we used 0 in our recipe), and the second is the comparison operator we want to use; the supported operators are =, >, <, >=, and <=. The third argument is the key value we want to search for. The optional fourth and fifth arguments set the maximum number of rows to return and the number of records to skip before retrieving records, respectively. If these arguments are not specified, the `execute_single` method will set them both to 0, which combine to return only the first matching record for our search. The results are returned as an array. Of the three calls to the `execute_single` method in our recipe, the first returns a single row, the second returns two rows, and the last returns all of the records in our example table. All are output as a multidimensional array containing a subarray of the resulting data. The returned values will look like the following command:

```
[0, [["1", "William", "Hartnell"]]]
```

```
[0, [["4", "Tom", "Baker"], ["5", "Peter", "Davison"]]]
```

```
[0, [["1", "William", "Hartnell"], ["2", "Patrick", "Troughton"], ["3",
"John", "Pertwee"], ["4", "Tom", "Baker"], ["5", "Peter", "Davison"],
["6", "Colin", "Baker"]]]
```

The complete output in the `irb` interpreter will look like the following screenshot:

See also

▶ The source code of the Ruby `handlersocket` library, along with examples, can be found at `https://github.com/miyucy/handlersocket`

Inserting data using HandlerSocket and Ruby

Now that we can read data (as described in the previous recipe), it's time to learn how to insert data using Ruby.

Getting ready

Complete the *Reading data using HandlerSocket and Ruby* recipe described earlier in this chapter prior to starting this recipe.

How to do it...

1. Launch the interactive Ruby interpreter in a terminal window as follows:

    ```
    irb
    ```

2. Open a connection to our database in the `irb` interpreter as follows:

    ```
    require 'rubygems'
    require 'handlersocket'
    hsw = HandlerSocket.new(:host => '127.0.0.1',:port => '9999')
    hsw.open_index(1,'test','hs_test','PRIMARY','id,givenname,surna
    me')
    ```

3. Still in the `irb` interpreter, insert a couple of new rows using the following statements:

    ```
    p hsw.execute_single(1,'+',[7,'Sylvester','McCoy'])
    p hsw.execute_single(1,'+',[8,'Paul','McGann'])
    ```

4. Then, read the rows we entered using the following statements in the `irb` interpreter:

    ```
    p hsw.execute_single(1,'=',[7])
    p hsw.execute_single(1,'=',[8])
    p hsw.execute_single(1,'>=',[1],20)
    ```

How it works...

Similar to reading data, we first open a connection with `HandlerSocket.new` to the read-write port (`9999`) when inserting data. We then use the `execute_single` method to insert data. This method takes three arguments. First is the number we used when calling `open_index` (we used 1 in our recipe), and the second is the + character, which tells the method we are inserting data. The third argument is a comma-separated list of the values we want to insert. These must correspond to the comma-separated list of columns we defined when calling `open_index` (we used `id`, `givenname`, and `surname` in our recipe). After successful insertion, the `execute_single` method will return an array with zeroes, thus specifying `true`. This will look like the following command in the `irb` interpreter:

```
[0, [["0"]]]
```

The last step in our recipe is to read the rows we entered and then read all of the rows in our table. The returned values will look like the following command:

```
[0, [["7", "Sylvester", "McCoy"]]]
```

```
[0, [["8", "Paul", "McGann"]]]
```

```
[0, [["1", "William", "Hartnell"], ["2", "Patrick", "Troughton"], ["3",
"John", "Pertwee"], ["4", "Tom", "Baker"], ["5", "Peter", "Davison"],
["6", "Colin", "Baker"], ["7", "Sylvester", "McCoy"], ["8", "Paul",
"McGann"]]]
```

The complete output of this recipe in `irb` will look like the following screenshot:

▶ The source code of the Ruby `handlersocket` library, along with examples, can be found at `https://github.com/miyucy/handlersocket`

Updating and deleting data using HandlerSocket and Ruby

Updating and deleting data is similar to but not quite the same as inserting data. In this recipe, we will use Ruby and HandlerSocket to update and delete data.

Getting ready

Complete the *Inserting data using HandlerSocket and Ruby* recipe prior to starting this recipe.

How to do it...

1. Launch the interactive Ruby interpreter in a terminal window as follows:

   ```
   irb
   ```

2. Run the following commands in the `irb` interpreter to open a HandlerSocket connection to our `test` database and the `hs_test` table:

   ```
   require 'rubygems'
   require 'handlersocket'
   hsu = HandlerSocket.new(:host => '127.0.0.1',:port => '9999')
   hsu.open_index(2,'test','hs_test','PRIMARY','givenname')
   ```

3. Then, update a row in the interpreter using the following statement:

   ```
   p hsu.execute_single(2,'=',[3],1,0,'U',['Jon'])
   ```

4. Read out the value of the column we just updated in `irb` to confirm that the data was updated using the following statement:

   ```
   p hsu.execute_single(2,'=',[3])
   ```

5. Open a connection to use for deleting data using the following statements:

   ```
   hsd = HandlerSocket.new(:host => '127.0.0.1',:port => '9999')
   hsd.open_index(3,'test','hs_test','PRIMARY','id,givenname,surna
   me')
   ```

6. Insert some junk data for us to delete using the following statements:

```
p hsd.execute_single(3,'+',[101,'Junk','Entry'])

p hsd.execute_single(3,'+',[102,'Junk','Entry'])

p hsd.execute_single(3,'+',[103,'Junk','Entry'])
```

7. Read all of the data in our table, delete the junk data, and then read our table again to confirm the deletion using the following statements:

```
p hsd.execute_single(3,'>=',[1],20)

p hsd.execute_single(3,'>',[100],10,0,'D')

p hsd.execute_single(3,'>=',[1],20)
```

How it works...

To update data, we first open a connection the same way we did when inserting data. In our recipe, we're only interested in updating a single column. So, when calling the `open_index` method, we only specify the `givenname` column.

We update data in step 3 using the `execute_single` method but with more arguments than what we use when reading or inserting data. First is the number we used when calling `open_index` (we used 2 in our recipe). The second is the comparison operator we want to use for finding the values to update; the supported operators are =, >, <, >=, and <=. The third argument is the key value we want to search for (3 in our recipe). The fourth and fifth arguments set the maximum number of rows to update and the number of rows to skip before trying to match records, respectively. In our recipe, we set these to 10 and 0, respectively.

The sixth argument is the character U that tells the method that we are performing an update. Seventh, is an array of the values we want to update the rows we find to. This array corresponds to the columns we specified when we called the `open_index` method; just fill the `givenname` column in our recipe. The sixth and seventh arguments set the maximum number of rows to update and the number of records to skip before searching records, respectively. We set these to 10 and 0 in our recipe. After a successful update, the `execute_single` method will return a comma-separated list containing a 0 if the command was successful and then the number of rows updated as an array. The output in `irb` will look like the following command:

```
[0, [["1"]]]
```

We then use the `.execute_single` method in step 4 to read the column we just updated. The output in `irb` will look like the following command:

```
[0, [["Jon"]]]
```

The complete output of steps 1 through 5 of this recipe in `irb` will look like the following screenshot:

```
daniel@pippin:~$ irb
irb(main):001:0> require 'rubygems'
=> false
irb(main):002:0> require 'handlersocket'
=> true
irb(main):003:0> hsu = HandlerSocket.new(:host => '127.0.0.1',:port => '9999')
=> #<HandlerSocket:0x00000000eb1ce8>
irb(main):004:0> hsu.open_index(2,'test','hs_test','PRIMARY','givenname')
=> 0
irb(main):005:0> p hsu.execute_single(2,'=',[3],1,0,'U',['Jon'])
[0, [["1"]]]
=> [0, [["1"]]]
irb(main):006:0> p hsu.execute_single(2,'=',[3])
[0, [["Jon"]]]
=> [0, [["Jon"]]]
```

To test the process of deleting data, we begin with step 5 of our recipe to call `HandlerSocket.new` again, this time defining all of the columns in our table instead of just the `givenname` column. We also give our connection a new integer identification number, (3), to distinguish it from the number, (2), we assigned to our update connect.

In step 6 of our recipe, we insert some junk data. Then, in step 7, we read our table, delete the rows we entered in step 6, and then read the table again to confirm the deletion.

When deleting rows in our recipe, we supply the `execute_single` method with six arguments. First is the variable we used when calling `open_index` (we used 3 in our recipe). Second is the comparison operator we want to use for finding the rows to delete (> in our recipe). The third argument is the key value we want to search for (100 in our recipe). The fourth and fifth arguments set the maximum number of rows to delete and the number of rows to skip before trying to match records, respectively. In our recipe, we set these to 10 and 0, respectively. The sixth argument is the character D, which tells the method that we are performing a delete operation. After a successful delete, the `execute_single` method will return a comma-separated list first containing a 0 if the command was successful and then the number of rows deleted as an array. Since we deleted three rows, the output of the delete operation in `irb` will look like the following command:

```
[0, [["3"]]]
```

The complete output of steps 5 through 7 of this recipe in `irb` will look like the following screenshot:

```
irb(main):007:0> hsd = HandlerSocket.new(:host => '127.0.0.1',:port => '9999')
=> #<HandlerSocket:0x00000000e8ae68>
irb(main):008:0> hsd.open_index(3,'test','hs_test','PRIMARY','id,givenname,surname')
=> 0
irb(main):009:0> p hsd.execute_single(3,'+',[101,'Junk','Entry'])
[0, [["0"]]]
=> [0, [["0"]]]
irb(main):010:0> p hsd.execute_single(3,'+',[102,'Junk','Entry'])
[0, [["0"]]]
=> [0, [["0"]]]
irb(main):011:0> p hsd.execute_single(3,'+',[103,'Junk','Entry'])
[0, [["0"]]]
=> [0, [["0"]]]
irb(main):012:0> p hsd.execute_single(3,'>=',[1],20)
[0, [["1", "William", "Hartnell"], ["2", "Patrick", "Troughton"], ["3", "Jon", "Pertwee
"], ["4", "Tom", "Baker"], ["5", "Peter", "Davison"], ["6", "Colin", "Baker"], ["7", "S
ylvester", "McCoy"], ["8", "Paul", "McGann"], ["101", "Junk", "Entry"], ["102", "Junk",
"Entry"], ["103", "Junk", "Entry"]]]
=> [0, [["1", "William", "Hartnell"], ["2", "Patrick", "Troughton"], ["3", "Jon", "Pert
wee"], ["4", "Tom", "Baker"], ["5", "Peter", "Davison"], ["6", "Colin", "Baker"], ["7",
"Sylvester", "McCoy"], ["8", "Paul", "McGann"], ["101", "Junk", "Entry"], ["102", "Jun
k", "Entry"], ["103", "Junk", "Entry"]]]
irb(main):013:0> p hsd.execute_single(3,'>',[100],10,0,'D')
[0, [["3"]]]
=> [0, [["3"]]]
irb(main):014:0> p hsd.execute_single(3,'>=',[1],20)
[0, [["1", "William", "Hartnell"], ["2", "Patrick", "Troughton"], ["3", "Jon", "Pertwee
"], ["4", "Tom", "Baker"], ["5", "Peter", "Davison"], ["6", "Colin", "Baker"], ["7", "S
ylvester", "McCoy"], ["8", "Paul", "McGann"]]]
=> [0, [["1", "William", "Hartnell"], ["2", "Patrick", "Troughton"], ["3", "Jon", "Pert
wee"], ["4", "Tom", "Baker"], ["5", "Peter", "Davison"], ["6", "Colin", "Baker"], ["7",
"Sylvester", "McCoy"], ["8", "Paul", "McGann"]]]
irb(main):015:0>
```

See also

▸ The source code of the Ruby `handlersocket` library, along with examples, is at `https://github.com/miyucy/handlersocket`

Using HandlerSocket directly with Telnet

HandlerSocket listens on two ports, `9998` and `9999`, for clients to talk to it. This means we can interact with it directly using `telnet`.

Getting ready

Install and configure the HandlerSocket plugin as described in the *Installing and configuring HandlerSocket* recipe earlier in this chapter. Launch the `mysql` command-line client and run the SQL commands from the *Getting ready* section of the *Reading data using HandlerSocket and PERL* recipe, described earlier in this chapter, to give us some sample data to read (and if we've already gone through the PERL, Python, or Ruby recipes, running the SQL commands again will reset the sample data to its default state).

We'll also need to install a `telnet` client. Most Linux distributions should have one either installed by default or easily installable from the system package repositories.

How to do it...

1. Open `telnet` and connect to the HandlerSocket read port in a command-line window as follows:

    ```
    telnet 127.0.0.1 9998
    ```

2. Enter the following commands (what looks like spaces in the following code are all tabs):

    ```
    P   0   test   hs_test   PRIMARY   id,givenname,surname

    0   =   1   1

    0   >   1   2   2

    0   >=   1   1   20
    ```

3. Disconnect by typing *Ctrl +]* and then `quit`.

4. Open a new `telnet` session; this time connect to the write port using the following command:

    ```
    telnet 127.0.0.1 9999
    ```

5. Run the following commands (remember to use tabs for all white spaces):

    ```
    P   1   test   hs_test   PRIMARY   id,givenname,surname

    1   +   3   7   Sylvester   McCoy

    1   +   3   8   Paul   McGann

    1   >=   1   1   20
    ```

6. Then, run the following commands in the same `telnet` session:

    ```
    P   2   test   hs_test   PRIMARY   givenname

    2   =   1   3   1   0   U   Jon

    1   =   1   3
    ```

7. Finally, run the following commands in the same `telnet` session:

```
P    3    test    hs_test    PRIMARY    id,givenname,surname
3    +    3    101    Junk    Entry
3    +    3    102    Junk    Entry
3    +    3    103    Junk    Entry
1    >=   1    1    20
3    >    1    100    10    0    D
1    >=   1    1    20
```

How it works...

To read data, we first open a connection using our `telnet` client and connect to the read-only port, `9998`.

In step 2, we first tell HandlerSocket about the database and table we want to connect to and the columns we are interested in. This command begins with the key letter, P, and then a number that is used to identify the connection. The number can be any positive number; we use 0 for simplicity. We then name the database (`test`) and the table (`hs_test`). Next, we specify the key we want to search on. In our example table, the only key is the primary key, so we use the key word, `PRIMARY`. The sixth argument is a comma-separated list of the columns we want to read. In our recipe, we name all of the columns in our example table (`id`, `givenname`, and `surname`). All of the arguments must be separated by tabs, not spaces.

With a connection defined, we are now able to read data. To do so, the basic form of the command takes at least four arguments, with an optional fifth argument. First is the identification number we chose when defining the connection 0. Second is the comparison operator we want to use; the supported operators are =, >, <, >=, and <=. The third argument is the number of index columns we are going to search. This must be equal to or less than the number of index columns we defined. As we only defined one index column (the primary key using the key word `PRIMARY`), we put 1 here. The fourth argument is the index value to search for. In the recipe, our first search command retrieves the row where `id` equals 1. The output will look similar to the following command:

```
0    3    1    William    Hartnell
```

The first field in the output is 0, which signifies success. The next filed will have each of the records that are being returned. We defined three columns when we defined our connection, so the number here is 3. Finally, there are the three fields of the record. Our search was for all records with `id` equal to 1, which, of course, only matches one record.

The second and third search commands in step 2 use the optional fifth argument, which sets the limit of the number of records to retrieve. By default, if this argument is not set, HandlerSocket will return only single records, which was fine for our first search. The second search is for the records where `id` is greater than 2. This could match many records, so we limit it to 27, which means we get records three and four back. The output will look similar to the following command:

```
0   3   3   John   Pertwee   4   Tom   Baker
```

When HandlerSocket returns data, it does so as one long string, so when it has finished giving us one result of the several, it immediately starts giving us the second, and so on. As the second field in the output is 3, we know the first three fields following it are the first result and the next three fields are the second.

The third search grabs up to 20 records where `id` is greater than or equal to 1. As our table only has six rows, this search has the effect of grabbing all records. At first glance, the output looks a little jumbled, but once we know what to look for, it is easy to parse.

In step 3 of our recipe, we disconnect so that we can reconnect on the write port. The complete input and output of steps 1 through 3 will look like the following screenshot:

```
daniel@pippin: ~
daniel@pippin:~$ telnet 127.0.0.1 9998
Trying 127.0.0.1...
Connected to 127.0.0.1.
Escape character is '^]'.
P        0       test    hs_test PRIMARY id,givenname,surname
0        1
0        =       1       1
0        3       1       William Hartnell
0        >       1       2       2
0        3       3       John    Pertwee 4       Tom     Baker
0        >=      1       1       20
0        3       1       William Hartnell        2       Patrick Troughton
3        John    Pertwee 4       Tom     Baker   5       Peter   Davison 6
Colin   Baker
^]quit

telnet> quit
Connection closed.
daniel@pippin:~$
```

In step 4 of this recipe, we reconnect to the read-write port, `9999`, this time so that we can insert, update, and delete records. In step 5 we insert some new rows. First, we define a connection, identifying the connection with the number `1` this time.

The command to insert takes three arguments plus the data we want to insert. The first argument is the connection identification number. The second is the `+` character, which signifies that we are inserting data. The third is the number of fields we specified when defining our connection (`3` in our recipe). In our recipe, we insert two rows. After successful insertion, HandlerSocket responds with the following command:

```
0   1   0
```

The first value is the error code. A `0` value means there was no error. The second field is the number of columns in the result set. The third field is the actual result. For an insert, the result of a successful insert is a single column with the result of `0`.

In step 6, we update a row. When defining our database connection, we only specify the `givenname` column because that is the column we are updating. The fields in the update statement are, first, the connection identification number and second, a comparison operator. In our recipe, we use `=` because we are looking for an exact match. Third is the number of columns in our table we are updating. Fourth is the primary key value we are searching for. Fifth is the limit of the number of rows to modify. Sixth is the offset from the first row in the table to begin searching from. Seventh is the key letter, `U`, to signify we are performing an update. Eighth is the new values, or in our recipe, value. All together the line looks like the following command:

```
2   =   1   3   1   0   U   Jon
```

The output looks like the following command:

```
0   1   1
```

As with inserting data, the first value in the response is the error code, with `0` meaning success. Likewise, the second value is the number of columns in the response. For an update, this will most likely be `1`. The third column in an update response is the number of rows modified; `1` in our recipe.

The complete output of steps 4 through 6 will look like the following screenshot:

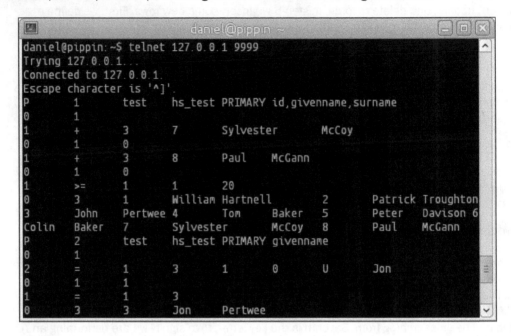

In step 7, we first insert some junk rows and then delete them. The insertion is the same as before. The syntax of the delete statement is similar to the update syntax, except for the fact that because we are deleting, we don't need to provide the new values at the end. We use D instead of U so that HandlerSocket knows we are performing a delete. The delete statement now looks as follows:

```
3   >   1   100   10   0   D
```

The effect of this statement is to search for up to 10 records that have id values greater than 100 and delete them.

The complete output of step 7 will look like the following screenshot:

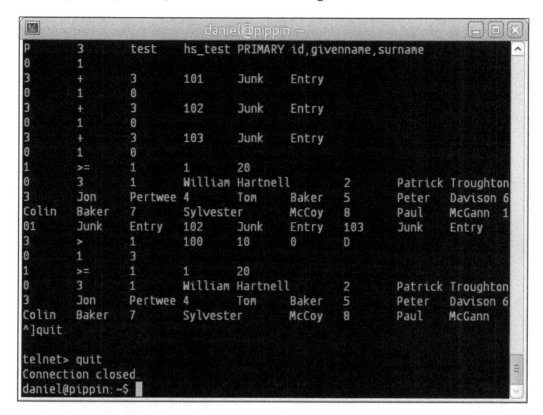

See also

▸ The documentation of the HandlerSocket protocol is available at https://github.com/DeNA/HandlerSocket-Plugin-for-MySQL/blob/master/docs-en/protocol.en.txt

12
NoSQL with the Cassandra Storage Engine

In this chapter, we will cover the following recipes:

- ▶ Installing the Cassandra storage engine
- ▶ Mapping data between MariaDB and Cassandra
- ▶ Using INSERT, UPDATE, and DELETE with the Cassandra storage engine
- ▶ Using SELECT with the Cassandra storage engine

Introduction

One unique feature in MariaDB is the Cassandra storage engine. This is a specialized storage engine, similar to the Connect storage engine featured in *Chapter 5, The CONNECT Storage Engine*. Like Connect, it allows us to access data stored outside of MariaDB. Unlike Connect, the Cassandra storage engine is specific to a certain type of data, namely, it lets us connect MariaDB to a Cassandra cluster.

In this chapter, there are recipes on installing and configuring the Cassandra storage engine, defining tables that use the storage engine to insert, update, delete, and query data.

The Cassandra storage engine in MariaDB is built and packaged only for Linux-based operating systems. As such, the recipes in this chapter assume that we are using a variant of Linux as we complete them.

Installing the Cassandra storage engine

Before we can use the Cassandra storage engine, we need to enable it.

How to do it...

1. On Red Hat, CentOS, and Fedora distributions, we may have to install a separate Cassandra storage engine package with the following command:

   ```
   sudo yum install MariaDB-cassandra-engine
   ```

2. Open the `mysql` command-line client, connect to our MariaDB server as a user with the SUPER privilege and run the following command:

   ```
   INSTALL SONAME 'ha_cassandra';
   ```

3. Still connected to our MariaDB server, run the following command:

   ```
   SHOW VARIABLES LIKE "Cassandra%";
   ```

4. Add the following code to the `[mysqld]` section of our `my.cnf` file:

   ```
   optimizer_switch = 'join_cache_hashed=on'
   join_cache_level = 7
   ```

How it works...

The Cassandra storage engine is included with MariaDB, but it is not enabled by default. To enable it, we will run the INSTALL SONAME command. This is a one-time operation.

The output of the SHOW VARIABLES command will look like the following screenshot:

```
MariaDB [test]> SHOW VARIABLES LIKE "Cassandra%";
+------------------------------+-------+
| Variable_name                | Value |
+------------------------------+-------+
| cassandra_default_thrift_host |       |
| cassandra_failure_retries    | 3     |
| cassandra_insert_batch_size  | 100   |
| cassandra_multiget_batch_size | 100  |
| cassandra_read_consistency   | ONE   |
| cassandra_rnd_batch_size     | 10000 |
| cassandra_write_consistency  | ONE   |
+------------------------------+-------+
7 rows in set (0.00 sec)

MariaDB [test]>
```

These variables can be set the same as any other MariaDB variable. They only exist, however, after the Cassandra storage engine has been installed; so we must not add these variables to our my.cnf file until after we enable the storage engine. If we add them before we run the INSTALL SONAME command, MariaDB will refuse to start.

In our recipe, we make two additions to our my.cnf file. These are used because Cassandra supports batched key access in no-association mode, which means that the SQL layer needs to do the key hashing. The settings we added do that.

There's more...

There are also several status variables that we can query after enabling the Cassandra storage engine. Similar to the Cassandra storage engine variables, they are all prefaced with cassandra_ so that we can search for all of them with the following command:

```
SHOW STATUS LIKE "Cassandra%";
```

The output of this command will vary based on how much we have used the Cassandra storage engine. For example, after first installing it, the values will all be zeroes as shown in the following screenshot:

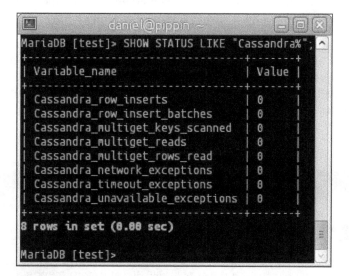

See also

▶ The full documentation of the Cassandra storage engine is available at
    https://mariadb.com/kb/en/cassandra-storage-engine/

▶ The full documentation of Cassandra is available at
    http://cassandra.apache.org/

Mapping data between MariaDB and Cassandra

To access data stored in a Cassandra cluster from MariaDB, we create a special table that defines where the Cassandra cluster we want to connect with is located, and how the data stored there should be treated in MariaDB.

Getting ready

We should complete the *Installing the Cassandra storage engine* recipe before starting this recipe.

Also, before we can complete this recipe, we need to have a running installation of Cassandra that we can connect to from our MariaDB server. The following are the instructions for installing a single-node Cassandra instance on the same host as we are running MariaDB on.

It is also worth noting that the Cassandra storage engine works better with Cassandra version 1.x than with Cassandra 2.0 and later. This is because of changes to the Cassandra data model and the introduction of password-based authentication. These changes will be addressed in future updates to the Cassandra storage engine.

On Red Hat, CentOS, and Fedora, first ensure that either Java 6 or Java 7 is installed. Refer to `http://www.datastax.com/documentation/cassandra/1.2/webhelp/cassandra/install/installJreRHEL.html` for instructions on downloading and installing the Java JRE. When installed correctly, the `java -version` command should output something similar to the following screenshot (the version and build numbers will most likely be different):

```
daniel@pippin: ~$ java -version
java version "1.7.0_51"
Java(TM) SE Runtime Environment (build 1.7.0_51-b13)
Java HotSpot(TM) 64-Bit Server VM (build 24.51-b03, mixed mode)
daniel@pippin: ~$
```

After Java is installed, create a `datastax.repo` file at `/etc/yum.repos.d/` and add the following code to it:

```
[datastax]
name = DataStax Repo for Apache Cassandra
baseurl = http://rpm.datastax.com/community
enabled = 1
gpgcheck = 0
```

We can now install Cassandra with the following command:

```
sudo yum install cassandra12
```

After installing, start Cassandra with the following command:

```
sudo service cassandra start
```

On Ubuntu and Debian, we will run the following two commands to add the signing key and the Cassandra repository:

```
sudo apt-key adv --recv-keys \
  --keyserver pgp.mit.edu 4BD736A82B5C1B00
sudo add-apt-repository \
  'deb http://www.apache.org/dist/cassandra/debian 11x main'
```

Then, run the following two commands to update APT and install Cassandra:

```
sudo apt-get update
sudo apt-get install cassandra
```

We are now ready for this recipe.

How to do it...

1. If we are running Cassandra 1.1, run the `cqlsh` command and create a Cassandra keyspace called `casstest` with the following commands:

   ```
   CREATE KEYSPACE casstest WITH
       strategy_class = 'org.apache.cassandra.locator.SimpleStrategy'
       AND strategy_options:replication_factor='1';
   ```

2. If we are running Cassandra 1.2, run the `cqlsh` command and create a Cassandra keyspace called `casstest` with the following commands:

   ```
   CREATE KEYSPACE casstest
       WITH REPLICATION = {'class' : 'SimpleStrategy',
         'replication_factor': 1};
   ```

3. Still in `cqlsh`, enter the following commands to create a Cassandra column family called `test` in the `casstest` keyspace:

   ```
   USE casstest;
   CREATE columnfamily test01 (
       pk varchar primary key,
       data1 varchar,
       data2 bigint);
   ```

4. Still in `cqlsh`, enter the following commands to create an additional Cassandra column family called `notes`:

```
CREATE columnfamily notes (
  note_id int primary key,
  note_note text
); Java support.exit
```

5. Open the `mysql` command-line client and connect to our MariaDB database server and connect to the `test` database (first creating it if necessary):

```
CREATE DATABASE IF NOT EXISTS test;
USE test;
```

6. Run the following commands to create a table in our `test` database that maps to the `test01` column family we created in step 3:

```
CREATE TABLE test01_cass (
  pk VARCHAR(36) PRIMARY KEY,
  data1 VARCHAR(60), Java support.
  data2 BIGINT
) ENGINE=cassandra
  THRIFT_HOST='localhost'
  KEYSPACE='casstest'
  COLUMN_FAMILY='test01';
```

7. Run the following commands to create a table that maps to the `notes` column family we created in step 4:

```
CREATE TABLE notes_cass (
  note_id INT PRIMARY KEY,
  note_note mediumtext
) ENGINE=cassandra
  DEFAULT CHARSET=utf8
  THRIFT_HOST='localhost'
  KEYSPACE='casstest'
  COLUMN_FAMILY='notes';
```

How it works...

There are two parts for mapping a table in MariaDB to a corresponding column family in Cassandra. First is the actual definition of the columns. These columns must be named the same as they are named in Cassandra and the data types must be compatible.

The second part is what comes after the table definition. This part is where we specify that we want to use the Cassandra storage engine and the connection parameters. We're connecting to a Cassandra instance hosted on our local server, so we specify `localhost` in the `THRIFT_HOST` parameter. The other two parameters that we need to specify are the `KEYSPACE` and `COLUMN_FAMILY` parameters we are using. These are `casstest` and `test01`, respectively.

There's more...

If our Cassandra instance is configured to use a non-standard port, we can use the `THRIFT_PORT` parameter to set what it is.

Also, if we set the `cassandra_default_thrift_host` variable in the `[mysqld]` section of our `my.cnf` file, we do not have to specify a `THRIFT_HOST` parameter (unless, of course, we are connecting to a different host).

Some data types in Cassandra and MariaDB are not directly mapped as they are not equivalent. The following table lists the mapping of Cassandra data types to their MariaDB equivalents:

Cassandra	MariaDB
ascii	BLOB, VARCHAR(n), and use CHARSET=latin1
bigint	BIGINT, TINY, SHORT (use which one fits the actual data in Cassandra)
blob	BLOB, VARBINARY(n)
boolean	BOOL
counter	BIGINT (this value is read-only in MariaDB)
decimal	VARBINARY(n)
double	DOUBLE
float	FLOAT
int	INT
text	BLOB, VARCHAR(n), and use CHARSET=utf8
timestamp	TIMESTAMP (for second precision), TIMESTAMP(6) (for microsecond precision), BIGINT (for the actual 64-bit Cassandra timestamp)
uuid	CHAR(36) (Cassandra UUID values are represented as text in MariaDB)
varint	VARBINARY(n)

Also, size limitations in Cassandra are more relaxed than in MariaDB. For those MariaDB data types specified in the previous table with values such as `VARBINARY(n)`, the value of `n` should be set large enough to handle whatever values are actually found in our Cassandra database.

We may run into instances where this is not possible. For example, Cassandra has a 2 gigabyte limit on its `rowkey` length. In MariaDB, the limit for unique key lengths is about 1.5 kilobytes. If the actual data in Cassandra goes beyond MariaDB's limits, it may not be possible to access it from MariaDB.

See also

▶ The full documentation of the Cassandra storage engine is available at `https://mariadb.com/kb/en/cassandra-storage-engine/`

▶ The full documentation of Cassandra is available at `http://cassandra.apache.org/`

Using INSERT, UPDATE, and DELETE with the Cassandra storage engine

Using a Cassandra storage engine table feels much like using any other table, but there are some important differences. This recipe demonstrates it.

Getting ready

We should complete the *Mapping data between MariaDB and Cassandra* recipe, before starting this recipe. Also, import the `isfdb` database as described in the *Importing the data exported by mysqldump* recipe in *Chapter 2, Diving Deep into MariaDB*, so that we have some data to use.

How to do it...

1. Open the `mysql` command-line client and connect to our MariaDB database server and then to the `test` database.

2. Insert some sample data into the `test01_cass` table, as follows:

```
INSERT INTO test01_cass VALUES
    ('rowkey10', 'data1-value', 123456),
    ('rowkey11', 'data1-value2', 34543),
    ('rowkey12', 'data1-value3', 444),
    ('rowkey13', 'data1-value4', 777666555);
```

3. Fill the empty `notes_cass` table with data from the `isfdb.notes` table using the following command:

    ```
    INSERT INTO notes_cass SELECT * FROM isfdb.notes;
    ```

4. Update the `test01_cass` `data2` value for `rowkey12` to `444`, using the following command:

    ```
    UPDATE test01_cass SET data2=454 WHERE pk='rowkey12';
    ```

5. Delete a row from the `test01_cass` table using the following command:

    ```
    DELETE FROM test01_cass WHERE pk = 'rowkey13';
    ```

6. Exit the `mysql` command-line client, launch the `cqlsh` client, and run the following commands:

    ```
    USE casstest;
    ```

    ```
    SELECT * FROM test01;
    ```

How it works...

As long as proper care has been taken when creating the Cassandra storage engine tables in MariaDB so that the data types are compatible (if not equal), the `INSERT` and `UPDATE` operations appear to work as we would expect. We can even perform the `INSERT INTO ... SELECT FROM ...` operations to move data from an InnoDB, Aria, or other standard MariaDB table into a Cassandra storage engine table and vice versa.

However, inserting values into Cassandra tables actually function as `INSERT` or `UPDATE` style statements. This is because of the way in which Cassandra's data model works. Rows can and will be silently overwritten if, for example, the primary keys match. This is how Cassandra is supposed to work, so it is not an error. We just need to be aware of it when using the Cassandra storage engine.

In the last step of the recipe, we switch over to the `cqlsh` client to show that the data we added is in our Cassandra database. The output of this step will look similar to the following screenshot:

```
root@test01:~# cqlsh
Connected to Test Cluster at localhost:9160.
[cqlsh 2.2.0 | Cassandra 1.1.12 | CQL spec 2.0.0 | Thrift protocol 19.33.0]
Use HELP for help.
cqlsh> USE casstest;
cqlsh:casstest> SELECT * FROM test01;
 pk,rowkey12 | data1,data1-value3 | data2,454
 pk,rowkey10 | data1,data1-value | data2,123456
 pk,rowkey13
 pk,rowkey11 | data1,data1-value2 | data2,34543

cqlsh:casstest>
```

There's more...

Cassandra has a feature that allows individual rows to have their own sets of columns. These columns can be accessed using MariaDB's dynamic columns feature. To do so, when we define our Cassandra storage engine table, we just need to define a BLOB column with the DYNAMIC_COLUMN_STORAGE=yes attribute. Refer to the recipes related to dynamic columns in *Chapter 10, Exploring Dynamic and Virtual Columns in MariaDB* for more information.

See also

▸ The full documentation of the Cassandra storage engine is available at `https://mariadb.com/kb/en/cassandra-storage-engine/`

▸ The full documentation of Cassandra is available at `http://cassandra.apache.org/`

Using SELECT with the Cassandra storage engine

As with the previous recipe, the SELECT statements are much the same when using the Cassandra storage engine tables.

Getting ready

First, we need to complete the *Using INSERT, UPDATE, and DELETE with the Cassandra storage engine* recipe.

How to do it...

1. Open the `mysql` command-line client and connect to our MariaDB database server and the `test` database.

2. Select everything from the `test01_cass` table using the following command:

   ```
   SELECT * FROM test01_cass;
   ```

3. Select ten rows from the `notes_cass` table using the following command:

   ```
   SELECT * FROM notes_cass LIMIT 10;
   ```

4. Select data with multiple WHERE clauses, an ORDER BY clause, and a LIMIT clause using the following commands:

```
SELECT * FROM notes_cass
  WHERE note_note IS NOT NULL
    AND note_id < 500
    AND LENGTH(note_note) < 30
  ORDER BY note_id DESC
  LIMIT 10;
```

5. Join the notes_cass table in the test database to the publishers table in the isfdb database with some WHERE clauses and a LIMIT clause, using the following commands:

```
SELECT publisher_name,publisher_wikipedia,note_note
  FROM isfdb.publishers INNER JOIN notes_cass
  USING (note_id)
  WHERE note_note IS NOT NULL
    AND publisher_wikipedia IS NOT NULL
    AND LENGTH(note_note) < 30
    AND LENGTH(publisher_wikipedia) < 40
  LIMIT 10;
```

How it works...

The SELECT statements for tables that use the Cassandra storage engine are much the same as the other SELECT statements. The main difference is that when the query is actually run, the Cassandra storage engine connects to a Cassandra cluster to fetch the data we are asking for instead of to a regular table on the local filesystem. We can use the LIMIT, WHERE, and other clauses to refine our results, and even join our data to other tables, just as if it was a regular MariaDB table.

The `SELECT` statement from step 5 of our recipe will look something like the following screenshot (the actual results may be different depending on the version of the `isfdb` database you are using):

```
root@test01:~
MariaDB [test]> SELECT publisher_name,publisher_wikipedia,note_note
    ->    FROM isfdb.publishers INNER JOIN notes_cass
    ->    USING (note_id)
    ->    WHERE note_note IS NOT NULL
    ->      AND publisher_wikipedia IS NOT NULL
    ->      AND LENGTH(note_note) < 30
    ->      AND LENGTH(publisher_wikipedia) < 40
    ->    LIMIT 10;
+-----------------------+----------------------------------+-------------------------------+
| publisher_name        | publisher_wikipedia              | note_note                     |
+-----------------------+----------------------------------+-------------------------------+
| FASA                  | http://en.wikipedia.org/wiki/FASA    | FASA Corporation.         |
| Presses Pocket        | http://fr.wikipedia.org/wiki/Pocket  | France                    |
| iUniverse Star        | http://en.wikipedia.org/wiki/IUniverse | an iUniverse, Inc. imprint |
| Granta Books & Penguin | http://en.wikipedia.org/wiki/Granta | A joint partnership       |
| Tor                   | http://en.wikipedia.org/wiki/Tor_Books | Other imprints: Starscape |
| Authors Choice Press  | http://en.wikipedia.org/wiki/IUniverse | Imprint of iUniverse     |
+-----------------------+----------------------------------+-------------------------------+
6 rows in set (0.01 sec)

MariaDB [test]>
```

There's more...

A big problem with NoSQL databases such as Cassandra is that they simply do not have easy ways to do relational-database-style things such as JOINs. This is a big reason why the Cassandra storage engine was created. Using the Cassandra storage engine lets us not only perform JOINs between the data stored in MariaDB and the data stored in a Cassandra cluster, but it also enables us to do so between two or more Cassandra clusters, keyspaces, or column families.

That said, the Cassandra storage engine is not really suitable for running analytics-type queries that sift through large amounts of data stored in a Cassandra cluster. There are plenty of excellent tools on the Cassandra side (such as Apache Hive or Apache Pig), which are designed for just those sorts of things. The Cassandra storage engine is merely an easy-to-use, convenient window from a SQL environment (MariaDB) into a NoSQL environment (Cassandra).

We should also be careful with the complex `SELECT` statements. A query that does a full table scan, for example, may work fine when all of the tables use the InnoDB or MyISAM storage engines, but they can take forever when a Cassandra storage engine table is included (for example, the complex `SELECT` statement from the *Using SHOW EXPLAIN with running queries* recipe in *Chapter 2, Diving Deep into MariaDB*).

See also

- ▸ The full documentation of the Cassandra storage engine is available at `https://mariadb.com/kb/en/cassandra-storage-engine/`
- ▸ The full documentation of Cassandra is available at `http://cassandra.apache.org/`
- ▸ More details on how the Cassandra storage engine handles JOINs can be found at `https://mariadb.com/kb/en/how-are-joins-handled-with-cassandra/`

13
MariaDB Security

In this chapter, we will cover the following recipes:

- ▸ Securing MariaDB with mysql_secure_installation
- ▸ Securing MariaDB files on Linux
- ▸ Securing MariaDB files on Windows
- ▸ Checking for users with insecure passwords
- ▸ Encrypting connections with SSL
- ▸ Using roles to control user permissions
- ▸ Authenticating using the PAM authentication plugin

Introduction

Security is important, but because the value of the data in a given database ranges from worthless to billions of dollars, deciding on how much and what type of security to employ varies greatly. The recipes in this chapter focus on a few common ways to enhance MariaDB's default security, but they really only scratch the surface of the topic.

Securing MariaDB with mysql_secure_installation

The simplest way to add a bit of extra security to our MariaDB installation is just a command line away.

How to do it...

To secure a default install of MariaDB, perform the following steps:

1. Open a terminal and run the following command:

   `mysql_secure_installation`

2. As prompted by the script, set a password for the `root` user, disallow remote `root` logins, and remove anonymous users.

3. Since we've been using the `test` database for various recipes in the current and other chapters, we may not want to remove it when prompted.

4. Reload the privilege tables when prompted.

How it works...

The `mysql_secure_installation` program is actually just a script written in PERL. Its sole purpose is to apply some basic security settings that nearly every MariaDB installation should have. This script should be run first thing after installing MariaDB on a server. It takes only a minute and should be considered as an essential step that we must perform whenever we install MariaDB.

There's more...

When installing MariaDB on Windows, Ubuntu, or Debian, we are prompted to set a root password. If we went ahead and did so, we would not need to set a root password when prompted by the script (and the script will tell us so). However, we will not be prompted to set a root user password when installing MariaDB on Red Hat, CentOS, or Fedora, so on those systems, running `mysql_secure_installation` is doubly important.

See also

▶ The full documentation of the `mysql_secure_installation` script is available at https://mariadb.com/kb/en/mysql_secure_installation/

Securing MariaDB files on Linux

Filesystem security is an important part of keeping the data in our databases safe. This is because MariaDB, like most programs, stores the data it handles in files on our filesystem. If those files can be read and copied by anyone who can log in to the server, then there's nothing stopping them from making a copy of those files and then accessing them with MariaDB on another server. This recipe is about securing our files on Linux.

Getting ready

Prior to starting this recipe, use the package manager to install the `tree` program.

On Fedora, Red Hat, or CentOS, run the following command:

```
sudo yum install tree
```

On Debian or Ubuntu, run the following command:

```
sudo apt-get install tree
```

How to do it...

1. Open a terminal window and run the following statements:

    ```
    sudo tree -puga /usr/lib*/mysql /lib*/mysql \
        /etc/mysql* /etc/my.cnf* /var/lib*/mysql
    ```

2. Stop MariaDB if it is running.

3. Change the ownership of all files that are not owned by either the `root` or `mysql` users to whichever of those is used for other files in the directory. For example, consider the following statement:

    ```
    sudo chown -v mysql: /var/lib/mysql/flightstats/ontime.frm
    ```

4. Remove the read and write permissions from the group and other users from all files and directories under the `/var/lib/mysql/` directory. The permissions of the `/var/lib/mysql` directory itself and the `/var/lib/mysql/mysql.sock` file (if it exists) are different, they should be 755 and 777, respectively. This is done using the following statements:

    ```
    sudo chmod -vR go-rw /var/lib/mysql/
    sudo chmod -v 755 /var/lib/mysql
    sudo chmod -v 777 /var/lib/mysql/mysql.sock
    ```

5. Start MariaDB again.

How it works...

For this recipe, we use the `tree` program to view the ownership and permissions of various MariaDB files on our filesystem. This same information could be gathered using the `find` or `ls` programs, but their output is not as easy to read as the output of `tree`.

The most vulnerable MariaDB directory on Linux is the one where our data is actually stored. By default, this directory is `/var/lib/mysql/`, but it can be configured to reside somewhere else. If there does not appear to be any data under `/var/lib/mysql/`, then check the value of the `datadir` variable in our `my.cnf` file or in the `mysql` command-line client as follows:

```
SHOW VARIABLES LIKE 'datadir';
```

The way to prevent access to our databases from people who otherwise have legitimate access to our database server is to limit the access of the data directory to just the `mysql` user. This user is created automatically when installing the MariaDB packages.

In this recipe, we use the `chown` command to change the ownership of a single file. We can also recursively change the ownership of all files in a directory (and directories under that directory) in one go using `chown` with the `-R` flag on a directory. This is shown in the following statement:

```
sudo chown -Rv mysql: /var/lib/mysql/
```

All files under the `/var/lib/mysql/` directory, with the exception of that directory itself, and the `mysql.sock` socket file (if it is there) can be set so that only the `mysql` user can access them. On Linux, this is typically set as 600 permissions for files and 700 permissions for the directories.

The socket file needs to have global read and write permissions so that remote clients can connect to our server. On some Linux distributions, this file is found under the `/var/run/` or `/run/` directory. So, we can lock down `/var/lib/mysql/` even tighter. However, on other Linux distributions, the socket file is found under `/var/lib/mysql/`, and if the directory is `/var/lib/mysql/`, it must be accessible to everyone (755 permissions), and the socket file must have global read-write permissions (777).

If we are on a Linux distribution where the socket file is located under `/var/lib/mysql/`, we can configure a new location of our choice and then lock down the data directory so that only the `mysql` user can access it (700 permissions). This is a good thing to do as anyone with read access to the data directory, while they may not have rights to the files, can still see the names of all of our databases.

We should also be careful to keep our server up to date with all of the latest security updates of both the operating system and MariaDB.

There's more...

On Debian and Ubuntu distributions, there is a special file under `/etc/mysql/` named `debian.cnf`, and like our data directory, special care should be taken to keep this file private. This file is automatically created when installing MariaDB. An example of this can be seen in the following screenshot:

```
# Automatically generated for Debian scripts. DO NOT TOUCH!
[client]
host     = localhost
user     = debian-sys-maint
password = w6mjSWGPPkabA5F4
socket   = /var/run/mysqld/mysqld.sock
[mysql_upgrade]
host     = localhost
user     = debian-sys-maint
password = w6mjSWGPPkabA5F4
socket   = /var/run/mysqld/mysqld.sock
basedir  = /usr
~
"/etc/mysql/debian.cnf" 12L, 333C                    1,1            All
```

The two `password` entries are randomly generated and will match each other. This file is used by the operating system to perform upgrades and other routine maintenance using the special `debian-sys-maint` user that is created automatically when installing MariaDB on Debian or Ubuntu. This database user has full access to all of our databases (if it didn't, it couldn't do the things it has to do). By default, this file is locked down so that only our system's `root` user has read and write access (`600` or `-rw`, if we're viewing the permissions with `ls -l`). We should never change this, and if we use a configuration monitoring tool, we might want to set up a check to make sure that this file's permissions stay locked down.

If an attacker gains physical access to our database server, meaning they can open it up and physically remove the disk drive, our only way to prevent such an access to our database files is if we encrypt our entire disk. If we elect to not utilize encryption, either because of the performance penalty or some other reason, we need to make sure that the physical security of our server is appropriate to the value of the data in our database. The type or amount of security that this entails will vary on a case-by-case basis.

Securing MariaDB files on Windows

Filesystem security is an important part of keeping the data in our databases safe. This is because MariaDB, like most programs, stores the data it handles in the files on our filesystem. If these files can be read and copied by anyone who can log in to the server, then there's nothing stopping them from making a copy of those files and then accessing them with MariaDB on another server. This recipe is about securing our files on Windows.

How to do it...

1. Using Windows Explorer, navigate to the MariaDB installation directory (in MariaDB 10.0, the default location is `C:\Program Files\MariaDB 10.0\`).

2. Right-click on the directory and select **Properties**, as shown in the following screenshot:

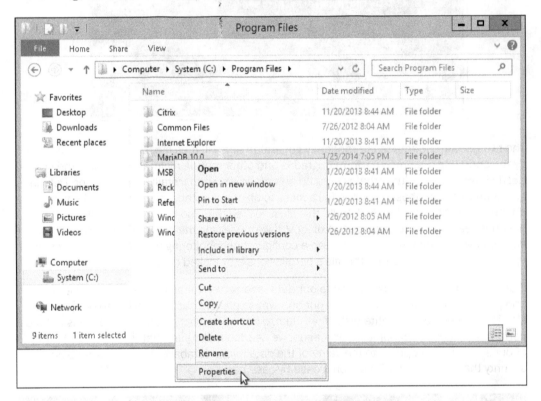

3. In the **Properties** window, click on the **Security** tab and check the permissions. The **SYSTEM** and **Administrator** accounts should have full rights to the directory, but standard users should only have **Read & execute**, **List folder contents**, and **Read** permissions. They should not have **Write** or any **Special permissions** as shown in the following screenshot:

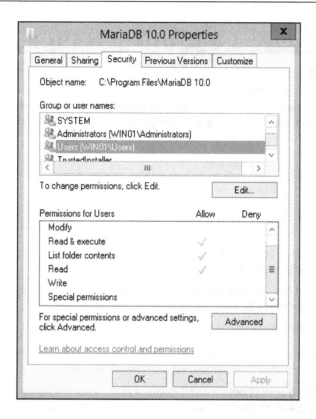

4. **Apply** any changes if necessary and click on **OK** to close the **Properties** window.

How it works...

By default, the MariaDB installer for Windows configures the installation directory to have proper permissions. This doesn't mean that we can just assume everything is all right and we should not check periodically to make sure that the permissions are still what they should be.

We should also be careful to keep our server up to date with all of the latest security updates to both the operating system and MariaDB.

There's more...

If an attacker gains physical access to our database server, meaning they can open it up and physically remove the disk drive, our only way to prevent access to our database files is if we encrypt our hard drive. If we select to not utilize encryption, either because of the performance penalty or some other reason, we need to make sure that the physical security of our server is appropriate to the value of the data in our database. The type or amount of security that this entails will vary on a case-by-case basis.

Checking for users with insecure passwords

Our actual MariaDB user passwords are not stored in plain text by MariaDB as it would be very insecure. Instead, a mathematical hash of the password is stored. When we are connected, MariaDB hashes the password that we enter and compares it to the stored hash. This is all well and good, but in MariaDB, there are actually two hashing options and one is definitely better than the other.

How to do it...

To discover the password hashing function used by MariaDB and to make sure all of the users on our server are using the more secure option, perform the following steps:

1. Open the `mysql` command-line client and connect to our MariaDB database server with a user that has the `SUPER` privilege.

2. Find out what the value of the `old_passwords` variable is by using the following statement:

   `SELECT @@old_passwords;`

3. If the value is not 0, inspect our configuration files and look for the setting. Remove any found instances (the entire line) and restart MariaDB.

4. Go back to the `mysql` command-line client and select the `Host`, `User`, and `Password` columns from the `mysql.user` table using the following statement:

   `SELECT Host,User,Password FROM mysql.user;`

5. In the output, look for any users with short (16 characters) or empty values in the `Password` column.

6. Contact the identified users and have them set a new password.

How it works...

A long time back, in MariaDB's past, the password hashes generated were only 16 hexadecimal digits long. This was fine back then, but these password hashes are no longer fine today. Password hashes in MariaDB today begin with a * character followed by 40 hexadecimal digits. These hashes are much more secure, and all the users who still have old password hashes should upgrade them to the new style.

Before we tell users to change their passwords, we need to ensure that the new passwords they set will use the new password hash. The `old_password` variable controls which hashing function is to be used. By default, it is 0, which means the new password hashing function will be used. If set to 1, the old hashing function is used. This setting was introduced for backward compatibility when the new hashing function was introduced so that the old clients could still connect.

Every modern MariaDB client application should support the new password hashes, so there is no longer a need to have `old_password=1`. However, there are old example configurations out there that people sometimes copy and paste which contain this setting and which means we may have it set and not realize it.

Using old-style password hashes is dangerous because they are so short. Modern computers can crack them fairly easily, so they should never be used.

Once we've verified that our MariaDB configuration is not setting `old_password=1` anywhere, we can have our users change their passwords (or change it for them). To identify users with old-style passwords, we can simply look at the hashes. We do this by selecting them from the `mysql.user` table using the following command:

```
SELECT User,Password FROM mysql.user;
```

The output will likely contain many more entries, but will be similar to the following screenshot:

The `badpass` user has an old-style password hash and the `goodpass` user has a current-style password hash. To properly identify the users, we would want to also select the `Host` column, but to make the output easier to read, it was not used in this simulated example.

See also

▶ The documentation of the `PASSWORD()` function is available at https://mariadb.com/kb/en/password/

▶ The documentation of the `SET PASSWORD` command is available at https://mariadb.com/kb/en/set-password/

Encrypting connections with SSL

When we are connecting to a MariaDB database running on our local workstation, there's really no need to think about whether or not the traffic between the `mysql` client and our database is secure. The traffic is all local and is confined to a single machine.

If, on the other hand, our client is running on one server and our database is on another server in some other part of the world, or even in the same datacenter, we should think about encrypting the traffic between the two.

Getting ready

This is a Linux-only recipe. To prepare for this recipe, we will need a set of SSL certificates. Certificates signed by a recognized and trusted certificate authority are preferred, but we can also use certificates we create ourselves. To create a set of self-signed certificates, we need to perform the following steps:

1. Create a temporary directory and navigate to it by using the following statement:

   ```
   mkdir -v ssl-tmp;cd ssl-tmp
   ```

2. Create a certificate authority key file using the following statement:

   ```
   openssl genrsa -out mariadb-ca.key 4096
   ```

3. Create a certificate authority certificate using the following statements:

   ```
   openssl req -x509 -new -nodes -days 9999 \
     -key mariadb-ca.key \
     -out mariadb-ca.pem
   ```

4. Answer the questions asked when running the command in step 3 using the defaults or our actual information. Do the same when asked in subsequent steps.

5. Create a key and certificate files for our MariaDB server using the following set of statements:

   ```
   openssl genrsa -out mariadb-server.key 4096

   openssl req -new \
     -key mariadb-server.key \
     -out mariadb-server.csr

   openssl x509 -req -set_serial 01 -days 9999 \
     -CA    mariadb-ca.pem \
     -CAkey mariadb-ca.key \
     -in    mariadb-server.csr \
     -out   mariadb-server.pem
   ```

6. Create a key and a certificate file to use with the `mysql` command-line client using the following set of statements:

```
openssl genrsa -out mariadb-client.key 4096

openssl req -new \
  -key mariadb-client.key \
  -out mariadb-client.csr

openssl x509 -req -set_serial 02 -days 9999 \
  -CA    mariadb-ca.pem \
  -CAkey mariadb-ca.key \
  -in    mariadb-client.csr \
  -out   mariadb-client.pem
```

7. Move the certificates and keys to our MariaDB data directory using the following statements:

```
sudo mv -vi mariadb*.pem /var/lib/mysql/
sudo mv -vi mariadb*.key /var/lib/mysql/
```

We are now ready to start the actual recipe. The names used in the recipe will match the names of the certificates and keys we just created here. If we have other certificates and keys we want to use instead, we just need to modify the recipe to match their names.

How to do it...

1. Edit our configuration and add the following statements to the bottom of our `my.cnf` file or to an `ssl.cnf` file under the `/etc/mysql/conf.d/` or `/etc/my.cnf.d/` directories:

```
# SSL configuration for mysqld and the mysql client

[mysqld]

ssl-ca=/var/lib/mysql/mariadb-ca.pem

ssl-key=/var/lib/mysql/mariadb-server.key

ssl-cert=/var/lib/mysql/mariadb-server.pem
[mysql]

ssl-ca=/var/lib/mysql/mariadb-ca.pem

ssl-key=/var/lib/mysql/mariadb-client.key

ssl-cert=/var/lib/mysql/mariadb-client.pem
```

2. Restart MariaDB.

3. Connect to MariaDB with the `mysql` command-line client and run the following commands:

   ```
   STATUS;
   SHOW VARIABLES LIKE 'have_ssl';
   SHOW STATUS LIKE 'Ssl%';
   ```

4. Create a user that requires SSL by using the following statement:

   ```
   GRANT ALL on test.* TO 'ssluser'@'localhost'
     IDENTIFIED BY 'ssluserpassword'
     REQUIRE SSL;
   ```

5. Exit the client and then reconnect as `ssluser` (this should succeed):

   ```
   mysql -u ssluser -p test
   ```

6. Exit the client and then reconnect as `ssluser` using the `--skip-ssl` flag on the command line (this connection attempt should fail):

   ```
   mysql -u ssluser -p --skip-ssl test
   ```

7. Exit the client and then reconnect as a different user that does not have `REQUIRE SSL` as part of their `GRANT` statements using the `--skip-ssl` flag (this connection attempt should succeed).

   ```
   mysql -u root -p --skip-ssl
   ```

How it works...

SSL is supported in MariaDB Linux packages using whatever the system default version of OpenSSL is. Enabling support on the server side for SSL connections is simply a matter of adding the `ssl-ca`, `ssl-key`, and `ssl-cert` variables to a `[mysqld]` section of our MariaDB configuration. On the client, we can choose to specify the information every time we connect, as shown in the following statements:

```
mysql -u ssluser -ssl-ca=/var/lib/mysql/mariadb-ca.pem \
  --ssl-key=/var/lib/mysql/mariadb-client.key \
  --ssl-cert=/var/lib/mysql/mariadb-client.pem test
```

However, it is far easier for us to add these to a `[mysql]` section of a configuration file.

Once SSL support is enabled, we can verify if it is working using the `STATUS;` and `SHOW VARIABLES LIKE 'have_ssl';` commands.

The `STATUS;` command contains an `SSL` line, which shows us the SSL cipher being used to encrypt our connection to the database. An example of what this line looks like is shown as follows:

```
SSL:       Cipher in use is DHE-RSA-AES256-SHA
```

The complete output of the `STATUS;` command will look similar to the following screenshot:

If SSL can be used and it is enabled, the output of the `SHOW VARIABLES LIKE 'have_ssl';` command will look like the following screenshot:

If our installation of MariaDB supports SSL, but it is just not configured, the value of the `have_ssl` variable will be `DISABLED`. If SSL is not supported or built-in in our installation of MariaDB, the variable will be set to `NO`.

The `SHOW STATUS LIKE 'Ssl%';` command shows us all of the various SSL status variables. The complete output is too large to show in a screenshot, but the following is an example screenshot showing just the `Ssl_session%` status variables:

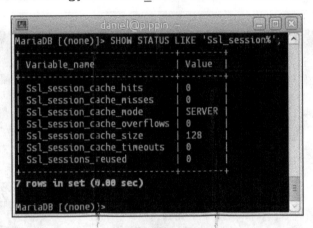

When creating users, we can add a `REQUIRE SSL` option to the end that will force that user to connect using SSL. Users who don't have the `REQUIRE` option are free to connect with or without using SSL. To connect without SSL, we can add the `--skip-ssl` option to our command line. If a user with `REQUIRE SSL` tries to do this, they will get an error when they try to connect, as shown in the following screenshot:

```
daniel@pippin:~$ mysql -u ssluser -p test
Enter password:
ERROR 1045 (28000): Access denied for user 'ssluser'@'localhost' (using password: YES)
daniel@pippin:~$
```

The error is exactly like the error for a mistyped password.

There's more...

We can restrict a user's SSL connections to require specific certificates and specific ciphers if we want to. This is done as part of the `GRANT` command, but instead of simply saying `REQUIRE SSL`, we can use the following statements:

```
GRANT ALL on test.* TO 'ssluser'@'localhost'
  IDENTIFIED BY 'ssluserpassword'
  REQUIRE ISSUER '/C=US/ST=NC/L=Raleigh/O=MariaDB'
  AND CIPHER 'ECDHE-RSA-AES256-GCM-SHA384';
```

The information after `REQUIRE ISSUER` must match our actual certificates, and `CIPHER` needs to be the one supported by MariaDB. The `Ssl_cipher_list` status variable has a list of all supported ciphers. We can also specify the name and force the use of a valid `X509` certificate.

Another thing we could do would be to get our certificate signed by a recognized third-party signing authority like we would for an SSL-enabled website. The actual encryption is no different (SSL is SSL), but the fact that the certificate is verified adds a measure of trust.

See also

- ▶ SSL system variables are documented at:
  `https://mariadb.com/kb/en/ssl-server-system-variables/`
- ▶ SSL status variables are documented, along with other status variables, at
  `https://mariadb.com/kb/en/server-status-variables/`
- ▶ Per account SSL options for `GRANT` statements are documented at
  `https://mariadb.com/kb/en/grant/#per-account-ssl-options`

Using roles to control user permissions

Roles are an alternative way of managing permissions. They are used to give users permissions as a group instead of individually. For example, all users from the finance department could be assigned to a `finance` role with permissions specific to the tasks they need to perform.

Roles were first introduced in MariaDB 10.0.

How to do it...

To create an example role and demonstrate how roles work, perform the following steps:

1. Launch the `mysql` command-line client and connect to our MariaDB database server.

2. Create a `test` database, if it doesn't exist, using the following statement:

   ```
   CREATE DATABASE IF NOT EXISTS test;
   ```

3. Run the following command to create a role:

   ```
   CREATE ROLE read_only;
   ```

4. Grant the role some permissions using the following statement:

   ```
   GRANT SELECT ON test.* TO read_only;
   GRANT USAGE  ON test.* TO read_only;
   ```

5. Display the permissions granted to the role using the following statement:

   ```
   SHOW GRANTS FOR read_only;
   ```

The output of the preceding statement is shown as follows:

```
daniel@pippin ~
MariaDB [(none)]> SHOW GRANTS FOR  read_only;
+-------------------------------------------------+
| Grants for read_only                            |
+-------------------------------------------------+
| GRANT USAGE ON *.* TO 'read_only'               |
| GRANT SELECT ON `test`.* TO 'read_only'         |
+-------------------------------------------------+
2 rows in set (0.00 sec)

MariaDB [(none)]>
```

6. Create a test user using the following statement:

   ```
   CREATE USER test_user@'localhost'
      IDENTIFIED BY 'testpassword';
   ```

7. Display the permissions granted to test_user using the following statement:

   ```
   SHOW GRANTS FOR test_user@'localhost';
   ```

8. Assign the read_only role to test_user, as follows:

   ```
   GRANT read_only TO test_user@'localhost';
   ```

9. Display the permissions granted to test_user again using the following statement (they will be different than when we ran the statement previously):

   ```
   SHOW GRANTS FOR test_user@'localhost';
   ```

   The output of the preceding statement is shown as follows:

```
daniel@pippin ~
MariaDB [(none)]> SHOW GRANTS FOR test_user@'localhost';
+----------------------------------------------------------------------------------------------------------+
| Grants for test_user@localhost                                                                           |
+----------------------------------------------------------------------------------------------------------+
| GRANT read_only TO 'test_user'@'localhost'                                                               |
| GRANT USAGE ON *.* TO 'test_user'@'localhost' IDENTIFIED BY PASSWORD '*9F69E47E519D9CA82116BF5796684F7D0D45F8FA' |
+----------------------------------------------------------------------------------------------------------+
2 rows in set (0.00 sec)

MariaDB [(none)]>
```

10. Log out of MariaDB and log back in as test_user using the following statement:

    ```
    mysql -u test_user -p
    ```

11. Try to use the test database using the following statement (we will get an access denied error):

    ```
    USE test;
    ```

12. Set the role to `read_only` and try to use the `test` database again using the following statement (this time, we will be able to access the `test` database):

```
SET ROLE read_only;
USE test;
```

13. Show the current role and the current user, as follows:

```
SELECT current_role();
SELECT current_user();
```

14. Display the permissions granted by using the following statement:

```
SHOW GRANTS;
```

How it works...

The roles feature is included and enabled in MariaDB by default. There's nothing that needs to be done before we can start using it.

Roles sort of exist in the same area as users, and we use the same commands (such as GRANT, REVOKE, and SHOW) with roles that we use for users. However, they are not users; for example, roles can't log in. Instead, roles are a collection of permissions that we can grant to a user.

Granting a role to a user doesn't automatically apply it to the user whenever they are logged in. The user has to use the SET ROLE command to enable a given role and the permissions that a role provides. We can see the currently enabled role with the SELECT current_role() command.

The output of steps 12 and 13 will look similar to the following screenshot:

```
MariaDB [(none)]> SET ROLE read_only;
Query OK, 0 rows affected (0.00 sec)

MariaDB [(none)]> USE test;
Reading table information for completion of table and column names
You can turn off this feature to get a quicker startup with -A

Database changed
MariaDB [test]> SELECT current_role();
+---------------+
| current_role() |
+---------------+
| read_only     |
+---------------+
1 row in set (0.00 sec)

MariaDB [test]> SELECT current_user();
+-------------------+
| current_user()    |
+-------------------+
| test_user@localhost |
+-------------------+
1 row in set (0.00 sec)

MariaDB [test]>
```

When a role is enabled, the `SHOW GRANTS` command will show both the default `GRANT` permissions assigned to the user and the `GRANT` permissions provided by the currently applied role. The output of this command will look like the following screenshot:

```
MariaDB [test]> SHOW GRANTS;
+-------------------------------------------------------------------------------------------------------------+
| Grants for test_user@localhost                                                                              |
+-------------------------------------------------------------------------------------------------------------+
| GRANT read_only TO 'test_user'@'localhost'                                                                  |
| GRANT USAGE ON * * TO 'test_user'@'localhost' IDENTIFIED BY PASSWORD '*9F69E47E519D9CA82116BF5796684F7D0D45F8FA' |
| GRANT USAGE ON * * TO 'read_only'                                                                           |
| GRANT SELECT ON `test`.* TO 'read_only'                                                                     |
+-------------------------------------------------------------------------------------------------------------+
4 rows in set (0.00 sec)

MariaDB [test]>
```

See also

▶ The complete documentation of the roles feature is available at
    `https://mariadb.com/kb/en/roles/`

▶ Information about the development of the roles feature in MariaDB is available at
    `https://mariadb.atlassian.net/browse/MDEV-4397`

Authenticating using the PAM authentication plugin

We're not limited to using MariaDB's built-in authentication system. We can also authenticate users using Linux's **Pluggable Authentication Modules** (**PAM**) system. Using PAM can enable authentication schemes far beyond what MariaDB provides, including things such as using biometric scanners, authenticator token generators, and so on.

Getting ready

The PAM authentication plugin is only available on Linux, so the server-side portions of this recipe are Linux-only. The `mysql` command-line client on Windows can make use of the PAM authentication on a Linux-based MariaDB server so that part of the recipe is cross-platform.

How to do it...

1. On Debian or Ubuntu systems, add the system `mysql` user to the `shadow` group using the following command:

    ```
    sudo adduser mysql shadow
    ```

2. Create a new system-login account named `pamuser` using either the `useradd` or `adduser` commands and set the user's password using the following statements:

```
sudo adduser pamuser
```

```
sudo passwd pamuser
```

3. Launch the `mysql` command-line client and connect to our MariaDB database server.

4. Install the `auth_pam` plugin using the following statement:

```
INSTALL SONAME 'auth_pam';
```

5. Create a user that matches the name of the system user and is authenticated using PAM in the following manner:

```
CREATE USER pamuser@'localhost' IDENTIFIED VIA pam USING 'common-password';
```

6. Grant the user privileges to our `test` database using the following statements:

```
GRANT ALL ON test.* to pamuser@'localhost';
```

```
FLUSH PRIVILEGES;
```

7. Open a new terminal window and use the `mysql` command-line client to connect to our server using the `pamuser` user we created using the following statement:

```
mysql -u pamuser
```

8. Enter the password when prompted and then issue the `SHOW GRANTS;` command to view the privileges granted to `pamuser`.

How it works...

Like many other plugins that ship with MariaDB, the PAM authentication plugin is disabled by default. This plugin can be easily enabled using the `INSTALL SONAME` command. The `INSTALL PLUGIN` command can also be used if desired.

Once installed, we can create users that are identified via PAM instead of via the standard password option. When identifying users in this way, we need to tell MariaDB what type of PAM authentication to use. These are defined using PAM configuration files. The existing ones can be found under the `/etc/pam.d/` directory. To keep things simple with this recipe, the standard `common-password` authentication was used. It checks the password entered with the passwords stored in the `shadow` file, but it could be any sort of authentication that PAM supports, including LDAP, Active Directory, smart cards, or even biometric scanners.

The PAM authentication plugin simply hands authentication duties off to PAM and then waits for a response. This is why we are still prompted for a password even when we didn't specify `-p` on the command line when logging in. After PAM has checked our credentials, if it comes back with an OK, then our user is authenticated and given the rights granted to them. If not, the login fails as expected.

The output of steps 7 and 8, assuming we enter the password correctly, will look similar to the following screenshot:

```
daniel@pippin:~$ mysql -u pamuser
[mariadb] Password:
Welcome to the MariaDB monitor.  Commands end with ; or \g.
Your MariaDB connection id is 121
Server version: 10.0.8-MariaDB-1~saucy-log mariadb.org binary distribution

Copyright (c) 2000, 2013, Oracle, Monty Program Ab and others.

Type 'help;' or '\h' for help. Type '\c' to clear the current input statement.

MariaDB [(none)]> SHOW GRANTS;
+-------------------------------------------------------------------------------+
| Grants for pamuser@localhost                                                  |
+-------------------------------------------------------------------------------+
| GRANT USAGE ON *.* TO 'pamuser'@'localhost' IDENTIFIED VIA pam USING 'common-password' |
| GRANT ALL PRIVILEGES ON `test`.* TO 'pamuser'@'localhost'                     |
+-------------------------------------------------------------------------------+
2 rows in set (0.00 sec)

MariaDB [(none)]>
```

There's more...

We don't have to rely on the existing configuration files or even the existing PAM plugins when using PAM to authenticate users. We can easily create our own plugins and configurations. The following *See also* section contains links to the documentations that describe how to do this.

See also

▶ More on the PAM authentication plugin can be found at
   `https://mariadb.com/kb/en/pam-authentication-plugin/`

▶ An excellent blog post on writing your own PAM authentication plugin can be found at
   `https://blog.mariadb.org/writing-a-mariadb-pam-authentication-plugin/`

Index

PERL
used, for deleting data 197-200
used, for inserting data 195, 196
used, for reading data 192-195
used, for updating data 197-200
PERL client library
URL 195
PIVOT data type
URL 103
PIVOT table type
using 100-103
Pluggable Authentication Modules (PAM) 258
plugin names
versus filenames 34
pool-of-threads
URL 53
progress reporting
disabling 23
in mytop 23
used, in mysql client 22, 23
progress_report_time variable 23
Proxy table type
URL 100
pyhs
used, for reading data from database
202-204
pyhs library
URL 202
Python
used, for deleting data 206-208
used, for inserting data 204, 205
used, for updating data 206-208
Python pyhs client library
installing 200, 201

Q

queries
optimizing, with subquery cache 55-57
QUOTED option 91

R

rankcol variable 105
read_only variable 115
relay logs
versus binary logs 116

REPLICATE_EVENTS_MARKED_FOR_SKIP
variable 126, 127
replicate_ignore_db option 120
replicate_ignore_table variable 121
replication
setting up 112-116
replication failure
causes 115
repository configuration tool
URL 133
require handlersocket command 210
roles
used, for controlling user permissions
255-258
roles, feature
URL 258
row event annotation
binlog event, enhancing with 122-124
URL 124
rt indexes
URL 168
Ruby
used, for deleting data 216-218
used, for inserting data 214, 215
used, for reading data 211-213
used, for updating data 216-218
Ruby handlersocket library
URL 214
running queries
SHOW EXPLAIN, using with 27-31

S

search command 164
Security 22
SELECT
used, with Cassandra storage engine
236-238
SELECT command 66
SELECT current_role() command 257
semijoin subqueries
optimizing 57, 58
semijoin subquery optimization
in MariaDB, URL 58
server_audit_incl_users variable 145
server_id variable 115
service command 157

Thank you for buying
MariaDB Cookbook

About Packt Publishing

Packt, pronounced 'packed', published its first book "*Mastering phpMyAdmin for Effective MySQL Management*" in April 2004 and subsequently continued to specialize in publishing highly focused books on specific technologies and solutions.

Our books and publications share the experiences of your fellow IT professionals in adapting and customizing today's systems, applications, and frameworks. Our solution based books give you the knowledge and power to customize the software and technologies you're using to get the job done. Packt books are more specific and less general than the IT books you have seen in the past. Our unique business model allows us to bring you more focused information, giving you more of what you need to know, and less of what you don't.

Packt is a modern, yet unique publishing company, which focuses on producing quality, cutting-edge books for communities of developers, administrators, and newbies alike. For more information, please visit our website: www.packtpub.com.

About Packt Open Source

In 2010, Packt launched two new brands, Packt Open Source and Packt Enterprise, in order to continue its focus on specialization. This book is part of the Packt Open Source brand, home to books published on software built around Open Source licences, and offering information to anybody from advanced developers to budding web designers. The Open Source brand also runs Packt's Open Source Royalty Scheme, by which Packt gives a royalty to each Open Source project about whose software a book is sold.

Writing for Packt

We welcome all inquiries from people who are interested in authoring. Book proposals should be sent to author@packtpub.com. If your book idea is still at an early stage and you would like to discuss it first before writing a formal book proposal, contact us; one of our commissioning editors will get in touch with you.

We're not just looking for published authors; if you have strong technical skills but no writing experience, our experienced editors can help you develop a writing career, or simply get some additional reward for your expertise.

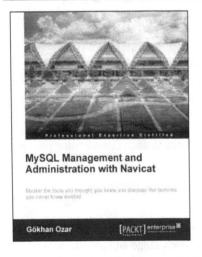

www.ingramcontent.com/pod-product-compliance
Lightning Source LLC
Chambersburg PA
CBHW060526060326
40690CB00017B/3400